Portraits c
Black Achievement:
composing successful
careers

To Agatha
With love from
Rachel

There's a space here that is just
your shape. All the best in getting there.

Jacqui MacDonald

Portraits of Black Achievement: composing successful careers

Published by Lifetime Careers Publishing, 7 Ascot Court, White Horse Business Park, Trowbridge BA14 0XA

ISBN 1 902876 21 0

Printed and bound by Cromwell Press Ltd, Trowbridge

Cover design by 3SIXTY Internet Ltd

Our deepest fear is not that we are inadequate. Our deepest fear is that we are powerful beyond measure. It is our light not our darkness that most frightens us. We ask ourselves who am I to be brilliant, gorgeous, talented and fabulous? Actually, who are you not to be? You are a child of God. Your playing small doesn't serve the world. There's nothing enlightened about shrinking so that other people won't feel insecure around you. We were born to make manifest the glory of God that is within us. It's not just in some of us; it's in everyone. And as we let our own light shine, we unconsciously give other people permission to do the same. As we are liberated from our fear, our presence automatically liberates others.

Excerpt from the inaugural speech by Nelson Mandela, South Africa 1994 - quoting from Marianne Williamson's book *Return to Love*.

This book is dedicated to my son James Davis. The future is yours for the taking.

And to my parents, who showed me the way.

Contents

Acknowledgements

I would like to offer my sincere thanks and appreciation to Jill Sharp. External funding allowed me to employ Jill in a number of roles which she filled admirably as my administrator, project researcher and joint-editor of early transcripts. Jill's support and perseverance proved invaluable throughout this project.

Funders: without their belief in this area of work and financial backing this book would not be possible – thanks to:

Calouste Gulbenkian Foundation

Department for Education and Employment

London South Bank Careers

Diverse Heritage Trust, Liverpool

My sincere gratitude to Yvonne Ryszkowska, Eileen Carnell and Patricia Thomas for re-reading and commenting on the text.

I would also like to acknowledge the support given by: Celia Harrington and Lorna Barker for tirelessly re-typing transcripts

Members of my PhD Support Group for acting as a sounding board

Members of my academic group (Assessment Guidance and Effective Learning) at the Institute of Education, University of London who were supportive and encouraging throughout

Compton Davis who encouraged my early thoughts and was supportive throughout.

And finally, my special thanks to the individuals who agreed to be interviewed for this publication. Without them, this book would not have been possible.

Photography

The photography in the book is by Robert Taylor, except:

Pages 9, 10, 26 Ron Whitfield, 47 Derrick Santini, 97, 129, 133 Trevor Leighton, 205 Manchester Evening News, 267, 282;

all photographs used with permission.

Contributors

Editor

Jacqui MacDonald is a lecturer at the Institute of Education University of London; in Careers Education and Guidance (CEG), the Institute's staff development facilitator for academic staff, and Project Director of the Business Links Unit.

Jacqui has a wide experience of co-ordinating careers work in schools, colleges, at local education authority level and in higher education. She is also a consultant for several careers services.

Her areas of interest include target setting, work related activities, vocational education, careers training for teachers and issues relating to career management.

Jacqui's publications have included chapters on equal opportunities, action planning, careers resource centres and careers and the whole curriculum. Her most recent work includes a DfEE publication *Careers Education and Guidance: what every teacher needs to know* (Hoffbrand, MacDonald and Thomas, 1998); *Effective Management for Careers Work: Reform through Open Learning* (Law, Edwards and MacDonald, 1999); and a chapter on *'Student views on careers education and guidance - what sort of feedback to careers co-ordinators'* (ed: Askew, S. Routledge 2000).

She is a member of several professional bodies including the NACGT, NICEC, BBC Secondary Education Committee and is a business advisor for the Prince's Youth Business Trust.

Administrator/Project Researcher

Jill Sharp has worked both in journalism and education, her experience in the former includes time as a freelane on-screen sub-editor and as assistant editor on a girls' magazine. Her most recent publication work includes research, writing and editing for London LEAs and GOL.

She has also worked extensively in education as a teacher of English and humanities in mainstream schools, in centres for excluded students and at evening classes for adults. She currently works with disaffected teenagers and is an Associate Lecturer with the Open University.

Photographer

Robert Taylor is a freelance photographer and artist. He came to photography via the RAF, training and qualifying as a barrister, and five years in educational publishing.

He has exhibited widely in the UK and internationally, illustrated several books and has work in the collections of the National Portrait

Gallery and the Victoria and Albert Museum. Whilst photography remains his main interest, he has also enjoyed co-production of a Channel 4 documentary about black divas (1996) and is currently working on a play.

Forewords

This book celebrates the success of black people in their chosen careers. It chronicles a determination to succeed often in the face of racism and other obstacles.

The experiences recorded here have important lessons for us all. For young black men and women who have not yet entered the world of work it shows that, despite qualifications and enthusiasm, success does not always come easily. For those of us in Government it is a reminder that many of our citizens face additional barriers to achieving career aspirations.

We have made some progress in tackling these barriers. But we recognise that we need to do much more to bring about the just and fair society to which all our people have a right.

Our common goal should be to prepare all our young people to meet the challenges facing them in the new millennium. To raise achievement to enable all young people to reach their full potential. And to create an environment where every young person can succeed, irrespective of background or origin.

This book shows us what can be achieved.

David Blunkett, Secretary of State for Education and Employment

Portraits of Black Achievement provides an insight in to the life-journeys of some very remarkable people and it creates a record of how the social and economic barriers to black people in Britain are being dismantled. The contributors to this book, by their very achievements, will ensure that those barriers can never be rebuilt. And so, this book is also an important and historical record of the development of multicultural Britain.

There is, of course, a long way to go. Black people are under-represented in positions of power and influence in Britain. Only 1.4% of MPs are from non-white ethnic minorities. Until the voices of all ethnic communities are heard in the Houses of Parliament, the decisions which are made there will continue to reflect only the experience of the majority community in Britain.

Discrimination in Britain is alive and kicking. Young black people are more likely to be excluded from school, more likely to be harassed by the police and are less likely to earn as much as their white counterparts. In Britain, opportunity knocks less often if you are young and black and that is why many of us continue to campaign in order to make sure that it knocks more often. However, the most important thing is to ensure that when it does knock, our young people are ready to open the door and seize it with both hands.

When black people achieve positions of influence in British society, they have the ability to develop practices and structures which value ethnic diversity. What is more, they promote equality and ensure that the opportunities for black people are increased through positive example.

The murder of Stephen Lawrence, and the resulting McPherson report, identified and accepted for the first time that institutional racism exists throughout British society. Those black people who achieve their goals and become more visible within British organisations bring their experience and understanding, they influence decisions, and they ensure that goal posts are more equally positioned. In short, by example, they challenge the history, culture and conventions of institutional racism.

As the first black trade union leader in Britain, my belief in equality has motivated me throughout my life. In the T&G, we see empowerment of black people as the key to tackling institutional racism. Frankly, there is no substitute for black people having an independent and articulate voice speaking and achieving for themselves.

It is important that we recognise and register the achievements and contributions of black people to the economy, as well as British culture. And it's not just about high achievers - black people in Britain support the very fabric of our society. Our public services, including transport and the National Health Service, have always been heavily dependent on ethnic minority professionals.

By the contribution of black achievers, both those in this book and the many thousands of others, we have demonstrated that we are not a community of economic migrants but a community of positive contributors to British Society. We have, all of us, given much more than we have taken from the country we call our home.

Bill Morris, General Secretary, Transport & General Workers' Union

Introduction

As a black person, born in South London of African Caribbean heritage, I am concerned with the emphasis on black under-achievement and the paucity of acknowledgment of black success. This book redresses this lack and aims to inspire young people in their career and life choices. Jill Sharp and I interviewed successful African and Afro-Caribbean people working in a range of different occupations. These interviews demonstrate the positive contribution that black people are making in Britain whilst pursuing a path to personal fulfillment.

The book is based on seventy two interviews. The interviewees speak to you, the reader, in their own words. They discuss life experiences including family, education, work, the idea of a black community, and what it means to be black and professional in the UK. Some of the material and views expressed challenge beliefs and attitudes held by both white and black communities.

The accompanying black and white photographs by Robert Taylor capture each interviewee's individuality and character.

The first person accounts provide a revealing glimpse of the experiences of these individuals as they explore what has motivated them to compose their careers.

For the majority of those interviewed, life has not been plain-sailing, but one of struggle and dogged determination. They, like the generation before them, have helped pave the way for subsequent generations to open up more chances and opportunities to realise their potential.

The reasons some black people achieve against the odds are complex. A number of questions might be considered. What sort of individuals succeed? Is it to do with their personality or general characteristics? Is it serendipity, or the era in which they were born? Is luck a factor? Is it the professions they choose? Is there networking going on behind the scenes? Understanding this complex set of factors is of great importance to me as a black woman, particularly as a teacher, as someone who worked within the youth service and as a consultant to the careers service. My particular interest is in the position and status of black people in Britain and the stories these individuals tell.

Reflections

This book challenges the assumption that oppressed people cannot be empowered, and are therefore incapable of being successful.

There are many black people living in the UK who have achieved status in their professional lives. This success has not been easy for most. It has occurred as a result of individuals composing their own careers and successful profiles. Their individual strategies have led them to their current success.

But what is success? The Oxford Concise Dictionary defines it as "outcomes of undertaking, the accomplishment of what was aimed at, the attainment of wealth or fame or position". Many of the individuals featuring in this book have had a number of work experiences before opportunities, perhaps even luck, guided them to their current professions.

What is interesting about their reflections is how they have defined their success. For most of them, whilst recognising they are successful, one or two felt that had they been white and/or male, their achievement would have been much more significant. Success is seen as being very much about personal gratification.

Different perceptions and definitions of success emerge in the interviews:

Success is .....where I am today, achieving against all the odds (JC)

Real life opportunities, about accidents, trying to cope with difficult situations and succeeding most of the time - and sometimes only just (Prof. GP)

Not being afraid to make mistakes (ES)

The people we spoke to do not regard themselves as role models. Far from it; they are individuals who have worked hard and kept focused despite conflicting pressures. With sheer determination they have achieved respect and recognition in their field. As some of the interviewees put it:

I have succeeded because no one who could have influenced my life negatively had the opportunity or power to do so. The best protection against those who dislike you is to be ready (Prof. GP)

It's a long game. But we have to be patient and play (MB)

It is certainly harder to be recognised as a leading authority in a field that is predominantly white (CL)

Being the only black person makes you incredibly strong and resourceful. You don't need anyone else's acknowledgement that you're okay because you know you've fought and you've got this far (KK)

People don't float into positions they stride or fly or scramble into them. You have to make a positive commitment to jump. It means also that you don't weep when it goes wrong because it sometimes does (TP)

Self worth, hard work and confidence enables you to succeed even in the face of adversity. (Dr SPA)

What is striking is that none of the people we talked with are complacent about their achievements. They do not want to dwell on the fact that they are black, but wish to be recognised first and foremost for their achievements in often challenging climates.

These conversations have allowed individuals perhaps for the first time, to reflect upon the process they went through and continue to experience. They speak from a black perspective, but do not represent all black experiences.

...there is no one story that encapsulates the black experience, there is no one black experience any longer. There are black experiences[1]

---

[1] Stuart Hall as quoted in a book review by Margaret Busby of *Windrush: The Irresistible Rise of Multi Racial Britain* by Mike and Trevor Phillips. Review article in Sunday Times 31 May 1998: Book Section.

These individuals have different histories. Whilst there are some commonalties, they do not reflect a homogenous group; they are individuals who have constructed careers for themselves. Factors including class, identity, the professions chosen and, simply when they were born, have all contributed to their success. We can all learn individually from these accounts, which also contribute to a wider debate on access to achievement.

These black achievers share a number of common features; they seek acknowledgement, respect and a chance to get on like anybody else. Their dreams, hopes and ambitions are no different to that of any other ethnic group. Some told of their humble beginnings and the strength and importance of extended families. The strict upbringing, of which some spoke, did not hinder their success; in fact it may have contributed to it. Whilst some came from middle class homes, all came from backgrounds where there was an expectation that they would at least try their best and recognition that this might be against the odds.

These conversations explore their occupational experiences, the factors contributing to their success, and highlight the complexities of being black and successful. They consider what success means and what they perceive as the benchmarks for measuring success.

All recognise there is racism within society, but do not wish to dwell on it. The key question for them is: what can you do about it? They had used a number of strategies to overcome their obstacles and these are described in the interviews.

A number of themes emerged in the production of this book. These include:

◆ Identity
◆ A power-point culture
◆ A black elite as well as a black middle class
◆ Professional success
◆ Making choices
◆ Strategies
◆ Education
◆ Race and racism
◆ The existence of a black community
◆ The role of parents and families
◆ My own experiences.

◆ Identity

How individuals identified themselves in terms of colour and their profession, depended upon who one spoke with. Is this individual a professional who happens to be black or a black person who is also a professional and successful? Does identity really matter and, if so, for whom?

This country is a multicultural and multi-national society. Let other factors determine your sense of worth and of belonging, rather than your nationality. (Dr SPA)

People need to remember their community, where they are coming from, who they are, it's no use pretending. (SB)

One of the biggest differences is the difficulty of defining who you are and what it means to be black in Britain today and I think the important thing for young people to understand is that the most important definition is their own, they define it. (BG)

Being black is important, but it's not the most important thing. (ZA)

I think it's a rather schizophrenic identity we have to play in the UK. (Rev RN)

◆ A power-point culture

Towards the end of the research I felt that for some individuals there was what one can only describe as a 'power-point culture', the need to be presented in a particular way to the public and thus reworking their narratives. One could interpret this action as a fear of judgement but there is also the question - what does this tell us about the society in which we live?

An example of this emerged when two individuals withdrew from the project because they felt that the text did not reflect them and that the content was factually inaccurate (even though their interviews were taped and transcribed accurately). They were also offered the opportunity to change what had been written, yet they still declined.

Further examples include those who have not simply amended their transcripts but changed them beyond all recognition, to the extent that I felt the richness of their experience was lost. And some people deleted what I believed to be very powerful statement, because perhaps it was not in keeping with the sort of statement, that given their public profile they should be making. For example, a deleted statement contained the following quote:

There is negative pressure on black men when trying to define their identity. The pressure from society often makes them aggressive towards how they see themselves; they internalise a very negative attitude about themselves.

Which seemed to me as rather unfortunate, particularly as such views need to be aired publicly.

◆ A black elite as well as a black middle class

Are we seeing the public emergence of a black elite? Is there a black middle class or merely a black professional group? Many felt uncomfortable being referred to as 'black middle class' whereas others clearly saw themselves as a member of that group.

There is a black middle class and they don't bother to signal it because they don't need to. (YB)

I'm part of a black middle class but there isn't a public perception of a black middle class in Britain. (CW)

I don't accept that the qualities of hard work, excellence and striving after achievement are confined to any one class. (PB)

There is a black middle class...but not the same as the white middle class. (ES)

◆ **Professional success**

Professional success brings its own complexities. There is also an issue of gender and race and how one is treated at work as well as the games people play in order to succeed.

> *There are many examples of having to play the game as I remember, but there are two ways of doing it: either you get sucked into it, or you know that you're playing the game. But for me I've always maintained that the ultimate end is positive achievement. (PC)*

> *My job title doesn't guarantee your acceptance. (HR)*

> *Many people are offered opportunities, particularly women, and they turn them down because they think I have never done this before; this is too good for me. (VA)*

> *When you're playing away from home, don't expect the supporters of the home team to applaud you; but don't let that stop you from playing to the best of your ability. (DO)*

◆ **Making choices**

No single factor influences the career choices that individuals make, that is, whether to aim high or to give up and give in to the stereotype of black under-achievement.

> *One of my realisations about life was accepting earlier on that things don't always go right; you just have to do your best and enjoy what you're doing. You just can't afford to be indifferent. (CW)*

> *The Will Does It (CH)*

> *I took the opportunities that were offered to me, even though sometimes they didn't look so attractive and though other people might have scorned them. (TP)*

> *Making choices means never saying I can't, you've got to believe in yourself. (AA)*

Educational attainment, family background, gender, race, opportunities (serendipity) as well as economic and social structures are all factors that contribute to determining the direction an individual will take.

Family or school networks allow some individuals to access certain jobs, but not for the individuals in this book. Most grew up in an era when media coverage indirectly influenced their conceptions as to the jobs that were open to people like them.

Several commented on the objective and fair advice given to them in schools by teachers. For most their dreams and aspirations remained almost closely guarded secrets with little parental understanding or support. For others their school experiences and significant individuals inspired and sometimes served to spur them on in their determination to prove themselves.

The ideal scenario that involves planned decision making was certainly not the case for the individuals we interviewed. There were those whose plans bore little resemblance to actual outcomes; many reacted to serendipitous opportunities and turned them to their advantage. What is intriguing about these accounts is that whilst their experience is perhaps no different to other groups, they saw and seized opportunities and proved success was possible.

◆   **Strategies**

These accounts demonstrate the importance of knowing how to play the game, gaining the skills to play the system to one's advantage rather than surrendering before the end of the first round.

Turning the situation round to my advantage (EM)

You have to be careful how you present yourself because it could be misinterpreted. (CV)

Using race (in a positive way) to your advantage. (DE)

You've got to associate with people who are going the way you want to go. (WS)

Other strategies used by individuals in their pursuit of success included self-employment, becoming independent of a structure that ultimately restricts, as a result enhancing their creativity and status.

...being able to do more or less what you want to do and being able to call the tune. (BO)

Self-employment has allowed me to develop a different kind of strength, spiritual strength, to reach somewhere deep to be able to cope. (CN)

◆   **Education**

There are those who feel that we expect too much from schools and those who feel that schools are not doing enough.

Education has failed so many of our young people. Political correctness is not preparing young people for the real world. (JC)

What is required are role models, a sense of history for black kids and a sense of citizenship. (JC)

If you want to get on in life then you have to put the work in yourself.

Let's not expect too much from schools. They are institutions of learning and what they are doing should be complemented by what is happening at home. (CH)

The most important thing is the interaction between the teacher and the child. (Dr CV)

When you're in difficult circumstances you can be tempted not to take responsibility: to blame the system or parents - anyone but yourself. (Prof. LY)

Every kid is waiting for a button to be pushed. (LH)

◆   **Race and racism**

Race did not emerge as a central theme in the interviews. Most did not make explicit reference to it at all but where they did their views were forceful.

At the moment because there is no rioting on the streets, society would have us believe that there is no racism. Racism is under-reported, the illusion is there is so much harmony. (MB)

Paradoxically, it's the invisibility of blackness that becomes an issue. (JA)

I want to show what black people can do if they put their minds to it rather than just complain about how bad things are. (MH)

Racism continues to be a scourge to contend with, even though the people of the Commonwealth in Britain are one of its greatest assets. (AP)

Institutional racism, it's not illegal, that's what makes it more pernicious. (Prof. GP)

◆ The existence of a black community

Some would argue that there is not a singular black community. We group things together because we talk about them in that way, but it's more complex. There is not one community but different sorts that come together and function effectively for different purposes.

There is a black community but we don't support each other enough. (DM)

I don't feel part of the black community: I never have... (PD)

There is a black community...with a growing level of confidence. (BE)

I don't think there is a black community: there are black communities. (MH)

I don't confine myself to one community. (CL)

Whilst all those interviewed recognised racism within society, they spoke more or less with one voice when they suggested that the black community must fight its own corner. They believed that the black community needs to be more unified, and should not expect too much from outside; it is not enough to demand what society needs to do, but there is a need to address more importantly what black people need to do for themselves.

◆ The role of parents and families

All participants were unanimous in their belief that parents/families have a role to play in the positive experiences and achievements of their children.

My mother and certain other people around me had a strong influence. They had a work ethic and they were decent people. They believed it was right to work in order to succeed and to do the best for the people they cared for. A lot of that rubbed off on me, even though I didn't know it at the time. (Sir HO)

...quite a lot of black families have been disadvantaged for a long time. Some affirmative action has got to happen, but it's got to be in tandem with community responsibility. (JS)

It's important to me that I'm a loving example to my family. (VT)

When you have your own children...you understand how important it is to preserve a little bit of certainty for them and some sanctuary. (JB)

We need parental support - space without suffocation. (SB)

◆ My own experiences: strict, clear boundaries and high expectations

I had, until this research, deliberately distanced myself from work that I perceived to be about black issues. This was not because I felt that these were not worthy, but I was frustrated with what I saw as the continual negative media profile of black individuals, the type-casting of black actors/actresses or the complete transparency of black people; unless associated with crime or expulsion from school.

I was also anxious not to be seen as an academic receiving financial gain through endless research on the hard done by black youth at the hands of a reckless system.

Whilst recognising and having experienced racism (albeit subtly) I was brought up with parents whose question was always "so what are you going to do about it?"

I knew if I were to explore this area it would have to be from an approach not attached to a blame culture. My experience at school and college was not over-inspiring. I had one or two teachers who were really encouraging, but on the whole I couldn't leave the confines of such institutions fast enough; yet I loved learning.

I come from a family of five girls, from a family headed by a father who was and remains a staunch nationalist (of Jamaica), who instilled in us the value of hard work and deferred gratification. We had a mother who would continually come out with Caribbean sayings which I still remember: her most famous being "silver and gold will vanish away, but a good education never decays". I did not look to schools to provide me with black history: I got that from home as well as from regular trips to Jamaica "for exposure and cultural awareness".

My home was an open door to many friends who came to see my parents as their parents and still visit them if they are on the island (my parents took early retirement several years ago).

Some of these narratives reflect the accounts of my parents, but I would not dare to pretend that I have first hand experience of some of their plight.

My career as a teacher was about trying to inspire young people and now I try to do it with adults.

What Next?

Through the accounts of these individuals, a range of learning, career and life experiences, the complexities of being a black professional in the UK are emerging.

There are no quick fixes, but we can't lose hope.

By rendering invisible the quiet achievements of black women and decent black men, the media cult of the black delinquent prevents young Afro-Caribbean men from seeing themselves as succeeding in any arena other than the criminal street[2].

There are lessons here for a number of agencies; schools need to acknowledge the prevailing economic and social structures, and to use this knowledge in the planning and delivery of a more progressive curriculum which includes a comprehensive careers education and guidance programme for young people.

---

[2] Janet Daley newspaper article *The racism, sexism and violence of rap culture* in response to Tony Sewell's research on black boys and black culture. The Daily Telegraph Tuesday 22 August 2000

Parents have a role to play in encouraging and supporting their children, even when they too might be unclear as to what is at stake or are struggling to make sense of the system for themselves. It is not sufficient to expect schools to provide all the encouragement and direction that will allow young black people to aspire to prestigious and fulfilling work.

Our participants talked of the need to challenge low expectations and encourage high expectations and for all agencies to find ways in which young people can be empowered, develop their self respect and confidence. Some spoke of the need for families to maintain contact with their ancestral links and to encourage exploratory visits. In fact, one or two argued that it is not the role of the school to go out of its way to teach black history, but something that the home should be addressing. The school's role is to provide a curriculum which would nurture young people towards success.

Professor Errol Miller argues that there is no single factor to explain institutional inequalities. It is the interaction between a number of social criteria such as gender, race, class, religion and geographical location which influences the development of individuals. Miller argues that it is impossible to completely level the playing field, which will always be tilted in favour of the dominant group.

All we as educators, family and others can do is to help young people address the issue of power structures..... It is not the hand that the individual is dealt that is important, but how they deal with that hand.

What has been missing for many years has been a positive portrayal of black achievement. This is not to deny the discrimination that black people continually face, but to promote the achievements and successes which are overlooked by schools, the media and society in general. There is a need to positively demonstrate that black people can and do achieve at the highest level.

I hope that young people will gain motivation from reading these accounts, and that the reflections will trigger discussion on institutional expectations and the role of hierarchy, race, gender, culture, class and power in creating opportunities for social participation.

Young people must be helped to construct their own future, recognise the disadvantages, but be helped to be creative and productive in their thinking in order to move on......We have underestimated what is required to be successful.[4]

This book examines not only the ways in which this group of black professionals composed their careers, but also pinpoints the complexities of being a black professional in the UK and how their success masks issues of inequality in our society. How do we move from the diagnosis that inequality exists to identifying specific contextual treatment?[5]

I describe this plight of black people as the five Ds of black youth: disadvantaged, disaffected, disillusioned, disruptive and disappeared. I hope this book dispels this blanket view of black people.

---

[3] Prof. Errol Miller. as part of his open lecture at the Institute of Education, University of London, 17 October 2000
[4] ibid. Prof. E. Miller
[5] ibid. Prof. E. Miller

Dr S Prince Akpabio

Dr S Prince Akpabio OBE is a dental surgeon, a specialist in dental public health and Founder President of the Commonwealth Dental Association (CDA).

Date of birth: 30 June 1924
Place of birth: Eket, Nigeria

'Be honest with yourself and determine if you would like to serve your fellow human beings irrespective of nationality, social status or financial rewards. Be prepared for honest hard work and give sympathetic understanding.'

I am an Honorary Research Fellow at London University and was a Consultant in Oral Health for the World Health Organisation for several years. In May 1991, I was appointed Visiting Professor, Faculty of Dentistry, University of Chiang Mai, Thailand. Awarded the British Dental Association's (BDA) "Role of Distinction for outstanding services to UK dentistry" on 29 April 1999.

We formed the CDA in 1991. Many problems on oral health are directed to the CDA from many National Dental Associations of the Commonwealth. That is one part of our work. Because I used to be a World Health Organisation Consultant, I still have commitments in East and West Africa and in South-East Asia. I go to Chiang Mai, Thailand, to lecture quite often. I also run a small private dental practice, three mornings a week in London, which means that I keep abreast of new developments in Dentistry that are taking place. Dental articles are also sent to me to review. What I find most enjoyable is the international connection that I have. I know many people on the dental and health scene in many parts of the world, and there is therefore a constant exchange of views on professional matters internationally.

The most challenging aspect of CDA's work is that dentistry and oral health in the developing Commonwealth countries have always been given a low priority. When you compare this with such life-threatening diseases such as NOMA and HIV/AIDS this is now changing. What people tend to forget is that the cost of treating dental diseases is extremely high. Many common dental diseases such as dental caries and periodental diseases can be prevented by simple inexpensive preventative methods. Developing countries must be helped to realise that oral health is an important, essential component of general health. I find this challenging and important because people seem to think that "it doesn't matter". Also, you have constantly to persuade companies and organisations to provide funding support for oral health. Now, I am seeing many of the things that I had dreamt of, and wanted to get done, beginning to be dealt with seriously, in many developing countries and by many Governments.

I was born near Eket, in South East Nigeria. My father was a big Chief. One of the important things brought home to me, at a very early age, was a sense of service to the community. My family home was always an open house. You knew that because you belonged to such-and-such a family, you owed certain obligations to your people. I knew that I had always wanted to serve the community, but never imagined that my path in life would lead me to the international scene and to form and serve the Commonwealth Dental Association. When you start something in life, this may open up. You then go for more, and this may open up, more and more. You may then find yourself involved in major international activities and commitments. You must be able to respond effectively to these demands and obligations.

'Success requires you to work hard, to have total commitment and to be prepared to make sacrifices.'

I had very happy school days! I was lucky because I was sent to one of the best schools in Calabar, Nigeria, which had a Scottish headmaster. He was demanding but very scrupulous, and expected the best from his students. When I passed my exams and left school, I studied Pharmacy at Yaba Higher College, Lagos. On qualifying as a Chemist and Druggist, I was sent to the Northern part of Nigeria, which is in parts rather rural, to work with a doctor. He and I had to run the hospital between us. There, I came face to face with personal and community ill-health and tragedies for the first time. That really shook me. At that point, I applied for a scholarship to study Pharmacy in the UK. After studying for a year, I decided that I preferred to do Dentistry. Whilst in Northern Nigeria I'd become aware of the difficulty of getting dental treatment for patients.

'I am intensely Nigerian but at the same time I am British.'

Unfortunately, it meant that I had to give up the six years Government Scholarship. Everyone thought that I was 'crazy'. I worked for a year, doing anything to earn a living. Because I had given up the scholarship, I could not ask my parents to support me.

I studied Dentistry at University College Hospital, London, where I qualified in 1956. After qualifying I was appointed as a General Duty and then as Resident House Surgeon, and eventually a Registrar. Then I undertook postgraduate courses at Guys and Kings College Hospitals, London, and also at the Eastman Dental Hospital. My period at King's, Guy's and the Eastman Hospitals brought me into contact with other disciplines, which opened my mind enormously.

When looking for accommodation in London, I obviously came across some discrimination, as a coloured student. In some cases, I actually had doors slammed in my face. But this did not really affect me. I competed for dental appointments, on equal terms, with my fellow white professional colleagues. I made several personal friends. In my early days, apart from the housing problems, we did not get the racial overtones, nor the social problems that we see today. One soon learns, in life, that "Happiness consists in giving and serving others". I have learnt this, over the years.

I belong to two or three worlds. I am intensely Nigerian at heart, and I think this is very much to do with my family background. At the same time I am British, and I am married to an English wife. It has never crossed my mind about whether she is African or European, or Asian. Also, I feel extremely international in my thinking and actions, and have many international friends and professional colleagues. This is good for my CDA's work.

'You pay a price if you want to be at the top.'

I am sure that my London family feel that I have devoted far too much of my time to my professional work, at the expense of time I should have given to them. You do pay a price if you are at the top, because you have to maintain a standard and quality that enables you to stay there. You must be very well read in your special field, and be completely up to date. This does mean that, sometimes, you may have to cut yourself off from the family to be able to sit and read widely, and reflect quite seriously.

'In this country we are a multi-cultural, multi-national society. Let other factors determine your sense of belonging rather than your nationality.'

'Schools need to be motivating places.'

When the Queen gave me the OBE "for services to dentistry and medicine" in 1996, that meant a great deal to me. It meant a recognition of my services, but also implied important obligations. Being entrusted with this honour, it meant that you should work hard and encourage others. It meant also giving much to the Commonwealth and the world.

I do not think it is helpful for coloured people to think in terms of ghettos. This country is a multicultural and multinational society. Let other factors determine your sense of worth and of belonging, rather than your "nationality".

I believe that the family, as a unit, is an important factor in a black person's future in this country. From the moment a child is born, the family must give the child their total support, encouragement and some direction. Choose the school very carefully for the child. The child should then work hard! Young black people must understand that they do have enormous opportunity, if they apply themselves diligently.

Self worth, hard work, and confidence enables you to succeed even in the face of adversity. Try to serve the community, to the very best of your ability, because in the final analysis, this is what brings the greatest inner satisfaction, fulfillment, and happiness to you.

Ziggi Alexander

Date of birth: 5 November 1951
Place of birth: Dominica

'Let the world know what you want and persuade others to help you get it.'

Independent Management Consultant.

I became an independent consultant because I wanted more control over my life. I have a simple philosophy: let the world know what you want and persuade others to help you to get it. In my first year in business I won two major contracts, hired two associates and had one of my products made available on the Internet. Previously I had worked in senior management positions in the NHS and Local Authorities, including Head of Human Resources for the largest City Government in Europe.

I have always been interested in public sector work. After university I thought I should be a teacher. There were too many black children failing in our schools, then and now. It is a national disgrace. However, when I did my teaching practice placements I thought, this isn't about teaching, it's about containment. So I became a community relations officer, with responsibility for education. At the time I was the youngest CRO in the country. That job gave me a great deal of satisfaction and a really good grounding in community development.

After a spell working in Japan teaching English as a foreign language, I returned to the UK and entered local government as a community librarian. It was at this point that I realised my ambition to publish work on black British history. I co-edited the modern version of Mary Seacole's autobiography and co-researched the *Roots in Britain* exhibition comprising over 250 photographs exploring the history of black and Asian settlers in the UK from Elizabeth I to Elizabeth II. During that period, I went to the USA for 3 months on a Winston Churchill Travelling

'I enjoy making a contribution where it is recognised that were it not for me sustainable change would not have been achieved.'

Fellowship to look at African-American community education projects. From senior jobs in libraries I moved sideways into strategic Personnel roles. Before I left London for a senior management post in the West Midlands, I was an Assistant Controller of Personnel in an inner city local authority.

I enjoy making a contribution where it is recognised that were it not for me sustainable change would not have been achieved. I am happiest when I am leading from the front. There comes a point when you can no longer follow mediocre people, whatever their organisational position. It is time to move on when it is obvious to everyone concerned that you know more and have more to offer than the top person or people. Under those conditions I cannot be effective because I want to develop, improve and experiment; this is hard to do when other people want to play it safe by acting as caretakers of the status quo. If I were to return to an organisational setting I would need to be somewhere where I could try out my ideas, utilise my leadership skills and implement my vision. Of course, this has to be done collaboratively, engaging everyone involved in the enterprise.

I was born in Dominica and came to England when I was four. My parents are ordinary working people but I was brought up with middle class aspirations. I went to a junior school in West London. In fact, I grew up in the area where the Notting Hill riots took place in 1958. I remember spending months with no natural light coming into the house because all the heavy furniture had been piled up against the windows to protect us from attack.

'It was always being drummed into me that I had to be better than my peers.'

I passed my 11 plus and got a place at Chiswick Girls' Grammar School. I was the only African-Caribbean pupil until about the fifth form. I went straight from grammar school to university. I gained an Honours Degree in American Studies from the University of East Anglia. I returned to London to study for a Postgraduate Certificate in Education at the Institute of Education, followed by a Masters Degree at Sheffield University.

As soon as I started school I remember being aware that I was black and different. However, I was lucky. My parents and my teachers encouraged me. They had the expectation that I would do well and any time I stepped out of line they had only to raise an eyebrow and I would get back on track. I was always ambitious for myself. It's more an issue of attitude than anything else. It was always being drummed into me that I had to be better than my peers and that if anybody disrespected me I had to make them eat their words or acts. That has been a consistent theme throughout my life, throughout my career: not letting people get away with racism. As an adult, I don't have sleepless nights about it. Over the years I have learned how to deal with those people who nurture a negative mindset and can't see past the colour of my skin.

When I act as mentor I encourage people to look for opportunities. If they have a career plan, it is easier for them to identify projects, committees and other avenues where they can gain useful experience. Unfortunately, some people see additional work as exploitation rather than as an opportunity to enhance their learning. At the end of the day, these experiences strengthen a CV and can help differentiate the exceptional candidate from the rest.

This is why I get involved in a range of activities. I used to do voluntary work in Saturday Schools and a Youth Club. At the moment I am the Chairperson of a Non-Departmental Public Body. This is a part time role and it is paid. I also sit on a Government Advisory Group, chair another UK organisation and sit on a major grants committee, all of which are unpaid. Other voluntary activities include membersip of the NHS Chief Executive's Leadership Strategy Group and I act as a mentor to people who want to get senior public sector jobs.

'Nobody has to like you, but they do have to treat you with a certain degree of respect.'

There are many white women senior managers in the public sector; but very few black people. Gender has never been the primary issue as far as I'm concerned. Clearly there are factors in play that impede women's progress, but in my experience 'race' is the *real* stumbling block.

Earlier in my career, I battled against racism on a daily basis. I routinely worked into the early hours to ensure that I could deliver. I could not always rely on my staff to do their jobs to a high professional standard. In fact, there were occasions when I identified blatant attempts to undermine me by producing sub-standard work close to the deadline. At such times if I hadn't stayed up all night working, it could have meant the end of a promising career. I command almost universal respect now and if anyone has unhealthy problems concerning my leadership, the onus is on them to find the way out. Nobody has to like you, but they do have to treat you with a certain degree of respect.

Outside of family and friends, my survival strategy has centred on networking, and identifying people who could help me if I got into difficulty. We need to surround ourselves with people who support us, not people who pull us down. Parents need to support their children: give them strong, resilient egos. We all know how tough it is to make our way in the world. If we do not have or develop the right tools at an early age, it is even harder to accomplish our goals. The strongest weapon in our armoury is belief in ourselves.

If as a young person I had had experiences of black people operating in a wide variety of professions and settings I would have made very different career choices. Perhaps I would have gone into business at the outset, who knows? Now, I am a businesswoman. My organisational experiences have given me the right background for being an independent consultant. I like being my own boss and being in control. I win contracts that are both satisfying and pay well and I have been able to maintain my commitment to the public sector.

'Being black is important, but it is not the only important thing in my life.'

For many years the experience of racism influenced all sorts of life decisions: the jobs I applied for, the friendships I made, the holiday destinations I selected. Not any more. Regardless of the obstacles that I encounter, I will continue to fight against injustice and unreasonable barriers. I have complete confidence in my abilities. This is how it should be. Being black is important, but it is not the only important thing in my life.

Baroness Valerie Amos

Date of birth: 14 March 1954
Place of birth: Guyana

'I want a society that is more inclusive.'

Parliamentarian and an overseas development and leadership specialist. Former chief executive of the Equal Opportunities Commission and currently a Government spokesperson in the House of Lords.

I came into the Lords in October 1997 and in July '98 was formally asked to come into government. My background prior to this was in local government and I was Chief Executive of the Equal Opportunities Commission.

I have been involved in politics most of my adult life. I have been involved in campaigning on race issues, on women's issues and on human rights. Social justice and equality have always been important to me.

I am a Baroness in Waiting and Government Whip in the House of Lords. As a Baroness in Waiting I represent the Queen, meeting heads of state and other dignitaries who come into Britain. As a Government Whip I am a Spokesperson on International Development, Women's Issues and Social Security and I am also part of a team involved in business management in the House of Lords.

There is something very positive about being part of the Party that is in government and trying to bring about huge social changes in the new millennium. Parliament is an important place to be. I want a society that is more inclusive; that has social justice at its heart, that has individual rights and responsibilities as well as wider institutional and government responsibilities.

The process of change can be quite slow, but that's part of the challenge. We've got the whole

*'The weight of those
expectations can be
overwhelming.'*

issue of the reform of the House of Lords, which
will have an impact on all of us who are part of
the second chamber.

In terms of ethnic minority women in the
House of Lords, there are seven: three Asian, three
African Caribbean and one Chinese. We are visible
and there is a responsibility to the communities
out there. There is an expectation that we will
raise the issues that concern ethnic minority
communities within the House. Regardless of
whether one sees oneself as having that
representational role, it is there.

The House of Lords had, until recently, 1200
members, so the small number of ethnic minority
peers is very visible. It is assumed that people
end up in the House of Lords because they have a
particular expertise. But community expectations
are not always realistic and because there are so
few of us the weight of those expectations can be
overwhelming. We are talking about big issues
here: education; development; health; the justice
system, all of which impact upon the way black
people live their lives.

There is a huge social status attached to being
in the House of Lords and because it is so unusual
for black people to be there I think there is even
more status attached to it, both nationally and
internationally. When I travel there is surprise at
my status, but there is also a great deal of
positiveness about it. Backbench peers receive an
allowance but they are not paid even though the
job takes up a great deal of time.

*'Home support was
extremely important.'*

I went to a girls' grammar school in Kent. I was
the first black girl there. I was pretty academic so
my school experience was positive and I
thoroughly enjoyed it. The fact of being the first
carries with it some burdens but also some
advantages. My parents were both teachers and
there was a lot of support at home for education.
They were both clear about the ways in which one
could challenge what was being taught and in
which one could maintain a particular cultural
identity. That home support was extremely
important.

It was always expected that I would go to
university. It was part of the way I was brought
up. My first degree was in sociology; then I did
cultural studies and finally research in education.

Race, Women and Social Justice have always been issues of particular interest.

I went into local government in the early 1980's, starting off as a special advisor on race issues and subsequently on women's issues. I was committed to the public sector and public sector values at a time when the public sector was really trying to grapple with equalities. It seemed a good place to go. My next role was going directly into management.

'My philosophy is about accepting challenges.'

Later, I was at the Equal Opportunities Commission for four years. I was Chief Executive responsible for running the organisation; managing relationships with government; positioning the organisation and developing strategy. It was a national organisation with an international impact.

My philosophy is about accepting challenges. I never say, I cannot do something because I have had no experience. What I tend to say is that I will have a go and see whether I like it and whether I am successful.

Many people are offered opportunities, particularly women, and they turn them down because they think I have never done this before; this is too good for me. But I will always say yes, I will do that.

I think that it is important that young people take education seriously because a sound education basis leads anywhere: there are more career choices than ever before.

Dr Jacqueline Andall

Date of Birth: 28 August 1963
Place of Birth: London

'Both my parents placed a high value on education.'

'The term 'black community' does not really tell you much.'

Lecturer in Italian Studies at the University of Bath

I loved school! I went to a former Grammar School that was mainly white, although there were three girls of African-Caribbean origin in my class. The school had an academic ethos with many people going on to university. I went around with a mixed group of girls from very different backgrounds.

I am part of a large extended family from Grenada. I grew up in Shepherds Bush in the heart of the Grenadian community and within walking distance of most of my relatives. My father was involved in various community organisations and both of my parents placed a high value on education.

The term 'black community' does not really tell you much. As a black person you will experience it differently depending on, amongst other things, whether you are male or female, your class position, your profession. In the 1970s and 1980s I experienced it as a cohesive community because I and other black people around me seemed to have similar experiences. As young black people born in Britain, we felt that we were not accepted as part of British society. We did not have black role models apart from a few sporting personalities. Beyond that, young black people were operating in a void. We developed a counter-position and asserted a black identity. For example, many boys became rastas. This was a time of the National Front, people being beaten up, the 'Sus' laws and police harassment. I remember the fights and the bottle throwing at Notting Hill carnival. I also remember going to the Black People's Day of Action in 1981 and feeling that this was a phenomenal event to be part of. Today, in London, everything is more dispersed and there are many different black communities. It is perhaps easier to identity where and who the black community is in smaller places like Bath and Bristol.

There is still discrimination in Britain and in Europe. In Britain, it was undoubtedly more blatant in the 1950s and 1960s, while today, despite improved levels of social and political integration for black people, it is expressed in more subtle ways.

'Discrimination is expressed in more subtle ways.'

I realised fairly early on that society did not expect black people to achieve. At my careers interview at school I expressed an interest in Law but was advised to consider an alternative career path as Law was 'apparently' too difficult.

I studied for a degree in French and Italian at Cardiff University. This included a year abroad in Paris and Rome. In my final year, the Italian department offered me the opportunity to study for a PhD. It was not something that I had previously considered but I was encouraged by one of my lecturers. When I left Cardiff, I began an academic career at the University of Bath as a lecturer in Italian Studies.

'I was encouraged by one of my lecturers.'

I hope my affection for Italy continues, even though my relationship with the country has changed over the years. When I first visited Italy in the late 1970s, I felt completely at ease with a Mediterranean culture. In those days, there were very few black people in Italy and the Italians I encountered were generally open and curious. The situation in Italy has since changed radically as it has now become a destination for African and Asian labour migrants. The change in attitude in Italy has been extraordinary and the current situation is reminiscent of stories my parents used to tell me of their early experience in Britain in the 1950s and 1960s.

I conduct research as part of my job. My research is mainly about the contemporary immigration situation in Italy. I have written a book which looks at black women's migration to Rome and their experience as domestic workers. At present, I am conducting a series of interviews with young black people who were born in Italy. This is the part of my work I most enjoy. It allows me to investigate new social issues and to travel to Italy extensively.

If you are used to the multi-cultural feel of London, it can be quite a shock to find yourself in a place like Bath. However, it does give you greater insight into aspects of Britain that many black Londoners might be unfamiliar with. There is a small black community in Bath and the Rainbow Steel Band, of which I am a member, does its part in promoting Caribbean culture in the region.

I currently work in a department where I am the only black member of staff. This is probably not an unusual situation for those black professionals frequently described as forming part of an emerging black middle class in Britain. Black people are certainly present in a much wider range of fields compared to thirty years ago and the black middle class, both similar to and different from the wider middle class, will no doubt become more established with time.

I do have a sense of belonging to Britain, but it is localised to Shepherds Bush and not bound up with a British national identity. In my teens, I would never have envisaged a time when I might describe myself as British. Then, I wanted to reject being British as, despite being born in Britain, I was treated as a 'foreigner'. Now there is a growing acceptance that you can be both black *and* British.

I want people to see me as black, because I am black! But being black is only one of my many identities.

'Black people are certainly present in a much wider range of fields compared to 30 years age.'

'Being black is only one of my many identities.'

Professor Charles Anyanwu

Date of birth: 8 August 1948
Place of birth: Nigeria

'Everybody has a contribution to make to society.'

'To do any activity well you need discipline.'

President of North London College, Professor of International Business at Enugu State University of Science and Technology, Nigeria, and Member of UN/ECE Experts Group Geneva.

'Hard work and perseverance yield great dividends. There's no short cut, no alternative route, to greatness'.

In Africa we believe that it is our duty to direct children and have them developed. Here, emphasis is to allow children to go their natural way. In the early 80s I went out into the black community in Stamford Hill and spoke with young black people of compulsory school age who were not doing anything. Some had been excluded from school; others felt older than their mates and couldn't fit in. So I started free classes for them in the local library, and this was the start of what is now the North London College, of which I'm President.

Success is the end of a ladder and starts with the ability to do something where the objective is set for a period of time: to reach that goal and to continue. I think that's an achievement. Everybody has a contribution to make to society. The moment somebody comes into the world he/she has their own beat to play. When the end of the ladder is reached he/she awaits others.

To do any activity well you need discipline and because of that you are sometimes constrained from doing certain other things. I do not have much of a social life; I am always here, designing a programme or doing things that need to be done. It becomes a habit. Discipline takes over ones whole life.

*'There is prejudice, we
must not hide this.'*

I went to a Christian school. When it came to
going to university my parents didn't have the
money so I went into industry and later to the
polytechnic. From there, I combined work with
study. I did my masters in business management
then began my writing and research, and moved
on.

In this life there is a misconception of what is
meant by enjoyment. People see lazing about and
being idle as enjoyment. That is wrong. Living and
working is enjoyment.

I can't remember how I felt when I was a
teenager but I know I was determined to have an
education. My philosophy has been based around
this need to be educated.

In this country, I don't think society expects a
black man to do well. There is prejudice, we must
not hide this. Whatever happens, even though we
call ourselves British, we are still foreigners. I am
a member of a UN sub-committee and they don't
immediately call me British even though I am a
delegate from Britain. But we must give room to
some prejudice; it is natural.

Society helps anybody here who wants to move
on. If you want to establish a business, there are
grants. It is up to us to prove our case. If we don't,
we are not building the foundation for our
children. Somebody has got to do it, to leave a
legacy. Perhaps our forefathers didn't do enough
to establish themselves in this society and that is
why we are suffering. It's not really to do with
society as such. So now we have to work harder.

*'We must not always
expect the easier
option.'*

We must not always expect the easier option.
Sometimes it is better to stop at the obstacle, find
another route and continue moving. It is not good
to stay in one place not achieving what you want.
Just by moving on you can learn more.

I think I was about twenty when I accepted that
I couldn't go into medicine. My second option was
to go into industry. At the end of the day it is
important to be doing something, to keep
building up. When I finished my computing
course I decided to move into accounting. I
finished my accountant's qualification and found
that there was a need to do a general management
course. After that I moved to the university where
my area became management, specialising in
quality management.

'We need to stop thinking about the stereotypes society gives us. Forget about it.'

'Young people need to have patience, perserverance and to work hard.'

'The education system should be redesigned to enable teachers to teach.'

We need to stop thinking about the stereotype society gives us. Forget about it. You have got to work hard and establish yourself. When you are well established people trust what you can do. These prejudices will disappear, will evaporate. Young people need to think positively. How they do now will make life easier for the next generation. They need to help create opportunities by working hard. And parents should encourage their children to study. Nobody is born stupid. Idleness leads to stupidity. Stupidity is the mother of underachievement.

Schools do not encourage everybody. If someone wants to be lazy, the school allows it. Often they assume children are not capable of working hard. The education system should be re-designed to enable teachers to teach. They are not teaching at the moment. What they do is guide. In teaching you change the total orientation of an individual from habit to a way of making a start. With guiding, you see the person moving and tell them to follow the road.

The hours that children spend in their schools are greater than the hours they spend with their parents, so the education system should take the body of education and create the society we want. It is this creative activity that is lacking.

The most important truth I've learnt is that there is no substitute for hard work. I don't believe there is such a thing as failure. I'd rather call it a delay. As long as we are determined, there is nothing that we cannot achieve.

Mervin Archer

Date of birth: 27 November 1952
Place of birth: St Lucia, West Indies

'My attitude's changed over the years.'

Mervin Archer is business manager for NatWest Bank at Hendon Business Centre. His role is to manage a portfolio of diverse businesses with a turnover range of £100,000 to £1m and more, providing lending and advice services.

My role in this job is to review business plans and match the needs of businesses to the bank's services. I try to add value to their business ideas. I've been doing this job for a number of years and with Nat West all my working life.

I fell into banking really. After A levels I applied for several jobs and banking seemed the best. I didn't have a particular affinity or love for it to begin with but it's subsequently become a career.

I passed my banking exams pretty quickly after joining the bank and soon after that obtained a law degree at London University in my own time. Since then I've had the opportunity to work in different areas of the NatWest Group and to broaden my knowledge of the bank generally. Also, my attitude's changed over the years. I recognise the need to work harder, to be more single minded, and to have an idea of where I want to go. That single minded approach has paid off and meant I've been able to realise my aims in certain areas.

When I started there were very few black people in the bank and many who joined at that time didn't stay on. The set-up then wasn't particularly supportive, and there were barriers to progress. But I wanted to have options to different career paths. Focusing my energies in a

*'We all have
tremendous potential
that we never develop.'*

certain direction wasn't part of any dramatic change: not a road to Damascus conversion or whatever. It was just the process of aiming at a particular goal and going for it.

The older and more experienced I've become, the more important I think that is because I've seen it work; from areas like physical attitude to moving an organisation forward. The first step is always to have your aim, your goal, clearly defined in your mind. We all have tremendous potential that we never develop. But this process of goal setting and achievement is open to every single person.

At the age of about seven I went from St Lucia to Barbados, so most of my primary schooling took place there. It's a country that values education highly. The methods were old fashioned but the whole environment was supportive. At eleven I graduated to one of the colleges for a year and then came to the UK to join my parents. At first I went to a comprehensive school that closed down because of high levels of violence and poor academic results. I'd moved from a very stable society in Barbados to slums in Islington. I did O levels and A levels, and then went on to work.

*'My parents are
traditional Caribbean
parents, very keen on
academic and career
success.'*

After the school closed we moved to Hornsey. My parents are traditional Caribbean parents,very keen on academic and career success. They paid for correspondence courses for me and my dad would take me and my brothers and sisters to museums and exhibitions. They had high expectations of us. Perhaps I wasn't aware of it until afterwards. My wife has always been very supportive throughout our married life of seventeen years.

The teachers here in the UK were generally positive towards me. They wanted me to be involved in the school magazine and in the school play. I was a prefect. The only time I remember school not being supportive was when a careers teacher suggested I should be a postman. But I just laughed and thought him absurd. I had my own ideas of the sort of career I should follow. I wanted to be a scientist: it was a subject I liked and so scientists tended to be my heroes and role models.

My parents' career knowledge was extremely limited. They didn't know where the real money was made or where the real power was held. Their career advice was based on individual knowledge that was limited because their knowledge and experience of the UK was limited. I think this is a particular disadvantage to black people and it's something I'm very keen on overcoming. Through the African and Caribbean Finance Forum, black professionals working in a variety of business sectors regularly visit schools to provide pupils with a first hand account of experiences in working in corporate UK.

The majority of people don't enjoy their jobs, they tolerate them. But if you're just going to tolerate your job you might as well make some money. Black people have tended to be pushed into areas where not a lot of money can be made, so what I've been trying to do is alert young black people to the opportunities to make money in careers that are outside the traditional areas.

I'm a founding member of the African and Caribbean Finance Forum (ACFF). It was started in 1990 to help black people gain access to UK and international corporations and rise through them. We run a number of support programs, seminars and a careers fair. We also mentor in schools. I'm extremely proud of my role in developing the ACFF and raising its profile to be the foremost organisation of its kind in Europe.

'Being single-minded and determined is what you need, and the continuing process of learning.'

Success is relative. It depends on the aspirations and sights you set yourself. I think success is a road and not a destination. One of the greatest things I've learnt is that you don't need anything from outside to solve your problems. Being single minded and determined is what you need, and the continuing process of learning. Every day there's something to be learnt even from the most negative of experiences. All sorts of situations present opportunities to learn.

I've always been in banking in one area or another up to this point. I don't know which other areas I would want to go into. I originally saw where I am now as a stepping stone, not as somewhere I would end up. At one stage I saw myself as a senior manager of a large branch somewhere, but they don't exist any more.

'Success is relative... success is a road and not a destination.'

I'm becoming increasingly interested in the creation of wealth in societies; how that is done and how the position of certain societies can be moved on in terms of wealth. As black people, we are too often stereotyped as not being very rich, not very bright, not very cultured: to be tolerated,

*'I don't like being
branded in such a
negative way by virtue
of being black.'*

as though we have very little to offer. The cultural changes that we've made are accepted grudgingly. We're not seen as having anything significant to offer in terms of wealth creation.

I want to change that. I don't like being branded in such a negative way by virtue of being black. There are a lot of positive cultural images we need to build on: we are bright, interesting, dynamic and creative. We need these new images of ourselves to change the agenda.

I don't think there's a quick fix. Start with the individual; with the self belief. Then start looking at where we want to go, recognising that we can get good jobs, we can lead industry, we can lead the public sector or be senior politicians. I would like to see leaders emerging from our young people. We need visible leaders, visible academic leaders, visible political leaders.

*'We are bright,
interesting, dynamic
and creative.'*

Mainstream education needs to be culturally aware. It sees us as being a problem. Expectations are low, there is the acceptance that certain types of negative or unhelpful behaviour is okay for black people. What's needed is a complete change of attitude.

*'Young black people must believe in the fact
that they can really achieve all that they
want with determination and focus'.*

Abiola Awojobi

Abiola Awojobi is currently producer of Everywoman, *a programme on the BBC World Service.*

Date of birth: 22 March 1967
Place of birth: London, England

'Success is setting goals for yourself and trying to achieve them.'

Everywoman is an international women's magazine programme, and the sister programme to *Woman's Hour* on Radio 4, which is where I worked previously. As a producer you're responsible for putting the programme together and deciding what items are going to be on. There are just two of us on the team but we try to get a balance, with a good spread of different women's voices from around the world. The job involves researching, setting up interviews, finding the right guests, writing a script. I feel content with my career so far because I've progressed from local radio to network radio and now to international radio.

Woman's Hour was very demanding to work on because of its high profile. There were about 25 of us at the table bouncing ideas around, inspiring each other. With only two it's inevitably more limiting, but at the same time it's more of a challenge and I've had the opportunity to act up as a senior producer on several occasions.

Over the years, in my capacity as a BBC Radio producer, I've often been told that I'm seen as something of an ambassador for the black community. People sometimes think that if they've got something to promote like an event or a book, I can automatically help out and get them on the radio – because I'm a black woman in the BBC. But of course I can't always – one still has to use one's editorial judgement as to what makes a good story. But if I can't take a project on personally I at least refer them to someone else who might be interested – that way I don't feel I've let anyone down.

I try not to let myself down, by being the best that I can – whether it's in my personal or my professional life. To me success is setting goals for yourself and trying to achieve them. It's a mantra which my parents instilled in me and something which they in turn, as Nigerians, had brought with them from Nigeria. I do feel Nigerian first and foremost but I also feel British. When I married I deliberately kept my maiden name for professional use because I want people to know I'm Nigerian.

For the early part of my childhood I grew up in the countryside in Lincolnshire, an all-white community. I was fostered, like many Nigerians in the 1960s, but we had a strong sense of identity. Although we were the only black children, we always felt proud of our heritage. We saw our parents regularly and they brought African food and clothing to remind us of who we were. So we never felt torn; we never felt ashamed to be black. Obviously there were instances when people called us names. But I remember feeling very Nigerian at the same time as fitting in here in England. My foster parents, who were also my god parents, were very good too at encouraging us to feel proud of our heritage. And that was important.

'The lower the stream, the more black faces were seen there.'

I was living back in London by the time I went to secondary school. There were only two black girls in my class. The lower the stream, the more black faces there were. I do feel that if I hadn't had such a good foundation from my parents I probably wouldn't have been recommended for the top set. Once you were in a lower stream, it was very hard to get out. With the friends I'd had at primary school there was now a divide because they were in a completely different world, channeled into things like typing and home economics when we were doing Latin and French.

But I felt I had to work very hard to stay in that top stream. At the end of the first year, you could be offered the chance to do Latin depending on how well you'd done in French. My parents received a letter simply saying that I hadn't been selected. There was no dialogue. I felt like a failure and it triggered something in me. I insisted that I wanted to study Latin. It was probably pride, but also I was indignant that we didn't even have a choice. In the end I did do Latin, took the O level and passed it. I'm still proud of that little achievement.

When I was growing up there was often friction between Africans and Caribbeans, although I hope and think things have improved for today's generation. But the friction that existed in the 1970s and early 80s played a fundamental part in my experiences at school. There were lots of negative vibes between blacks, between Africans and Caribbeans. It started when we were in primary school in London. In those days it wasn't trendy to be Afro-centric. Nigerians wear very bright clothes and our neighbours would always come out and laugh at us. In those days, Africans were seen as dark-skinned 'Zulus'. And other black girls used to accuse me of thinking I was something special because of my fair skin and because I didn't fit into the pigeon hole of what they thought I should be like. In the black community there is a perception amongst some people that the lighter you are the better you are. And so it got some girls' backs up that I was lighter than them – they thought I thought I was superior and I got bullied endlessly because of this. But the irony was that I had a very little self confidence and certainly didn't think I was better than anyone. But my friend and I were picked on – it was a nightmare at the time. But these were the sort of girls who sadly weren't going very far, who the system had labelled right from day one.

'Part of the way racism works is that there always has to be an underdog.'

Now I think there's greater understanding between the two communities and more people want to define themselves as African. Part of the way racism works is that there always has to be an underdog. If you're the victim of racism, then you in turn try to push someone else down. So ironically it wasn't through white people that I experienced my most negative moments. I think society has often operated on a divide and rule mentality.

I got into the media business oddly enough because ironically I didn't do as well as I'd hoped in my A levels. So before going to university I took a year out and worked. A teacher who knew I was interested in writing saw an 'ad' for a work experience position in a local publishing company and I was taken on as a trainee reporter. I was very shy, and my experience of being bullied hadn't helped, so this really brought me out of my shell. I was going round London interviewing people like Maya Angelou! I kept that job in the holidays while I was a student at university.

'It was important for me to be myself.'

I did a BA(Hons) in African studies because I wanted to learn more about my history. I've always been interested in learning more about the past and my culture. In fact one of my favourite novels is *Kindred* a sci-fi book by African American writer Octavia E Butler. It's all about how a young black woman in modern day America keeps getting transported to the past back to slavery times and where she is always called upon to save a curly haired young white boy from grave danger. It turns out that he's her great great great grandfather and she has to save him in order to be born herself. It's compelling and really makes you think about the impact of slavery and it's a good example of a black woman writing in a genre where they don't often feature.

After my degree I did a post graduate diploma in radio journalism. I do like to keep learning. Recently I did a six month creative writing course, geared at black women, learning how to write poetry and short stories. It was fantastic: a very positive environment where we didn't feel afraid to read our work out. And it helped me tighten up my writing for the freelance articles I do for Black Beauty & Hair Magazine.

'Having a quiet confidence in yourself gives off a positive vibe to other people.'

Having a quiet confidence in yourself gives off a positive vibe to other people. My favourite quote is from a black film maker. When asked how she'd made it to the top she said, Because nobody would let me in at the bottom! Other people will be very quick to put you down, so even if deep down you're feeling anxious, just pretend and carry on. That will give you the confidence to go on to the next step, and then the next.

Jazzie B

Date of birth: 6 January 1963
Place of birth: London, UK

'We developed our ideology.'

Jazzie B is a recording artist and producer, and founder of the band Soul II Soul.

The mind is a powerful thing. I think we've used all the power of our intelligence to take us to where we are today, and there's still that whole thing about maintaining it and being shrewd.

Daddae and I started Soul II Soul when we were in secondary school. It began as a sound system and then amalgamated both sound and fashion. Growing up in the seventies there were so many fantastic things happening, and obviously young people wanted to find their own niche.

We were playing sound and everyone else was playing Shakespeare. In woodwork classes, they were building stools and benches and we were building speaker boxes and amp cases. We put all our energy into the sound system and club culture. We developed our ideology: what we were going to do and the best way to go about it. We moved from depending on our parents into full time work, took all our finance and invested in a sound. We 'traded as' for a little while, then we entered into the Manpower Services Commission. They 'aided us with money and information' and the rest, in those immortal words, is history.

From there we went on to running our own promotions, our own venues – and we made a lot of money. We then took our urban sound into the West End where we had people from all over the world come together religiously on a Sunday night for three years.

We travelled extensively as DJs in a sound system – from Japan and Australia to America. I worked for the Royal National Institute for the Blind as an engineer making talking books and then into a recording studio as a tea boy, to develop more skills and get some knowledge of the business. Daddae stayed in printing and it worked out well because whenever we had a dance, he'd print the leaflets; whenever I needed dubs cut, I'd cut the tunes in the studio.

'Success is something for individuals to find within themselves.'

We were bombarded by offers for a recording contract and finally hooked up with Mick Clarke, a fantastic gentleman and real person in the business – and there are very few of them! We went on to sell nine million records. Now we're based in the Caribbean.

Between running the sound and the warehouse bit, we actually had a market stall. We designed T-shirts with our emblem, so that in the bars everyone would recognise who Soul II Soul was. Then we started to sell them at the dance. One night we had the same vision: to locks-up our hair. That's where the 'funky dreads' came from.

When I go back home – and I do have dual nationality – I'm known as English, and when I'm here I'm known as a – you know what. Look at the graffiti outside and all the National Front stuff. You're not really wanted. But it's where I call home because I was born and bred here and these are the backstreets that I know.

I've done various TV programmes, I'm a director of the Hackney Empire, and I've also worked with Bernie Grant. I'm not a politician or anything but I think all these things are important for the preservation of the youths. Many youths are spending time in jails or various institutions because they don't have as much offered to them as we did in our day. Because if you're not academically blessed or don't have that patience, you've got to do what you've got to do.

'It's children having children these days.'

When you have your own children like I do, you then understand how important it is to preserve a little bit of certainty for them, and some sanctuary. Things are much harder than they were back then. There are many problems with single parent families and that's a big thing for me because I was fortunate to have both my parents around when I was growing up, but many of my friends didn't. It's children having children these days.

I was in Newcastle a while back doing a gig. In the hotel, a lady who was slightly the worse for wear after a few drinks tried to get into the lift. When she saw me she said, are you going in that lift? I took a look at her, swallowed, and said, No, but you are. Things happen every day and in some ways it's a good thing because it helps keep your feet on the ground. There's the whole thing about over-reacting, and that just doesn't solve anything. All I can do is feel sorry for some of these people because it's ignorance more than anything else.

'I try and bring out the best.'

I try and 'bring the best out' and show as much positivity out there as possible. Honesty is really important to us. I take each day as it comes. Like they say: Tomorrow is not promised to any of us. I'm guided by the power of the Trinity and the fear of God alone. My spirituality prevails more than my business acumen at this time in my life because that's what draws me through. The mind is a powerful thing. I think we've used all the power of our intelligence to take us to where we are today, and there's still that whole thing about maintaining it and being shrewd.

'My spirituality prevails more than my business acumen at this time in my life because that's what draws me through.'

'A fool to catch a wise one.'

What we have to be as a race of people is a little bit clever, and be 'a fool to catch a wise one', because no-one likes a real 'wise guy'. What you've got to do is hold your corner.

You've got to do what you've got to do. But maybe most of us could use a little bit more 'decorum' when it's not worked out the way we anticipated. It sometimes happens that a youth who wasn't good at the job turns the whole thing on its head and starts to call them racist, which could have been the case. But how much more powerful if he held it down and used different measures to highlight the problem. Better still to take himself to the next stage and say, If I can't count the money, maybe I'll be able to pack the shelves.

'We all get tarred with the same brush.'

Where do you want to get to in your life? If you do the right things, someone's going to recognise those skills eventually. It's all about hard work, and hard work will prevail in most situations. But burning of bridges is a bad thing because the world is so small. That's why I say we could use a little bit of decorum when things go wrong for us because there's too much of the 'cry wolf' all the time, and I think it lets us down. We all get tarred with the same brush.

I actually wanted to be a teacher when I was at school. I had great relationships with most of my teachers and I was very flamboyant. I got involved in most things – good and bad. For me it was always about reputation because of the streets where I came from.

Education is very important. None of us are born with a silver spoon in our mouth. The power of the mind is the strongest weapon available to each one of us; if you use it properly and keep your temple pure, the world is truly yours.

'Life is what you make it.'

I'm no different to anyone else; I still get the same tribulations and I'm still offended when I'm stopped periodically ... A few years ago, somebody was apparently mugged in Kentish Town and they were wearing a Soul II Soul T-shirt, so where did the police come...? These things happen every day. All I can really say is, Look around you! Just take five minutes and if you're able to free your mind and listen to your heart you will see that life is what you make it. And it IS hard. Not all of us are blessed with inner strength. But you must be able to communicate and talk with somebody.

'I know I can't change the world but the world I'm living in is important and so is my contribution to it.'

It's about hard work, even just getting up in the morning from your yard. If you look back in history you see it doesn't come to anyone who's sitting down and waiting. You've got to go and get yours. I know I can't change the world but the world I'm living in is important and so is my contribution to it.

Success is something for individuals to find within themselves. From the point of view of our culture we don't pay enough attention to our successes. Jamaica going to the World Cup was a success; Bernie Grant was a success...

I drew the dole at one point in my life because I didn't have another option; I lived in a council flat because the housing trust 'lost my papers'. So I thought: I can't go on like this – it's not what I'm all about. Let me go and do something about it.

Everything starts at home: any kind of pride you have, or any nasty habits. Being a youth has always been difficult but we have to take it on ourselves and deal with these things properly. Maybe we create many of the problems ourselves, and instead of putting them into other people's hands, we ourselves should address them.

Sonia Bassey

Date of birth: 8 July 1965
Place of birth: Liverpool

'The education of young people is the key to empowerment of your community, support the development of your children in the communtiy.'

Sonia Bassey is co-ordinator of the Diverse Heritage Project in Liverpool, which records and celebrates the different cultures of the Liverpudlian community. Her role is to manage the project and its staff, secure funds and develop business and marketing strategies and develop educational resources for black and disadvantaged groups and individuals.

When I left school I did art at college and then I went to work in a bank, but I left because I didn't like it. So I became a freelance artist in the community. I joined a training course and through that I developed freelance skills and started doing logos, letterheads, posters, and leaflets for local community organisations. I specialised in positive imagery of black people because at that time there weren't any. I then took a job on a European project as information and publicity officer.

I was born in Liverpool and brought up here. I went to an all girls school in a predominantly white area. I felt out of place and when I first joined I was put in the lower class, which made me feel uncomfortable from the very beginning. I worked my way up to the top class but I felt they didn't expect anything of me. They assessed what they thought you were capable of and never pushed for a little bit more. Teachers who liked your work seemed to make an example of you, but

I didn't like that either because it set you out from the rest of the class.

I've had lots of support from my family. We were a single parent family but my dad was always around. They actually encouraged me to do my work. My dad's dad came to Britain from Africa, he was a seaman. My mum wanted her kids to achieve so she's the one who drove us. They never had any careers.

The most significant individuals for me have to be: Erika Rushton, Ibrahim Thompson, and Maria O'Reilly. Erika was my course tutor who gave me confidence in my ability, Ibrahim opened my eyes to adapting my skills for freelance work and Maria has been a constant advisor/supporter in times of need.

'They were all jobs that you never see any black role models in.'

There was careers advice at school, but they were all jobs that you never see any black role models in: the civil service, the army. When I got the job in the bank it was male dominated and you couldn't progress if you were a woman. Gender was more of an issue then race in that type of environment. I'm not dark skinned so my experience of racism is to be sitting in people's company and hearing them tell racist jokes without realising I'm black. So you have to challenge that and deal with it. I've also experienced racism through my kids who are darker than me.

Significant turning points were, writing a report for an O level English exam on the Toxteth Riots 1981, which inspired me to become active in my community. My job as an Information and publicity officer was a job I never thought I would leave but funding ran out. I loved it, but it was a turning point in my life because I then went into the field of management which I also love.

I've been able to develop my skills and bring them back to the community, to establish myself here as a community worker. A lot of people find it difficult to get jobs. Our "Journey of Discovery Project" gives people a level of skill to enable them to go on to college or university. We also make them aware of the barriers they might face when they get there. So giving them the option of becoming a freelancer allows them to control their own workload, it gives them the ability to make choices of their own. This course is a very new approach to community empowerment.

We teach report writing, letter writing, administration – so they can actually form partnerships with people. They can decide to be a freelance administrator and do administration for all the artists or people in the community who have not got access to computers.

'You can't empower your community, if you don't pass on that information.'

I don't understand people who learn and want to keep it to themselves. I find it difficult to come to terms with the people not wanting to pass out information and support each other. I'm all about passing on what I know and helping people to achieve. You can't empower your community if you don't pass on that information.

I'm not money orientated, although I have made sure I've secured myself financially. Because I've got kids and I have to provide for them, that's something I've got to do to survive. When I was expecting twins I had no job to go back to, and I thought what am I going to do now? I didn't want to live on benefits and bring my kids up like that. So I went and did a job I didn't really want to do. Because I had kids to keep I did it, and while I was there I was able to progress, because there were loads of opportunities for me to progress, through my own initiative. When I've heard people use words I don't understand, I've asked them to explain. That way you learn something instead of it going over your head.

'You can't rely on anybody but yourself.'

You can't rely on anybody but yourself, to get where you want to be. There are people in this world who want to help people and there are other who just want to help themselves. But in order for me to help other people I have to help myself first. You've got to be able to equip yourself to do that.

You can never stop learning, you'll learn till you die. I mean everything evolves doesn't it? Ways of working evolve also, such as the internet.

'You can never stop learning.'

Black kids don't get history lessons about their own cultures. History in school is about World War II, Medieval times, but they don't show you what part black people played in that history. I don't think young black people get realistic career choices, they don't get taught how to survive. You can't get benefits until you are eighteen so you have got to go on to further education. We've still got stereotypes like when black people wave their arms they are being aggressive or threatening.

'Success is being in a position where I can actually gain more skills and bring them back and use them in the community.'

If you don't make mistakes, you won't learn from them will you? You regret some things but if they didn't happen you'd never make sure they didn't happen again. There are ways around everything. There are times when you do have to give a little bit to get what you want, your minor compromise doesn't matter. There has got to be a bit of give and take, you can't get everything you want.

Patrick Berry

Date of Birth: 15 May 1952
Place of birth: Port Antonio,
Jamaica

'One's ambitions are never quite clear.'

'I think of myself as British.'

Patrick Berry is group managing director of Choice FM radio station and former director of Roots *magazine.*

'There is no easy route to success'.

I have the day-to-day responsibility for the London operation of Choice FM, overseeing all the workings of the company and making sure that the policies are carried out.

I think the whole thing started from leaving college in the 70s and not being able to find a job. In those days it was even more difficult to find a job than it is now if you were black, even with academic qualifications. It was that frustration that led me to do something for myself. So in 1979 I got involved with some other guys and started the *Roots* magazine. That's where I started to learn business and that developed into applying for the radio license and finally to getting this job.

One's ambitions are never quite clear. It is all part of a dream, and they always say that a person's business is never bigger than their dream. But I don't think so far in England we have achieved a solid black company that is a British institution. That is something I would love to create.

I was born in Jamaica and came to England when I was five, so this is where I have spent most of my life and I do think of myself as British.

There were aspects of school that I enjoyed just like anybody else. My parents always had high expectations: that was the whole point of bringing me from Jamaica to here. When I left school I went to work for an organisation called Minority Art, a voluntary group that was giving advice to ethnic minority arts groups on how to get funded. I was involved in reviewing their events in a monthly newsletter and it was that newsletter that gave me the idea of doing a black magazine. From there I linked up with my current business partner and started the magazine. I was lucky to come across something which I found I liked doing. Then I was lucky enough to link up with the right people who could give me that opportunity. But I'd drifted through many jobs until that time – even university hadn't provided me with the direction I had hoped for.

'If you have a passion for something, try to make it work for you.'

I wanted to be my own boss. I wanted to be master of my own time. I think that had always been an issue for me and why I found some things difficult. When you find something that you really enjoy doing you may be making sacrifices along the way but it doesn't feel like a sacrifice because you are so involved in what you want to do.

We are often compared with the Asian community, and I think this is unhelpful. Many of the Asians that came to Britain were already in business and had capital, so it was natural for them to remain in business when they settled in the United Kingdom. In contrast many of our parents came from a rural background that had kept them largely unskilled. Consequently we could not expect them to leap into business.

When we started the magazine we had a grand plan that if it was successful we would do radio and television and film. There was room for an expansion and the opportunity first came in the early 80s when three hundred community licenses were issued. We had made an unsuccessful application and so in preparation for our next bid we got together with some people who were really experienced in commercial radio. Then in '89, when the opportunity came to try again for a license, we finally managed to get it.

'I never expect to stop learning.'

As you progress you become bolder and better prepared to accept and deal with problems.

You find that people put some of their problems onto you and expect certain things of you. You have to adapt as you go along, and I never expect to stop learning.

'Education is like weight training.'

There is no easy solution for young people. Education is important. The best gift you can have are basic academic skills. It is like weight training: if you want your body to be a certain shape, you lift weights and you become strong. Education does this for the mind, and with a strong mind you will have a better chance of dealing with the difficulties you meet along the way. You need dedication and passion, but you also need luck and prayers.

If you find something that you are passionate about, then go for it. Try to make it work for you. Looking back, I would like to have taken my college experience more seriously and worked harder at my academic studies.

You have got to make the most of every opportunity.

Maurice Bessman

Maurice Bessman is a full time writer of radio, stage and television plays. He writes for Channel 4's Brookside, *BBC's* Holby City *and is a board member of Liverpool's Everyman Youth Theatre.*

Date of birth: 29 June 1953
Place of birth: Liverpool, UK

'It's about having sheer guts and determination.'

I spent the first few years of my life in Toxteth and then my family moved to Kirkby, a white working class area which was basically just one big estate. We were four black kids in a population of forty or fifty thousand. I remember at the age of six walking to the shops and a girl stopped me and said she was going to throw me in a thorn bush. I'd never even seen one before. I became terrified of going to school with all those white faces. You don't even perceive you're different at the age of six. I had a white brother so there was no problem. That incident made it quite clear I was different and some people didn't like it.

Later I went to one of the first comprehensive schools in the country. It was in Harold Wilson's constituency so there was a lot of pressure for us to succeed. I didn't have very many rewarding experiences with teachers. Maybe because the school was too big. There were one thousand two hundred lads and that's a raging vat of testosterone with all sorts of stuff going on. Some kids there hadn't seen a black person before so I stuck out like a sore thumb, and there was racist abuse. When Alf Garnett came on the telly the racist chants changed overnight from 'nigger' to 'silly coon'. School did however, get me my first writing commissions at the age of eleven when I used to get paid for writing sick notes to get kids off games.

When I left school I had no idea what I wanted to do, and I ended up working for a couple of years in advertising because I'd overheard someone else saying it was what he wanted to do. I started as an office lad and it was the best thing that could have happened to me, working with a bunch of anarchists. My view at the time was that adults tell you what to do. Now all of a sudden they were asking me questions and actually listening to what I said.

While I was with the advertising agency I trained as a photographer, then at eighteen I went into the RAF thinking I'd be able to carry on with photography, but it didn't happen. I wasn't cut out for the force at all, because there was always somebody telling me what to do. But I'd signed up for the minimum of three and a half years, so I did what I had to. I did athletics, played rugby, played footie. It's okay if you're good at sport because they'll train you to represent them, and that's what I did.

'I'd learnt very quickly how to either disarm a situation or withdraw.'

It has become a bit of a cliche, but if you're quick with words and you're funny, it disarms people and they don't know what they're dealing with. I did have fights while I was in there, but they were nothing to do with race. I was a bit of a smartarse, and being class clown people forget that, you know, 'he's a nigger'. I'd learnt very quickly how to either disarm a situation or withdraw. Sometimes you have to, and I think it's a question of personal safety, avoiding situations that are unpleasant or violent. I was a top recruit on the fast track, and they wanted to promote me. It might have made a difference that I wasn't jet black. You know, the thing about if you're black stand back; if you're brown stick around; if you're white, alright.

'I knew that what I wanted to do was write but I knew nothing about it.'

What I wanted at that time was a job where I wouldn't be made redundant and where I'd get decent promotion, so I chose nursing. The day I walked onto a ward I knew it was right for me. I felt absolutely comfortable there. Maybe it's about being able to communicate and have a laugh with people at their lowest moments. I could do it well and I enjoyed it from day one. When I worked in the hospital in Walton, I was a charge nurse on an intensive care unit. I'd go in, in the morning and have people let the door go in my face. Then they'd go into the unit and I'd be standing there with my uniform on. It was their loved ones life in my hands, and their attitude completely changed. But it only changed because they knew who I was. In the end I progressed on to teaching student nurses. That was

*'Don't limit yourself,
because the moment
you think you're
limited, then you've
accepted the
stereotype.'*

great for a while but I couldn't face having every day
mapped out for me. I knew that what I wanted to do
was write but I knew nothing about it. But I started
scribbling words, went to a writers' workshop and
began to read about writing drama. My head was
exploding with ideas.

I learnt early on as a newcomer to the writing
business that if you want to write you have to
read. Richard Wright, James Baldwin, Maya
Angelou, Arthur Miller; all these and many more
writers inspired me. I would read anything, I still
do. I'm a sucker for knowledge, and a nosey one at
that. Novels, newspapers, magazines, even notice
boards... anything that might give me a bit more
information or an idea that I could incorporate
into a story. I got my first break in writing drama
for local radio and used those scripts to help get
me into *Brookside*.

On *Brookside* I attend the storylines meeting each
month. For two days all the writers, the producer
and the script editor sit round and argue about
where the programme should be going. They do
twelve episodes at a time, then commission the
writers for each episode. As a writer, you really want
to see your work up on screen. You've got to have a
belief, almost an arrogance, that the world deserves
to hear what you have to say.

*'When in doubt write
the truth.'*

I don't ever see any limits. I just keep saying,
What next? Measures of success are intangible for
me so I keep wanting to do something else. But I
have to be careful I don't end up writing too much
and never seeing my family. With my other writing
there's a bit more headspace, and that's what I
like: to be able to think around the ideas and let
the characters grow in my head.

The thing about television is, it's so slow!
Something I might be writing now for TV won't
make it to the screen for two years at least. Some
years back, when I was putting a lot of effort into
getting something on telly with no joy, I thought
I'd write for theatre. I did something with a strong
narrative, you know – beginning, middle, end – for
four black actors. Out of that came Liverpool's
first black theatre company. There had never been
one in the city in all the time that black people
have been in Liverpool.

Theatre doesn't pay well at all. It takes up a lot
of time but it's a commitment I've made to black
theatre in Liverpool. The Everyman Theatre gave us

a chance, which was great, but there was a lot of pressure on us. If a black company does a play and it's no good when the next one comes along they'll say, "We've given this a go once and it didn't work". That would never happen to a white theatre company.

So I have my theatre work, and I do radio as well. I had a play on Radio 4, partly about Black experience in Liverpool going back to 1917. My main line of work is now *Brookside* and I've been there for about ten years. I'm also writing a screenplay for a feature film about the first black football player, who played for Spurs in 1908.

'You've got to study because there's always something new to be learnt.'

As a writer, I don't like anyone telling me to change things, but I do realise that another mind on the job might just help. After all, once you've written the first draft it then becomes a collaborative process. In order to stay 'fresh' one of my strategies is to keep studying. Sometimes when I read a play my jaw drops open in wonderment, and then it starts clenching out of envy, because I think, I'd love to write like that. So I try. But you've got to study because there's always something new to be learnt. You also have to learn from the people on their way up; the new icons are behind us.

If you're writing drama, I think you have a responsibility to examine conflict. Politics drives me. It teaches me all sorts about standing back in a situation and looking at it. I enjoy being able to put my own structure on something, whereas inside the big bureaucracies – the forces or nursing or teaching – the hierarchy is imposed. Writing then gives me a sense of control and freedom.

'A change is going to come.'

Despite gaining a personal sense of freedom and control in my writing I am very aware of the wider picture for black people. About twelve percent of Liverpool's population is black, but you won't see that represented in employment in the city. And you won't see Britain's black population represented in proportion on the television screens either. But the advertisers are now streets ahead of the drama producers because they are aware that there is a black pound. So you now see black faces in adverts and they're not just singing and dancing! "A change is gonna come", as Sam Cooke wrote, and as a writer who is black, I realise I'm playing the long game. While I'm waiting for a good result, I'll keep writing, studying and perfecting my skills in the hope that my success can help pave the way for the black writers of the future.

Syan Blake

Date of birth: 14 September 1972
Place of birth: London, UK

'Grab life and live it to the utmost.'

Syan Blake is a professional actor, best known for her role as Frankie in Eastenders.

Before *Eastenders*, I played some small roles on TV, including *Casualty* and *Frontiers*. I then had thirteen months of unemployment when morale was very low and I wondered if I'd made the right career choice. Then I landed the role of Frankie. Since leaving, I've done more theatre, a film in Amsterdam, and other TV and radio work.

At the moment I'm doing a weekly book review for a radio station, discussing black literature, both published and unpublished. That's something that I got together myself. In terms of regular work, I do whatever comes along that's appealing to me, not just for my career but for myself as a person, so that I'm doing things that will stretch me. I had a small role in a play at the Edinburgh Festival because I wanted to experience something different and be part of a huge international festival.

I always want more and I'm striving for better in everything. I'm moving in the right direction. Because I'm a recognisable person I feel a certain responsibility in the way I conduct myself and the choices I make. I want to give out a good and positive message. It's strange that you can do just one thing and because it's such a high profile television job, people think you're much more than you are. I'm honoured, but it's also a little sad because I haven't really done anything yet.

'I always want more and I'm striving for better in everything.'

'Because I'm a recognisable person I feel a certain responsibility in the way I conduct myself and the choices I make.'

'You need to take control.'

'At least I knew I'd tried.'

I've always been very single minded and my career has always come first. From as young as twelve or thirteen I sacrificed things to achieve my goal. In acting you have to be extremely disciplined because you are self employed, and every single day you have to live in a positive way so that when work does come along you're fresh and ready for it. You have to be physically well and mentally active.

I'm trying to get work off my own back, not necessarily relying on my agent. I wanted to get in on radio but doors were closing all around me, so I decided to put something together myself. It's obviously helped, having the profile I've had, and my aim now is to try and take some control of my career.

I had quite a hard time in my early teens at school. I was singled out and bullied, not physically but verbally, which I found very hard. I wanted to leave but my drama teacher persuaded me to stick it out. I did, and then went on to drama school. It wasn't until I'd finished drama school and started working that my family thought it had been a positive choice of career. They were concerned that I wouldn't have an academic qualification and knew the profession I was going into was very insecure. I was concerned about that as well but I felt that even if I came out of drama school and never worked, at least I knew I'd tried.

When I was at primary school I wanted to be a director so I used to put on adaptations in the school assembly. I had a brilliant head teacher who allowed me to do this whenever I wished. By the age of 16 I had decided I wanted it to become a full time profession and I was gearing myself up to subjects in the arts. Although they were dubious about a career in the arts my parents have always told my siblings and me "that whatever we wanted to do was up to us as long as we were happy". My family was very supportive of my amateur dramatics and took me to classes all over London. My sister, brother and I were given the freedom to make our own choices but our parents were always there to catch us when we fell.

Although I come from East London I don't have a strong accent so people tend to assume I am middle class and went to public school. They

'Never give up, follow your dreams.'

don't believe that I grew up in east London on an estate. I suppose my voice has opened doors for me. Often when I speak to people on the phone they don't realise I'm black and when they meet me they're surprised!

I lost a lot of self confidence as a teenager. I found A levels difficult and, although I obtained two Bs and a C, I didn't do as well as I hoped. The same thing happened when I started drama school. Being away from home in a highly disciplined environment and surrounded by some extraordinary people, was difficult. I took a lot of knocks in terms of confidence. Suddenly I was in a melting pot of people who had excelled, and that gives you a good kick up the behind!

A sense of community is important to me. I grew up in the East End and I do want to remain part of the area. I think it is a bit easier, just a little, than it was when I was at school. At that time there were very few role models and I didn't find anyone that I could identify with. Now, even in advertising, there are different hues where there only used to be one.

'There is a lot of our heritage that has been lost.'

I am only discovering now about black history – in my generation at school we had never heard of Mary Seacole. I have been deprived of so much knowledge. Unless you actively seek it out it's not going to be handed to you. There is a lot of our heritage that has been lost, it needs to be laid open for young people today so they can decide what they want to know and not be seen as radical in order to find out about their past.

There is a spiritual side to everybody: collective unconsciousness is a phenomenon that everyone should be made aware of in order to tap into and explore the spiritual side of their ancestry.

'There is a spiritual side to everyone.'

I couldn't name one book that was definitive in influencing me, for the simple reason that every book I enjoy leaves a lasting impression.

Finally: my definition of success is a life in which you regret nothing....

Kwasi A Boateng

Date of birth: 24 December 1961
Place of birth: Akimoda, Ghana

'As an architect you have to be both a businessman and a good designer.'

Architect and development consultant. He co-runs a private architectural practice and delivers programmes in mentoring within civil society to enable groups and individuals reach their full potential.

The profession of architecture does not expect black professionals to excel because it derives from a middle class structure based on patronage. Black people find themselves being boxed into more technical backroom activities. You are not perceived as someone who should be engaged in initiating. The role that I've been developing with my partner, Chris, is to make sure there is a path behind us for people to come through and to broaden opportunities for black architects. We both realised that to practise as an architect you have to be both a businessman and a good designer.

The expectation here is that you will return to your place of origin to practise. It's not even considered that you might stick your neck out and practise in this country. Institutions in the United Kingdom are responding to the needs of groups and professionals like me because we add value to this society. The basic skills that they acquire are relevant to every form of practice but they must be able to adapt it to any working environment.

My first four years of my architectural career were in the Civil Service. I was plastered

'It's knowing how and when to positively use race to your advantage.'

everywhere, in every brochure and on every poster. You can trade on it in terms of being asked to give talks and present a black perspective. It's knowing how and when to positively use race to your advantage. Sometimes you find that you're hitting a particular nerve and policy makers in this society find it frightening to be letting us in on their game. Policy makers wonder if we'll turn out to be really British, or sell out and go native. I don't think we have the luxury of just being who we are. Yet we did have an exhibition at the Royal Institute of British Architects (RIBA) so our Institute recognises our excellence.

I was educated in Ghana but came to Britain to go to university. My secondary school wasn't any different from that of most Ghanaians, but it was exceptional in that it bred a sense of belonging to a wider group. The school I went to prided itself on not just turning out students who were good academically, but rounded people who had a perception beyond the academic. So I slotted into British culture easily in academic terms. I went to the South Bank University at Stockwell, on the edge of Brixton. It was the first time I'd been in an urban environment and in fact the challenges were more social than academic. We black Africans learned to support each other at that time, but very informally. My architectural education was only made possible through the buttress of mentoring.

'Others would not be asked to justify themselves but we have to be prepared.'

Today we still keep in touch with one of our mentors. He introduced us to the practice of keeping design diaries, so that if we were ever questioned about the origins of our designs, we had the evidence to hand. We were constantly being told that Africans cannot think in 3D, so the design diary was our back-up. You've got to build a case. Others would not be asked to justify themselves but we had to be prepared.

I think it's true to say that we come from a background that is emotionally giving. You would open your heart and tell someone your concerns which that person would later use as a weapon to taunt you. After a while you begin to harden up: become a tortoise in a shell. I remember having to do group submissions and my group just disappearing. I would have to go and find them, and when the presentation was being done, even the body language showed their negative attitude.

Certainly in many ways being educated in Ghana gave me an advantage in the British class system, because no-one could place me in terms of my accent. When it came to technical information like putting together a submission that's where I sometimes faltered because too often I let my emotion carry me. But I learned how to control it. By the time I finished my first degree I knew when and how to keep cool.

'I'm interested in bullfighting.'

I'm interested in bullfighting. I think it holds an important lesson that people of black cultures must learn when we enter this society. Wherever the matador places his red cloak, that's where the bull thinks he has to go. The cloak is enticing him. The lesson for us is to be aware of where the 'cloaks' are being placed, so that whatever happens we face it with dignity. Maybe we encounter something that we cannot turn to our personal advantage at present; but we can make sure that no-one else will have to face it again in the future.

Sometimes, just to turn difficulties into a black issue is an ignorant approach, because often it goes beyond that. When a group carves out a niche for itself it sets its rules, and those who don't comply are out. We have to be aware of this. You find that if you are to enjoy the society, it doesn't help to be in a state of conflict all the time. It takes too much energy. It's like the bull again. The only time you ever see who is behind the cloak is when you are about to die. I intend to thrive and prosper.

'Being black is not just about colour.'

Being black is not just about colour. As Frantz Fanon wrote, it's about the way you think and perceive the rest of the world. I define myself as a pan-Africanist because it helps me to build bridges with people from the Caribbean, people from North America, people from the Pacific. But I don't lay my attitudes on my children. The worst thing you can do is to expose people to disappointment too early in their lives. There are times when perhaps it's more appropriate to look around you than to battle to get through this wall. Look around a bit; take hints from other people.

'Success is self discovery.'

I think success is self discovery. I now know exactly where I am in this society. I also know where I want to be, and to a certain extent how to get there. Britain is still a very tolerant society, and it's safer than most other places I've been to. I do have a feeling of being British. This country offers unique opportunities. People get through in Britain. Sure, they don't always get through very quickly, but they do get through.

Rt Hon Paul Boateng MP

Date of Birth: 14 June 1951
Place of Birth: London

'Politics enables one to make a difference to peoples' lives.'

Paul Boateng is a lawyer and a politician. He has been Member of Parliament for Brent South since 1987, is Deputy Home Secretary and a Privy Counsellor.

'Everyone has something to offer in terms of their own skills, in terms of their own talents and I think that you have a responsibility to make the most of it'.

My ministerial responsibilities are as number two to Jack Straw in the Home Office. I have specific responsibility for the prisons, probation and the voluntary sector. I have also been appointed Minister for Young People with responsibility across Government for the Children's Unit and Fund. At the same time I represent a multi racial constituency in north west London. This means that on a day to day basis I am involved in addressing the problems and concerns that affect the lives of around seventy thousand people.

I enjoy it enormously. It's challenging and interesting work. Politics enables one to make a difference to peoples' lives, and to that of the country as well. I see politics not as a profession but as a vocation, a calling. My profession, my career, is as a lawyer. First as a solicitor, then as a barrister. That's what I am: a lawyer, and a politician. There are of course some frustrations about the job, but they centre around time: the pressures of managing time so that you have

'I am: a lawyer, and a politician.'

'I see life as a series of opportunities, and you make the most of them.'

enough for the constituency, the Department and also so that you can have enough time for the family and for your wider interests.

I see life as a series of opportunities, and you make the most of them. You give of yourself, and you give of what skills and talents you have. Everyone has something to offer in terms of their own skills, in terms of their own talents and I think that you have a responsibility to make the most of it. That's certainly how I was brought up. In my family, it was expected that you use what you've got in order to make a contribution. With those abilities and the life chances and experiences that they bring, comes a responsibility to make a contribution.

My education began in West Africa, in Ghana, where my father is from and where I was brought up as a child and a young man. In Ghana, my father was a lawyer and Cabinet Minister. The significant turning point in my life was when my father was imprisoned without trial and my mother, sister and I were forced to leave Ghana and come to the UK. In Britain we were refugees, in very reduced circumstances. But school was remarkably similar in terms of what we were taught and the quality of the teaching both in Ghana and in Hemel Hempstead. I loved school. I worked hard, and I had a good time too.

I grew up in Britain in the late 60s and early 70s. It was a very exciting time politically. There was a sense of can do. The 60s seemed, at the time, to be breaking many of the established patterns in Britain and in the wider world. There was a struggle against racism and for peace. The political debate was alive and one lived on the cutting edge of that. It was a time of great cultural change.

'There are certain factors that contribute to where you are now in terms of direction and motivation.'

I didn't have a gap year. I didn't feel as a young black guy I could afford a year off. I didn't feel that I had that luxury, freedom or that choice. It wasn't an option. There are certain factors that contribute to where you are now in terms of your direction and motivation. The overriding factor for me has always been to do the best with the talents and opportunities one has. You had to get on with life. Getting a good degree, planning your career was simply part of that. I was fortunate to obtain articles and therefore a training opportunity with a remarkable lawyer called Benedict Birnberg.

'You had to get on with life.'

I became a lawyer because I saw the law as a useful tool to bring about the sort of changes that I felt are necessary in this world, in terms of its injustices and in terms of the prejudice and bigotry that confines and restricts the life chances of so many people. There came a time, in about 1980, when I was legal advisor to a number of grassroots campaigns, and I felt sick and tired of banging on doors, lobbying and making representations to local councillors and MPs. It's at that stage that I decided I wanted to be an elected representative. I had been a member of the Labour Party since I was fifteen but had not until then sought elected office. So I got selected, got elected, first for the GLC and then for Parliament and that's how I came to be doing what I'm doing.

'I don't accept that the qualities of hard work, excellence, and striving after achievements are confined to any one class.'

My family has had a big influence on my life. My maternal grandfather was a printer from Hoxton in East London. He left school at fourteen and yet he was the best read most literate man I've ever known. My paternal grandfather was a cocoa farmer, a man who got his hands dirty every day of the year on a farm in the Ashanti region of Ghana. But he had the foresight and knew the value and power of education. He made every effort to educate his son. This was done by hard work, by men who lived with their hands. I don't accept that the qualities of hard work, excellence, and striving after achievement are confined to any one class.

My mother loved, supported and encouraged me. My father's achievements never caused me to doubt that there was anything to which one could not turn one's hand. Paul Robeson is also a man I admire enormously. He sought to transcend stereotypes and he was destroyed for it. If you ask me for two, the most significant pieces of literature for me are the Bible: a source of God's love and purpose and as a novel, Howard's End, whose message is of the importance of human relationships, summed up in the phrase "only connect".

'Every black youngster has to realise that he or she will have to work much harder than their white counterparts.'

In Africa I was very conscious of being a youngster in a young nation. I was not particularly conscious of race which was not really an issue. In this country it was a different kettle of fish. Every black youngster has to realise that he or she will have to work much harder than their white counterparts, and that racism and discrimination will be an aspect of life which they will have to overcome. This is certainly what I teach my children.

'Racism is an interesting thing.'

Racism is an interesting thing. One of the ways that it has manifested itself is in a concerted effort over the years by racists to break black men. It is not for nothing that lynchings and racial attacks tend to be focused on us. That is not to say that racism has not impacted upon black women. Black women have experienced it in different ways: bent not broken by it. It's interesting to see how still, when a black man enters a lift, some white people will still clasp their handbags that little bit tighter, stiffen up and display a tension not otherwise present. There may come a time when they stop doing that, but it still happens. This is a stereotype, amongst others, that black men have to live with every day of their lives. Too many black boys experience a similar stereotyping in the classroom. Sad but true.

'If you're black and you're in Britain you have to work hard, because you are constantly asked to prove yourself.'

Racism and discrimination are unfortunately facts of life. My aim, my desire is to make a contribution that will make it easier for those who come after us. But lets also be quite clear: if you're black and you're in Britain you have to work hard, because you are constantly asked to prove yourself. That is the reality and I think to pretend otherwise doesn't do anybody any favours. That's not to say things aren't getting better. They are, but there is no room for complacency. Things are not as bad as when I was a young man, but it's still going to be tough and you have to prepare yourself for that. But, one mustn't give in. You must want to make the most of yourself. We have a responsibility to do that.

'But, one mustn't give in.'

What we can do is to go on living, go on working, so that blackness becomes something that is not a feature always to be remarked upon. We must not allow ourselves to be imprisoned in what the Barbadian author George Lamming called 'the castle of our skin'.

Young black men have an enormous influence on the youth scene. There is something dynamic and exciting about the impact of black youth on contemporary culture. It's bizarre and ironic that whilst to some to be black, male and young is threatening many in the wider white society find

'We must not allow ourselves to be imprisoned in what the Barbadian author George Lamming called 'the castle of our skin.'

in it something to emulate. Ali G of course satirises this.

I feel very much part of the black experience in Britain, but I am not to be defined by that experience. No one should be. We all have our own different experience and we all bring our own talents, skills and aspirations to the table.

Success is for me, living a full life in the knowledge that you've done your best and made the most of what you possess. Success is not to be confused with status.

Yvonne Brewster

Date of birth: 7 October 1938
Place of birth: Kingston, Jamaica

'The younger generation are essentially Black British.'

Yvonne Brewster OBE is the Artistic Director of Talawa Theatre Company, responsible for the overall artistic decisions, planning and direction of the company.

Talawa is 15 years old now. It began in those glorious days of the GLC (Greater London Council). I wanted to do something that I'd not seen in this country before; a large black production, properly funded, with top actors and doing something artistically important, but also sociologically and historically important, for the black community.

My job as Artistic Director is to look down the line, not to navel search. I've been quite careful in developing an artistic policy for the company. Some of the offshoots that have developed are the Women Writers Project, the summer school and our schools' workshops. They're a vital part of the work that we do and so they're attached to every production. Audience development is extremely important because if you don't engage younger people you are dead in the water. We're doing something that has come out of the process of living in Britain and we must make sure that it speaks to the younger generation of people who are essentially Black British.

I was the first black woman drama student in this country. I arrived on the Queen Mary with a chaperone. We arrived in Sidcup, she settled me in digs and said, "Farewell my dear, I hope you have a good time"! Then off she went. So there I was, in a ghastly little room with a one bar fire.

I went to the Rose Bruford Drama College in Kent. I was only 17: a terrified young woman. On the first day Miss Bruford said to me, "We'll take your money, but we must tell you, you'll never work". Well, I saw the writing on the wall, especially when they wouldn't let me do verse speaking in my own accent. I had to put on an extraordinary English accent. So, I went along to classes at the Royal Academy of Music and at RADA: I was doing three things at the same time.

'I don't give up that easily.'

I've always been a fighter and I've always remembered that I can do it. In England there was too much prejudice, as in pre-judgement, of what you should be trying to do, but I don't give up very easily. I felt that I was not going to give up, I didn't care what those English people thought because there were other places in the world that would allow me to work, like Russia.

'I refuse to be comfortable.'

I come from a very comfortable background. My mother's still alive and still working. Every day she gets up people's noses; she's my role model! We come from quite a distinguished Jamaican family. I'm not pretending that I came over on a banana boat, and I've ever been poor. Maybe I've just taken a lot of things for granted. I was privileged growing up and I think I'm privileged now. There is a black middle class and they don't bother to signal it because they don't need to. They go happily along, they permeate every area of English society. They crop up in the most unlikely places. But English people see black people as all the same. I always get treated like a bus driver, and there is a lack of recognition of what we could give to the society. That's England's loss, not ours.

'There is a lack of recognition of what we could give society.'

I sat on the London Arts Board for years. I was the only black person, and they kept renewing me so I had to be careful not to see myself as a token. When that happens, it's time to give up. You don't invade a society: you should persuade, not invade. My persuasive tactics are a bit invasive, I know! But I see them as persuasive.

'I do not like feeling sorry for myself.'

As a black woman in the arts, I had to strategise. I do not like feeling sorry for myself. So when Rose Bruford told me I would never work I thought, just watch me. I was the first student in my year to get my equity card. But then, when they were doing the casting it was, Oh there's nothing for you; you'll have to play the troll. Well, it's no good getting angry but actually I will not play the troll. So I convinced them to let me be the narrator! You have got to apply some intelligence to it and that's been the same all my life. If you haven't worked out what you want, don't blame anyone if you don't get it.

When I first arrived here, people used to either move from me on the bus or come and touch me. They did not expect intelligence from such as I. Okay, I'm not a Rhodes scholar, but I have native intelligence. I don't know where it reaches on the Richter scale, but it's not right at the bottom. And I'm not going to be a victim of lack of thought or planning either, so I plan.

I think that one has to give the next generation a leg up, but they need to look after themselves as well. I don't like the problem – and I know this is newspeak – but treat it as a challenge, not a problem. I think young black people should decide where their greatest influences stem from, whether food, dress, music or leisure and go with it. Don't make excuses, go with it. Then you'll know the ground on which you yourself stand. For some that will be African or Caribbean, for others it will be English.

There will always be people calling you this or that; and that's their problem. The essential factor is to be able to say, I cocked up this one, or I'm not very good at that, but without any false humility. If you can decide for yourself where your headscape is – and nobody else can decide it for you – then they'll never drive you mad!

Boundaries are there to be broken.

'If you haven't worked out what you want, don't blame anyone if you don't get it.'

'I'm not going to be a victim of a lack of thought or planning either, so I plan.'

Pogus Caesar

Director of Windrush Productions a company involved in TV and Radio production, art and design and media modules for schools and colleges.

Date of birth: 8 February 1953

Place of birth: St Kitts, West Indies

'I took a chance.'

We produced *Xpress* (1995-6) a multi cultural entertainment series (Certificate of Honour *Prix Circom Regional*), I also produced and directed *Respect* (1996) series on black sports people. *I'm Black in Britain* (1994) personal view on racism in Britain. *Drumbeat* (1999) entertainment series..all produced for Carlton/Central Television. Senior Producer/Director *The A Force* (1996) entertainment series. Throughout the years I have had the opportunity to work with people such as Lennox Lewis, Stevie Wonder, Jada Pinkett, Issac Hayes, John Singleton, Cathy Tyson, Paul McCartney, Dr Robert Winston, John Barnes, Denise Lewis, Henry Cooper, Prince, Rev Al Sharpton and Craig Charles.

During the late 70s I started painting. I became interested in Pointillist art, and started to produce pictures made entirely out of dots. The next seven to eight years saw me approach numerous art centres, colleges, schools, borstals and art galleries. In 1982 I went to New York armed with an instamatic camera. On my return to England I exhibited *Instamatic Views Of New York*, a gritty insight of Big Apple street life..exhibition venues include the Museum of Moving Image, Bradford and E.M Flint Gallery, Walsall, 1885. The pointillist paintings were also in one man and group exhibitions including Mappin Art Gallery, Sheffield and Ikon Gallery, Birmingham. Other exhibitions that were well received were *The Famous, The Infamous & The Not Yet* portraits exhibited at Wolverhampton Art Gallery 1987.

Caribbean Expressions In Britain group show at Leicester Museum and Art Gallery and *Into The Open* at Castle Museum, Nottingham 1984. Other exhibitions include *Songs Of Light & Other Secrets*, photomontages exhibited at The Symphony Hall Birmingham 1998. The year 2000 has seen the most recent exhibition *Downbeat,* a photographic homage to the singers and producers in reggae music. I would also like to give credit to Birmingham artists Keith Piper, Claudette Holmes, Donald Rodney, Sonia Boyce, Vanley Burke and Maxine Walker.

My art has been collected by numerous individuals and institutions throughout the world. During the 80s I was offered studio space at The Cultural Centre, Handsworth, Birmingham; Bob Ramdhanie an arts activist and probation officer openly encouraged the local community to use the arts/music facilities. The late Princess of Wales visited my studio where I was asked to present her with a painting called *A New Approach.* It was also during this time that I ran West Midlands Ethnic Minority Arts Service and edited it's magazine *Blackboard.* W.E.M.A.S was an organisation that worked towards promoting the richness of cultural activity that was being produced throughout the Midlands at that time.

At my last school there were only a few blacks and we really had to pull together during the early days in Birmingham. This was 1960/64, at the time I didn't really want to go to school; there were little or no studies relating to my culture, even then a few of us were very aware that our blackness was not being celebrated. Disruption and truancy was the norm, this can happen sometimes when there is nothing to hold your interest but Anglo-Saxons and Christopher Columbus.

'We were experiencing more and more alienation from the British system.'

At the time there were a lot of unreported incidents that were racially motivated, skinheads were a problem at the time, inside the clubs and dances they were happy to dance to reggae singer Max Romeo's *Wet Dream* a big chart hit at the time. As the clubs spilled out onto the streets there would be skirmishes: I remember one incident when an argument over a girl turned into a viscious fight with devastating insequences. Yet there was little rascism at school, there was just a basic lack of understanding from teachers towards the needs and expectations of young black people we were experiencing more and more alienation from the British system.

I left school in 1967 and worked as a die polisher at The Royal Mint, Birmingham, stacked shelves in a supermarket and eventually became a chef at the Holiday Inn, Birmingham. Being artistically inclined from an early age, I felt that 'cheffing' was the job that I could do: it required a high degree of artistry but with very little paperwork. I would sweat it out daily in the kitchen but at night I painted with vigour, pictures made out of thousands of tiny dots. As time went by the art was consuming most of my life, so I decided to give up the job. Eight days later I was standing in the Bull Ring and New St Station selling photocopies of my work. After a few months I had made enough money to hire a market stall. The money that I earned was used for buying frames, sending out letters to art galleries, travel and household bills.

'Throughout the years I tried to stay focused.'

Funnily enough I always wanted to be a graphic artist and go into advertising, but that didn't happen. Over the years I have been involved in a host of schemes and ventures, some have not worked while others have been frighteningly productive. The turning point for me was getting my first solo exhibition *Drawings And Prints In Dots* at The Arts Lab, Gosta Green, Birmingham, 1983. Another turning point was the broadcaster, Trevor Phillips; he had bought one of my pictures on an earlier visit to Birmingham, at the time he was setting up a new multicultural series for Channel 4. I was offered a production job based in Birmingham and my role was to research stories involving local people in the black community. One of the stories looked at how Handsworth had changed throughout the years. After it was broadcast on C4 I was approached by actor/producer Zia Moyheddin; he had seen the film: I was offered the role of presenter on *Here And Now*, Central Television's flagship multi cultural programme. It was now 1985 and I would spend many years at Central Television working on a number of productions and as a reporter for *Central News*. I also directed short film items on Nigel Benn, Rev Al Sharpton, Ska Music Special, Black Hair Designs and the rapper MC Hammer. I also had the privilege of directing some inserts for a Stevie Wonder video and interviewing Paul

McCartney at the NEC. During my years at Central TV I absorbed as much as possible, the valuable experience learnt prepared me for life as an independent director and producer.

Windrush Productions was formed in 1993. Throughout the years I tried to stay focused, I had no formal training: just took up the pen, camera or microphone and did what felt natural.

Both my parents were teachers in St Kitts, West Indies. When they came to Britain it was difficult to obtain the kind of employment that they were used to. My mother got a job as a nurse at the Birmingham Accident Hospital At night she made extra money by making clothes for local people. My father went to work at New Street Station. Shift work can play havoc with family life. My parents don't really talk much about the early days; but their memories are shared by many. One can only guess how the cultural fabric of Britain would have changed had they and countless others been given their just reward in the land of milk and honey.

'Throughout the years I have been involved in a host of things, many have not worked but some have been frightening successful.'

During the early 90s I was elected Chairperson of the prestigious Birmingham International Film and Television Festival, a position I held for many years. Other Birmingham initiatives I was involved with include: membership of Carlton Television Equal Opportunities Committee and Board Member of Media Development Agency, Birmingham.

I come from humble beginnings in Birmingham as a do a wealth of talented people involved in everything from commerce to sport and entertainment. If you are able to succeed then I would like to think that it can give others inspiration who can then in turn achieve similar if not greater results than we already have. I have always been involved in race relations and organisations which are concerned with the betterment of multiculturalism. The intention I believe is to set examples of good practice, the ultimate end is positive achievement, self empowerment; stretching your potential way beyond what you thought it could be.

'For every young black person who succeeds, there are others who will not tow the line; some give up while others will take what they want.'

For every young black person who succeeds, there are others who will not tow the line; some give up while others will take what they want. It is the old story; educationalists need to listen more to the voice of black youth, many feel that their pleas are falling on deaf ears. Not all of us are strong, no matter how it seems sometimes. It's about giving people the space to grow. Sometimes you have to rewrite certain elements of the school curriculum.

I have never known an ethnic group in Britain take so much battering, mental and physical. But no matter what seems to be written on the wall, it will get better because it has to; it's so obvious. Just keep your third eye open and you will see a light, you will gain strength from it's glow, and you will keep shining. If the eye flutters to a close, then you're in trouble.

'Educationalists need to listen more to the voice of black youth, many feel that their pleas are falling on deaf ears.'

During 1999 Windrush Productions completed *Reflections* a 30 minute film charting the lives of three West Indians who came to Britain during the 40s and 50s. It is a project I had wanted to do for a long time; the opportunity to document the proud heritage of our parents, their hopes, dreams and aspirations. People who under strenuous conditions, survived, and 50 years later were able to hold their heads high and say "We did it".

In the words of Windrush E. Smith "the angels gave us armour the moment we were born..few know how to wear it...."

There are several books that I frequently return to. They include: *Rasta and Resistance from Marcus Garvey to Walter Rodney* by Horace Campbell. *Collected Poems* by Derek Walcott. *Mamma* by Terry McMillan and *Black Child* by J. Cape.

'Success isn't about excess financial reward; it's about achievement'.

Janet Campbell

Date of birth: 19 November 1962
Place of birth: London

'I don't have a degree but have returned to education several times in order to gain further qualifications.'

'I don't think that you can afford to leave school or college without some kind of career plan - nothing specific but with some ideas would be good.'

Janet Campbell is director of human resources Europe at SCO Ltd.

I don't have a degree. I left school at 16 with O levels and I found a summer job. I was supposed to go back to do A levels but I'd had enough of education. So, I jumped at the offer of a full time job. It was in the merchandising office of the Scotch House store in Knightsbridge.

We had to check when things came in: do the paper work and make sure the right goods had been received with the right reference numbers. Then a friend who worked at an oil company told me they had a job opening in the legal department. I got an interview but they felt I would be more suited to employee relations, so that's how I got into personnel. Where I am now isn't where I'd planned to be. I was going to be a nurse but I spent two weeks of my summer holiday on a geriatric ward and realised that nursing wasn't for me.

Had I done my A levels and gone to university, I think I would have ended up in law, but in personnel work I do feel I have found my niche. I've done a lot of training on the job and I also have a Diploma in Management Studies.

I really enjoyed what I was doing at Marathon Oil and progressed fairly quickly in the early days, but then there were fewer opportunities for me, which is why I made the decision to move on. I didn't have a career plan as such. I think if I were sixteen today I would have a career plan because it is much more difficult than it was twenty years ago. So many more people go to university these days and there are many more people with the right qualifications.

Whilst I have a great sense of achievement for what I have done, I did have a couple of lucky breaks. It was a risk for my boss, who is senior vice president of human resources world-wide, to put me in this job. He could have hired somebody from outside with more experience than me; but his risk paid off. My next post will be a senior human resources role, maybe in a different industry, or I'll go into consultancy.

'I had an absolutely superb teacher, he was encourging and supportive.'

I thoroughly enjoyed school. I did go through a bit of a patch when I hit my early teens, when I wasn't a particularly nice person, but I got through it largely because my mum persevered and because of one superb teacher: Mr Backhouse. He really was supportive, and the two forces combined meant that I had no choice but to pull myself together. At that time I was involved with a crowd and who led me astray, but I was able to get back on track and pass my exams. My mum took a great deal of interest and was always at parents' evenings. She did shift work and she would always arrange the shifts so that she could be there.

Mr Backhouse had very high expectations of me and when I went off the rails he said, I'm not putting up with this because you can do better. He was one of those teachers who cared passionately about all of his students. I think the racial mix when I was at school was pretty balanced. Some teachers had different expectations of black students, and by and large the sports teams were made up of black kids.

I realised that racism affected me personally when I was older and at work. I had always known that there was a difference between me and a white person, but my mum's mantra was, 'There is good and bad in every race'. She always told us that you have to work twice as hard as the white person sitting next to you because it is going to be twice as hard for you to get a job and keep it. That came from her experience. She was one of the immigrants into this country from the West Indies in the early sixties. Many had very good qualifications but ended up doing menial jobs.

The expectations people sometimes have of a black person are largely due to the negative images and stereotyping they see in the media.

'All this political correctness is not helping our black kids.'

Usually, they expect you to react badly or aggressively in certain situations. They don't understand the cultural background or body language. For example, when I was younger, to look someone in authority or older directly in the eye was the height of disrespect. If you don't understand this, it's easy to misconstrue someone's reluctance to look directly at you as something else – arrogance or a "chip on the shoulder".

In one sense you live two lives. You have your life at work and your life at home and you do different things. Sometimes you even speak in a different way. I have found myself taking on more and more work just to prove myself – I'm black but I'm also a woman. When I joined Marathon Oil as a clerk typist I wanted to be a secretary, the next rung up the ladder, but I was told I needed shorthand. So I went off and learned shorthand but it took them another two years to promote me. Constantly doing things to prove people wrong is quite a struggle because you are forever fighting against deep-rooted stereotypes.

Once I was walking down the street pushing my son's pram wearing tracksuit and trainers, very casual. As I passed an elderly white woman she clutched her handbag. I had to stop and ask her why she thought I needed her handbag. She was really embarrassed and apologised, but I was so angry I couldn't let it pass.

'Success is achieving against the odds.'

I believe those attitudes come from negative stereotyping and institutionalised racism. The education system must do better. It fails many black children. Too many are marginalised at school, or excluded. Sadly most large organisations are inherently racist. Look at the BBC and *EastEnders*. The programme is supposed to represent real life – but only when it suits them. Every ethnic group that's been in the soap has had problems and has never lasted.

Success for me is where I am today, human resources director responsible for Europe, Middle East, India and Africa, against all the odds: I'm black, I'm a woman and I don't have a degree.

I don't feel British. I always say I'm English because being "British" is something altogether different. I'm thirty seven years old and I was born here. How can I feel British when people still ask me where am I from and won't accept north

'When you are focused you can move forward.'

London as the answer? I suppose I don't like the term British as I associate it with the Union Jack and the whole skinhead thing of the 70s and 80s. I identify more easily with being called English.

Maybe someone would look at me and say I'm black middle class but it's not a label I've given myself. I identify myself more strongly with the black community. Most of my friends are black, and I'd like to think that I am part of a community because I actually believe that's important. In my professional life I am part of a community of human resources professionals that are mostly white, whereas in my personal life my friends are quite mixed: Asian, black and white. But I guess the focus of what I do is within the black community. So there is a division but it's not one that I deliberately sought.

'You've got to believe in yourself.'

All this political correctness is not helping our black kids. In fact, I think this flood of political correctness has done them a disservice. In the real world we do talk about black coffee and blackboard and baa baa black sheep. When kids are ready to make their choices about what they want to do, give them positive images, positive role models. It's not about changing who you are but learning that there are different ways of behaving in different situations, compounding the stereotype.

'Education is everything.'

The world's much more competitive now. So I would say, leave school with some qualifications and better still go into higher education. Whatever you do, understand IT because that's the way the world is going. When you are focused you can move forward but if you have nothing to focus on, then you stand still.

Chris Cleverly

Chris Cleverly is a barrister, the head of Trafalgar Chambers. He was called to the bar in 1990 and became head of chambers in 1996, at twenty nine, the youngest head of chambers in the bar. He is also involved in the media as a writer and presenter.

People think that being a barrister is all about arguing, but in actual fact it's more about being able to listen and empathise. It's only by listening to what is happening that you can see where people make mistakes or inconsistencies and it's only by empathising that you can bring a jury to understand someone else's story in terms of their own.

The hardest thing about becoming a barrister is having to study law. It's very dull reading through lots of old cases when you are starting out. It becomes more interesting when you become a barrister and you're actually applying it to real life events, and to real people.

'We have to serve a form of apprenticeship.'

Because it was so dull, I nearly dropped out of being a barrister altogether, and I spent a year selling advertising space, but I'm glad I went back to the bar as it's been a very fruitful and satisfying career for me. Looking back on those years of study I realise that in anything we do we have to serve a form of apprenticeship, a period where we don't seem to get much reward, certainly no reward that we can immediately see or experience. It's only by going through that period of time when we may not be paid very much or paid at all, that we learn patience.

*'Seek and you shall
find.'*

I decided to become a barrister very early on,
when I was about six years old. I met a distant
uncle, from Africa, and was very impressed by
him. I asked my mother what he did for a living
and she told me he was a barrister. So I thought,
well, that's what I want to do. I think the most
important thing about role models is that if you
cannot imagine yourself doing a thing, then you
can never actually do it; you have to dream the
dream, before you can live it. If you can see
yourself in what somebody else is doing, or
striving to do, then you can learn from what
they're doing. You can see that you can do
something more than you are doing. You must
keep hold of the truth about you, and perhaps try
and show people the truth about themselves.

*'You have to dream the
dream, before you can
live it.'*

I look at role models, such as Malcolm X. When
you see someone like that transform themselves,
it doesn't really matter what from to where, then
you know that your past does not necessarily
affect your future. You can change things in the
present to make a better future. Just because you
were one thing once, doesn't mean that you will
always be that way. In my comprehensive school
there were very few black people, and there was
quite a lot of violence in the early eighties to do
with racism, quite a few people that I went to
school with were in the National Front or the BNP.
The oppression that I may have felt then doesn't
mean that that's the oppression I have to live
with. Because I was quite an aggressive lad at that
time, it doesn't mean that I must always be that
person. And it's that transformation, that change
of where we are, that's part of the human
experience. And if we can change, then life
becomes much richer.

It's important to stop and think, this is where I
am, and this is what I'm experiencing. Not to be
too wrapped up in the past or the future.

I think a helpful phrase is, 'Seek and you shall
find.' That means to me that everything is out
there, if I am patient enough, persistent enough, if
I am fortunate enough (and I think that fortune
comes from time to time to everyone). Then I will
find it, whatever it is that I seek. The most
important thing to seek is knowledge, and the
most important thing to know is love.

Des Coleman

Des Coleman is an actor, best known for his part as Lennie in EastEnders.

Since I left drama school I've had eight good years. I've been quite lucky as an actor. My first job was in the musical *Chicago*. After that I did a couple of minor plays and then *Big* at the Birmingham Rep. Finally I did *Miss Saigon*, in which I understudied the lead. I left that to join *EastEnders*.

I used to be a welder. I'd always had aspirations to go into some sort of entertainment but I didn't quite know what. I wanted to be a singer. I wanted to be a comedian. Then I went to drama school and homed in on acting. I enjoy it but it takes a lot of getting used to because the entertainment industry isn't one I feel many people can live with. I'm glad that my rise to notoriety hasn't been meteoric. The level of pressure at the top must be extraordinary. And I can easily see how the desire to remain there can lead to some people burning out. I'd like to think that the years I have spent trying to achieve my goals have given me some form of grounding as to what is important in my life.

'I'm not the sort of guy who will sit back on my laurels and think that the world owes me a living.'

I like to think I'm intelligent. If I lose a job – and anyone can lose a job at the next contract – I've got the guts to get out there and find another one. I'm not the sort of guy who will sit back on my laurels and think that the world owes me a living. I enjoy the challenge, and even if things get boring I feel you've got to look inside yourself and try to find a new way.

I've always been what you might call a 'show off'. I've always had a sort of zest. At first I wanted to be an engineer because my dad was an engineer. But after a few years I thought, "This is my life; what do I really want to do"? And it was either to be a pilot or to go into entertainment.

'Nothing is fair.'

As an actor you are self-employed so you can't just go spending. You've got to look after your accounts. It's a very disciplined job, and it's even harder if you're struggling. You don't realise how many talented people are out there who don't make it. It's unfortunate; unlucky. But then, nothing's fair.

I really enjoyed school and didn't really want to leave, because I knew what the reality would be: waking up at eight to get to work for nine, working till five and then home to sleep. I was always good at sports and I didn't really find schoolwork difficult. I realised as a kid that if someone was about to tell you off, you just had to smile and you got away with it. I used to play on that a lot!

I come from a family of six and we're all very close. I always knew that if I failed, my mum, brothers and sisters would be there. So it didn't matter what I did because I knew that I would have their support.

'It's pointless complaining. You just have to try and forge ahead.'

I held several jobs, never being quite sure what I wanted to do, then I went to Guildford College to train to be an actor. It used to be very elitist but anyone can go to drama school these days. But of course there are not enough roles. Out of all the actors in Britain, how many people could name even three black actors? All those TV channels are running, and even black people can't remember a black actor's name! That's a bad state, but it's pointless complaining. You just have to try and forge ahead.

It takes a lot of will power. People tell you you'll never do it, so it takes a lot of inner strength. There are so many people who want to do it but the pressures prevent them.

'Success requires a positive outlook on life.'

Success requires a positive outlook on life. I'm too young to be able to say whether I'm successful. These last few years have been good but there's a long way to go. Maybe I'll be able to say when I'm sixty five and all my dreams have been fulfilled.

Young people have to want to do things themselves. There's a lot of peer pressure but young people must make decisions for themselves, not for others. There weren't any black role models around when I was a kid. But you cannot walk around with a chip on your shoulder. It's part of life and you've got to deal with it. Because things might be a bit harder it would be very easy to sit back and not try. But to me that's just not an option.

'Not trying , is not an option.'

I don't need to see myself as part of a black community. I'm from Derby, so I see myself as a Derby lad. Full stop. I've got this far without any group as such behind me.

There's nothing as cruel as folk. There's nothing that will shock me in another human being. You can't save the world; just do your own little journey with the people you're involved with.

I'd like to have written *Wake me up before you go* and *Walking on sunshine*. They're songs that meant a lot in my past. I see myself going on to write in future. I'd like to get into the mental side of it.

Eastenders is a huge learning curve that can make or break your character, I'm lucky in the fact that I have moved on from the show and continued to enjoy success in the different fields of the industry. I joined the cast of *Rent* in the West End and went to Hollywood Black film festival to promote a film I starred in. Most recently, I completed filming *Is Harry on the Boat in Ibiza* due out spring 2001. My book, *So you finally got into drama school*, will be published in 2001 so hopefully I'm taking that learning curve onwards and hopefully upwards.

Dr Morgan Dalphinis

Date of birth: 1950
Place of birth: St Lucia,
Caribbean

'Expectation was inherent - never articulated.'

Dr Morgan Dalphinis is an executive manager in academic development for Handsworth College, Birmingham. He will shortly be taking on the role of director and chief executive of the Urban Learning Foundation.

'Education stood me in good stead. Caribbean writers had a lot to tell me about myself'

I grew up in the town and in the country though the dominant influence was being on the land. This gave me lots of freedom which I wasn't then really aware of. At the time I felt aggrieved and thought all the good things were happening in the city.

As a child my job was to feed the pigs and tie up the animals. You could have a lot of fun; eat all the bananas you wanted. But at the back of my mind I still thought the city boys were having more fun.

My mother was the dominant one in our household. She was a teacher and expected us all to do well. This expectation was inherent – never articulated, we were also conscious of the migrant dream of going to England if we got the opportunity.

When you're at school in the Caribbean you pick up the core principles very fast. I liked the clear discipline and the clear work that you have to do. And success is valued. So there was no contradiction between receiving education and aspiring to do as well as you could. Learning was ongoing in school and out of school, with proverbs and stories often being told at home.

'I began to develop a conscience which made me think about my behaviour.'

When I came to England the most profound initial impact was being attacked by racists. But if you're used to walking five miles with mangoes on your head you're stronger than other people. So I was able to defend myself extremely well. On the negative side, for ten years I became very animal in my reactions. Whatever people said I responded in kind and just hit out. But then I began to develop a conscience which made me think about my behaviour. Education gave me a thread of continuity and stood me in good stead.

My mission at secondary school in England was to try and understand what was being taught and to do it well. In some cases I didn't like it but I knew I had to see it through. I knew it was a wonderful opportunity to have free secondary education. In my St Lucia you had to pay for education after primary school.

I had some good teachers, for example, there was Mr Robertson who brought along a rucksack full of books and told me I'd enjoy reading them. He gave me the mental food I needed. And Mr Giles who punished a guy who'd stuck electrodes on my leg in science. So, if you like, there were fewer reasons for me to fight; they were sorted out by others.

'When I started to read Caribbean writers - such as Braithwaite - that was a trigger for me.'

When I started to read Caribbean writers – such as Braithwaite – that was a trigger for me. I realised they had a lot to tell me about myself. I lived in Shepherds Bush then with lots of other young black people. We did things together and had an all black basketball team. There was a feeling of solidarity and influence.

I think the priority for young people whoever they are, but particularly for black kids, is to make a clear decision about what is important. That means getting a good education and enjoying learning. It's important to learn to love yourself and through loving yourself, other people. I think some black people get involved with the negatives which have been pushed at them. But it's possible to evolve a positive response and go after what is important. If people want to bring you into a place of hate and emptiness it's the way they are. It's their problem. The issue is who are you and what do you want to do with your life?

'I think the priority for young people whoever they are, but particularly for black kids, is to make a clear decision about what is important.'

I don't carry this delusion about being a member of the middle class. All of us rely on our skills to keep the employment which gives us the

'The issue is who are you and what do you want to do with your life?'

appearance of being middle class. But we have no power here. Through most of our history we've been decimated by colonialism and collectively enslaved. But we got free and came to England looking for a job. Now some people may believe we're safe and middle class.

I think having links with our countries of origin is incredibly useful. It's good to go back if only to look and be a tourist and to see that there are different environments. I think the same principle applies between Britain and Europe, so it's important that we get out there and explore what Europe has to offer.

Paul Dash

Date of birth: 25 June 1946
Place of birth: Barbados

'Painting for me is a way of life.'

Paul Dash is a lecturer in education at Goldsmith's College, University of London and a painter.

'Being successful must to some extent be about being happy. It's doing things that have meaning to you'.

I wear two hats; I am an artist and I am an educationalist, a teacher. My research focus is Caribbean Children in Art and Design Education. I work on the secondary PGCE course at Goldsmiths, and contribute to MA courses. I also give talks at various centres around the country, sit on the boards of two galleries and work as a GCSE moderator for Edexcel. You could say that I am very involved in education.

I enjoy my work at Goldsmiths, and I love painting; research is a stimulating challenge. What I don't enjoy is boring paperwork. I have a fairly wide administrative commitment at Goldsmiths, which can take up a lot of time. I guess I wear too many hats.

Art making is part of a contract I have with myself. It is a way of life, a vocation; I have to make art. I trained as a painter and have exhibited in various contexts including the Summer Show at the Royal Academy, the Whitechapel Open and the Commonwealth Institute.

I came to this country in 1957 at the age of 11. In those days you were taught directly or indirectly, to believe that black people were inferior to whites. So on being thrown into British society, I was traumatised. I had to make sense of a new environment and a whole new set of relationships and experiences that were overpowering.

'The school I went to was awful.'

The school I went to was awful, a two form entry secondary modern staffed by disenchanted, racist teachers. I never took the eleven plus. I went straight into that dreadful place without any formal testing. When I first went there they took one look at me and decided I should be placed in the lower stream, even though I was a year ahead in maths and had a better grounding in history and geography than most. Over the next three years I did well in school exams but instead of being promoted to the A group, as several boys below me were, I was kept in the B stream. This whole scenario played on my mind. My entire career at that school was spent in what was effectively a remedial band populated by pupils in need of serious educational and even psychological support.

'My parents instilled in me a great love of academic learning.'

My parents instilled in me a great love of academic learning. So, concerned about the poor education that I knew I was receiving, I tried to educate myself. I started with a foreign language, French, which was horrendously challenging because of the difficulties I experienced with pronunciation. Then I tried Spanish, which to the English speaker is a more straightforward language to learn. Today I can speak enough Spanish to get by in Spanish speaking countries. I also taught myself Blues piano, appearing upstairs at Ronnie Scott's Jazz Club on several occasions in the 1970s with a band called Protoplasm. I also played with Curved Air, though they weren't called that at the time. I was ambitious but not in an aggressive way. I just wanted to fulfil those ambitions my parents had for me. I didn't want to let them down.

Returning to my days at school, I developed an interest in painting Oxford cityscapes. My art teacher took a keen interest and was very encouraging. I painted other subjects at home. My mum bought sketchbooks and paints with money set aside from her meager housekeeping. I made pictures based on memories of Barbados: market scenes with people jostling for fruit and vegetables; pastorals with black-belly sheep and lowing cows; cane fields at harvest, that kind of thing. I also painted carnivals. Most of my pictures were crowded. It was almost as if I needed to reclaim the Caribbean by painting lots of people and busy tropical landscapes.

'I had to find my own way.'

My art enabled me to make sense of this new challenging school environment. Gerald, my brother, and I were the first black or Asian children to go there. He left within a year, at the age of fifteen. I had to fend for myself. My art was critical to me: it helped me through that very difficult time period. Over time I went to the local art school, which was great, then Chelsea School of Art, which was a nightmare. I was very much on my own there, not like the black youngsters going to college today. There wasn't another black undergraduate in the building. I had to find my own way in what was a very avant garde, hard edge art environment – Caribbean pastorals and Oxford Street scenes didn't attract much interest. I simply couldn't settle.

On leaving college I did a few odd jobs but kept my painting going. Eventually I registered to become a teacher and was contacted by Mary Metcalfe, the head teacher of Haggerston Girls' School in Hackney. So I went into teaching part-time.

A few years later I got married, started a family and became a full time teacher. Eventually I was appointed Head of Art at Haberdashers' Aske's School in South London. While there, I started looking more seriously at pedagogy and curriculum content. This came out of the frustration of not finding material for project development with a Caribbean base, apart from carnival that is. There was a lot of multicultural work going on in schools but very little of it was inspired by Caribbean cultures. The ILEA took an interest in my work and I was invited to participate in various initiatives. I gave talks at Brighton Polytechnic and contributed to the AEMS project (Arts Education in a Multicultural Society). I did an MA at the Institute of Education based on my interest in the curriculum. I was employed at the Institute and stayed there for three years before moving to Goldsmiths in 1994.

'I don't feel part of a black community.'

This may be controversial but I don't feel part of a black community. While in Barbados I was certainly part of a black community but I have never felt that way in Britain. To my mind a community is a group of people who share several cultural characteristics, meet in communal 'spaces' and interact with one another. British Caribbean people are dispersed throughout this

'Our youngsters are confused.'

country. We lack institutions that could bring us together. Were we to develop an ability to utilise, say, information technology and have 'conversations' on the net, we could create digital communities. But it would be difficult to focus minds on that concept, so I don't see it happening. We get information through the media which is usually distorted because it is produced by others for their own purposes. They construct us to fit the stereotypes they have invented. As yet we haven't found effective ways of debating such issues or concerns around identity and representation. As a consequence our youngsters are confused; they're constantly bombarded by messages that indicate they are either thick or a problem. There's plenty of information about black dysfunction – corruption in Nigeria, beheadings in Uganda – but there is little celebration of black achievements outside of sport or music.

'There's a lot more going on in Africa, LA and Kingston than we are told in the media.'

It's very difficult to construct institutions when you are a minority. It's even more so when you are from the Caribbean because of our allegiances to former island communities, and a history that is locked into western culture. We are part of the West yet separate from it: a strangely ambivalent position. They don't appreciate our need for space where we can deal with issues of common concern to blacks, particularly issues around race and racism, identity, etc. Some of us are fortunate: we go to university, where we share experiences and ideas. But even in such environments there is an issue over communication. We write academic papers, but they're read mostly by white academics. We don't successfully reach a black audience.

'We have to be active agents.'

We have to be active agents in the re-education of our people, and the re-education of the white population. To that end we need to recruit progressive black teachers who can engage with issues, teachers who are willing to put their neck on the line for what they believe in. Just having a black face isn't enough.

African peoples have given much to the world and will contribute much more in the future. I want to be part of an educational programme that puts that message across to young people, both black and white. That for me is the challenge for the 21st century.

Brenda Emmanus

Date of birth: 7 June 1963
Place of birth: London, UK

'With television, either you're in vogue or your not.'

'I've been creating my own opportunities.'

Brenda Emmanus is a freelance journalist, and TV and radio presenter. She is also director of Showplay Television, an independent production company.

"Luck is when opportunity meets preparation, or persistence overcomes resistance!"

My career has been quite diverse. I've certainly been fortunate in that some varied opportunities have come my way. While I was doing my degree I freelanced at *The Voice* newspaper, and immediately after graduating I started there full time. When they started *Black Beat International*, a music magazine, I did some work on that, and also on *Chic*, a black women's magazine that they brought out. So I veered away from news and into arts and entertainment.

My first television job was as a researcher on *Kilroy* for two years. When that was off air I worked on *Breakfast Time*, finally becoming an assistant producer there. Then when Janet Street Porter came in to do youth programmes at the BBC she took me on as a researcher and reporter. I did a series called *Reportage*, a youth current affairs programme; I did *The A to Z of Belief*, and also *David Bowie Specials*, and an animation series. I did tackle a diverse range of subjects!

When I moved to Channel 4, it was as an arts and entertainments reporter, but I also started to produce, research, report, direct and cut my own short films. My skills developed and I learnt to edit and write scripts.

When my contract at Channel 4 finished I wondered what I'd do next. I'd heard about *The Clothes Show* looking for an ethnic minority contribution, so rang them to say I was interested. In the end, I was with them for five years. More recently, I did some work on *Black Britain* at the BBC, presented the Midweek National Lottery and reported on 'Celebrity' for Carlton Television.

I've also done a lot of radio work over the years; everything from GLR to the BBC World Service. I still keep up my magazine journalism, and I'm also currently working on a novel. As a freelancer you have to juggle! That can be exciting, but also stressful, because you never know what's coming up when. There have been times when I've panicked, thinking nothing is happening, and worrying about my finances.

With television, either you're in vogue or you're not. We've had a long spate of blonde and busty women presenters, linked in with the 'lad' culture, I think. So I've had to sit back and wait for the tide to change. In the meantime, I've been creating my own opportunities by developing a production company, and making the most of all opportunities.

'My teachers nurtured me and advised me.'

My parents instilled a work ethic in me from the beginning. My father, particularly, was strict. He always made sure I'd done my homework before I went out. They helped me to understand about deferred gratification: work now, reap your rewards later. As a child, you sometimes feel resentful, but I needed that kind of discipline. I did like school, and I liked being the first to get my homework done. I still want to continue learning new things and having my brain stimulated. I was lucky because my teachers nurtured me and advised me.

I don't remember experiencing any racism at school, but when I was fifteen and went for a Saturday job I was told, "Thanks for coming, but we've already got a black person working here."

'I didn't want to set myself up for rejection.'

My drama teacher encouraged me to audition for the National Youth Theatre, but I wasn't sure. I thought they'd be all white, and wouldn't want me. I didn't want to set myself up for rejection. But she made me apply and helped me rehearse the part of Eliza Doolittle in *My Fair Lady*. I was shocked that I got in! I had a great time there, but was always self-conscious about being black.

There were all these middle class girls and I felt very cockney and very black. Also, I realised there were only certain parts I was getting: I was always the maid, or playing less fruitful roles.

'I'm stilll on a journey.'

All the time, people are telling me I'm a success. But I think success is relative, and personal. I'm seen as a role model, but you don't choose to be a role model; people choose you. I've not done all the things I'd like to do. I'm still on the journey. I'm still juggling, and waiting for the next job to come through. I'm still panicking about long-term security. When I feel I have control over my own destiny, then I will feel I'm a success.

'I don't feel completely embraced.'

I'm very conscious that I'm treated differently because of who I am. People are always polite when they recognise me. I almost feel guilty declaring that I'm British, because I don't feel completely embraced. I feel I've a right to be British because I was born here. But there have been times when I've felt so frustrated with things not happening here for black people that I've considered going off to America. It's surprising how many black people here think that way. At least you'll be given an opportunity in the States. But there's the fighter in me that says I have a right to make it here, so I'm going to stay and make it work. I'd feel guilty, I think, running away to the States.

I'm also aware when I'm chosen for a programme that they're choosing a black person either because they've got a minority slot to fill or they want something different. Well, I am different, and I'm proud to be black, but I don't want to be somebody's novelty all the time.

'I'm proud to be black.'

I never really feel that I'm allowed to develop. I was told by *The Clothes Show* that I had to go because I'd 'peaked'. That shattered my confidence at the time. So you're always watching your back and trying harder. There's always a level of insecurity when you've got a job: when are you going to be out of favour? Who will be next?

Black men generally have a bad image, but black women are more easily accepted. Yet in the media black men are there, and they're doing well. Andy Peters, for example, is also an executive, and he's done exceptionally well. On television though, personalities are sometimes far more important than competence.

I suppose I would now be deemed 'middle class', but what it means to be 'black middle class' I don't really know. In America the black middle class are part of the decision-making process. If they make a noise, they're listened to. But here we don't have a power base in the same way. There's a strong black *presence* in many professions, but not a strong black *influence*.

'Everybody is struggling to make their mark and get their bit.''I didn't want to set myself up for rejection.'

There is, though, a growing level of confidence within the black community. There's a confidence about our culture, and that'll grow with each generation. But in terms of the essence of community, of being together and supporting each other, I'm not sure if we've got it right yet. We're not unified, and we don't hold hands enough. Everyone's struggling to make their mark and get their little bit. If everyone could pool their resources, pool their ideas, at least we'd have one solid power base.

The Stephen Lawrence case has made a difference. Stephen was almost an angel from God sent to teach us a lesson. His parents have shown the kind of will and determination which I imagine was around during the days of slavery, when slaves were ready to break their shackles and escape, they were dignified and determined. What happened was tragic, but the positive side is that it shows what great people there are within the black community, and that we can pull together when we need to.

'You've got to take personal responsibility for your own fate.'

In the end, you've got to take personal responsibility for your own fate. Parents, teachers and friends can only do so much; in the end, it's a long journey and you have to make it on your own. It's helpful to acknowledge that, and to realise that every action has a consequence. Fear has held me back a lot: fear of rejection because I'm black and I'm female, or sometimes the fear that I haven't got what it takes. I realise now that a rejection letter is not going to kill me! What it should do is fuel the fire even more, and make you even more determined to show them you can do it.

'Surround yourself with people who are positive.'

It's also been important for me to develop a strong network of friends and family. Without them I wouldn't be where I am now. Surround yourself with people who are positive. If you surround yourself with negativity then it will hold you back. Being with positive people is as

'In the end, education is the key, particularly for black kids. They must realise that raving and music and boyfriends and designer clothes can wait.'

important as making sure you get the qualifications.

In the end, education is the key, particularly for black kids. They must realise that raving and music and boyfriends and designer clothes can wait.

What we all need is a better understanding of other cultures. If you understand where someone's coming from then you have more hope of communicating with them. West Indian parents put a lot of responsibility on the school, but I think they have to take some of that back: keep a check on what their kids are doing and make sure they're doing their homework. There's a lot of turmoil in the school system and its hard work being a teacher. Everybody has to play their part in nurturing and supporting the child. It can't just be left to the school. Children should also be encouraged to take some responsibility for themselves. They've got to be given a sense of self from the beginning.

Denise Everett

Denise Everett is senior embryologist at the Lister Hospital, in charge of the day to day running of a very busy in vitro fertilisation unit in the middle of London. She is the first black woman to hold such a position in the UK.

My job consists of collecting, culturing and growing human eggs, sperm and embryos. These are used in a patient's treatment cycle. I've been in the field for ten years. My embryology career started at the London Bridge Hospital where I was for three years and now I am at the Lister.

Date of birth: 24 January 1965
Place of birth: Finchley, London

'My personal achievement was studying part-time for a degree and holding down a full-time job.'

After leaving school I worked as a lab technician for a NHS biochemistry laboratory, and then went into research for a drug company because I thought I'd like it – but I didn't! I stuck at it for a year, though, so I could put it on my CV, and in the meantime saw a job in *New Scientist* for a junior embryologist. I didn't know what it was and had to look it up. Then I phoned them, went for an interview and got the job. I've been doing it ever since.

I went to an all girls school in Hackney. It was a traumatic time for me and before O levels I missed nearly three months having my tonsils out. I still got seven O levels and then went to college to do A levels. I didn't learn anything in the classroom at college but I learned everything socially! So I had to retake them the following year.

I knew I wanted to work in a hospital but that I didn't want to be a nurse. I also didn't want to go to university, so I took the job as lab technician, going to college one day a week to do the BTEC National Diploma. Then, foolishly, I waited until I was at the Lister before I decided to do a degree. I studied part time whilst doing a full time job. It was hard!

My parents are both from Jamaica and they came over in the late 50s. I was brought up in what would be seen as a single parent family. But, there was an extended family network behind my mother. The key to the family was a strong and supportive grandmother who was present for the best part of my childhood.

'Young people need to remember that they're black but not use it as an excuse. Use it to your advantage, because you've got to focus. Nothing falls into your lap, you've got to go and fight for it.'

I grew up understanding that I needed to be independent, not to follow the crowd. My grandmother was the most significant individual in my life she would say, "If you are going to do something, do it well".

I don't see myself as a British citizen. I don't fancy the idea of being old and alone in England. But I wouldn't give up on England totally – I do like England otherwise I wouldn't be here. They have invested in me and in my education. I used to meet people who'd paid thousands of pounds to come here to do A levels and I'd think, "wow, I get it for nothing". So I'll stay here and do as much as I can.

When you hear about someone on the news getting mugged or whatever you breathe a sigh of relief it it's not a black person involved.

Young people need to remember that they're black, but not use it as an excuse. Use it to your advantage, because you've got to focus. Nothing falls into your lap, you've got to go and fight for it. Think ahead. Because you're black you also need to have that piece of paper, those exam results.

'Success means being able to make a choice. Being your own person.'

Just because it hasn't happened yet doesn't mean it won't. It might just take a bit longer than you scheduled. You've got your whole life ahead of you to muck around later. It's important that you try not to make the same mistake twice.

My strength indirectly comes from reading autobiographies such as Eartha Kitt, Oprah Winfrey, Malcolm X. Just knowing how they struggled and how they've achieved what they've achieved. Success to me means being able to make a choice. I didn't do what was anticipated. I'm not part of the stereotype. Being a woman and being black probably made me more determined.

Yvonne Foster

Date of birth: 6 August 1958
Place of birth: Jamaica

Yvonne Foster is the managing director of a company she established in 1994, specialising in the delivery of vocational education programmes to the private and public sectors.

I have total responsibility for how the business develops and whether it develops, though I do have a team of four people who work with me. I tender for work, give presentations, meet clients, then I delegate different parts of the work to staff and to subcontractors. It's always a challenge and you're always learning. I do want to see it grow significantly over the next few years. Quite a lot of status goes with being a business owner.

One of the things I've had to strive for is to be really professional in the way I approach my work. I gained an academic background as a mature student and went on to obtain professional qualifications in the area of training and development. You must really know the system that you're operating in, in order to compete. You may not be on a level playing field, but at least you're on the field. I wanted to operate within the mainstream, adopting the professional values that were appropriate. My strategy's been about understanding the society, and giving what I can to it in the hope that I will get something back. Things have been very tough, but I couldn't say they've been more difficult because I'm a black woman.

'There were opportunities here in England that I wasn't taking.'

One of the reasons I decided to set the business up in the first place was my experience of being employed. As a training manager for a construction company I was fortunate to have gained that position, but I realised that I'd go no further with that organisation despite having a lot of abilities. I realised that in order to achieve my potential I needed to be in a position to create my own destiny, and that meant outside of the employed situation. It was a conscious decision.

I entered a polytechnic as a mature student with a small daughter. My family was a really good support network. I kept focused and made some strong decisions about the goals I was working for. I've also felt satisfied that I've taken my life into my own hands. What's important to me is sustaining and developing what I've set up. This meant that for the first three years of the business I had very little social life.

My schooling was a disaster! I remember vividly always wanting to achieve and always feeling that I was a bright child, but at one point I was in a group of children who were educationally subnormal. I shouldn't have been there, and that experience has driven me to take charge of my own career. My parents were first generation immigrants and my mother had six children. My parents worked very hard, but they didn't understand the education system; didn't understand the support we needed. Educationally I was lost at school. I had no good advice and I left thinking I just needed to get myself a job. It wasn't until I started doing my first degree that I met someone who believed in me academically. This tutor was effectively my mentor for three years.

'Despite the obstacles that may assail you, keep focusing on your main goal and take consistent action towards it.'

After school, I went to college part-time and did a secretarial course, then worked as a secretary for Philips for a few years. I became pregnant with my daughter at nineteen. It wasn't something that was planned. I left home when I was 20, found myself a flat, and started to bring up my daughter. I continued to work full-time, and went to evening classes to do some A levels.

It was going back to Jamaica for two months and seeing the poverty and deprivation there that made me realise there were opportunities here in England that I wasn't taking. That was an important lesson. It was when I came back that I started to do evening classes, and I stayed on the education track for about seven years.

For five years I worked for the Open University part-time. I loved working with mature students. At the time, the OU didn't have many black tutors and they were actively encouraging them. It was a very good experience for me. There are many institutions that recognise the barriers that prevent black people coming forward and make a conscious effort.

'There is no point in dragging the past with you.'

I've felt well supported by many white colleagues. There's no point in dragging the past with you because often it's not very constructive. I didn't have a very good start in life but I've been able to change positively. There have been times when I've felt angry and let down, but I picked myself up and moved on. People will support you if you're seen to be supporting yourself and getting on with it. You've got to be diplomatic, but it's also important to verbalise things so that people know you're there.

I think parents now are often much more aware of the contribution they can make to their child's education; that they need to play an active role. There are a lot of opportunities but a large section of the black community is still not going to access them for a whole host of reasons. It's not just about racism. I think a good mentor would do wonders for many black kids. My mentor at college wasn't black, but she was brilliant and really believed in me.

'Education is important.'

A very sound academic basis has been the foundation of who I am today. It's given me incredible confidence to know that I can achieve academically. I think education is the single most important factor. It doesn't matter how tough it is out there; get yourself a good education and doors will open up. You've got to push some open: they won't necessarily be there saying, "Come right in". But first you've got to get that foundation. Without it, you're not going to stand a chance.

Luna Frank-Riley

Luna Frank-Riley is director of MATRIX which specialises in Information Technology – marketing, business development and e-commerce applications in collaboration with major corporations. MATRIX also specialises in fund-raising and the development of bids for key ICT projects funded by the European Commission, UK government funding schemes, international trusts and other financial institutions.

Date of birth: 13 December 1964

Place of birth: Rep. of Trinidad and Tobago

As we are working in the IT sector, we try to utilise as much technology to ensure that work is done efficiently, and professionally. With technology such as video-conferencing and email, distance is much less of an issue.

My other area of interest is in economic development and the regeneration of communities and inner cities – again with a strong emphasis on IT. We provide small business support.

I'd like to have a role with the UN at some time in the future, and because of my interest in IT, I would like to be involved in the development of UN policies on the information society and universal access. I believe that we need to ensure that all individuals; especially children have access to technology to support their education and leisure, and enhance their general quality of life.

My first job in England was with Leeds Building Society as a part-time cashier. I was also reading for a degree in Economics and Social Policy. As my personal circumstances changed, I switched to doing the degree on a part-time basis so that I could work and continue with my studies. Also I could see first-hand and understand about money, interest rates and the general impact on economic policy.

Then a full-time job came up at *Commonword*, a community publishing house which published anthologies by black writers, across the north west. This is where I learned my first fund-raising skills, when having to deal with arts officers from the Arts Council, local authority and some charitable trusts and foundations.

'Believe in yourself and your God - that all things will be possible.'

The next challenge for me was at FullEmploy. They needed someone to run the resource centre. I'd done a course there so I knew the organisation and its work; which is why I could show others how to construct a business plan. I became resource centre manager, talking to unemployed black people who wanted to start their own businesses. It was a matter of working one to one on their business plans. There were some real gems. One woman started a chicken and chips business which still exists today. She has her own shop now.

'We need to see black people in positions.'

At that point Manchester Polytechnic (now Manchester Metropolitan University), wanted somebody who could start up a consulting facility within Hollings faculty so that staff could develop links with the corporate sector for research and student placements.

Another turning point was at Manchester Business School as Corporate Relations Executive. Here was the first time that I met a male boss who mentored me through my work and career because he recognised my skills and capabilities and offered the support and advice as needed. From MBS, I was seconded to the Moss Side and Hulme Task Force to help build the foundations for small business development in this inner city area.

'My bosses were confident men, so it was natural for them to support me to achieve more.'

I went to an independent all girls school, St Augustine Girls' High School, and was a loner; I was the only girl who wanted to be a politician. The expectations were that you would be able to think for yourself, but also you had to conform to a large extent. I fitted in by fitting out: as long as you didn't bother me I didn't bother you. I was on the school hockey team and badminton squad – so I did have team skills.

The support came from my parents when it came to choosing subjects. I really wanted to study economics at that time because I wanted to go to the UN, but the school didn't teach economics so I opted to go to a state St Augustine Senior School. A few people said I'd regret it but it was great because it was a mixed school. It was fun to do battle with the boys at that point because I hadn't had that opportunity before.

'Be fearless, even when all the odds are against you.'

Doing my own thing has always been my coping strategy. If someone blocks me I fight back, but then I move on to the next chapter. My mother, a nurse, would always encourage me to read about Black heroes like Dr Martin Luther King, Mahatma Gandhi, Angela Davis and Malcolm X. She would help us to understand about Black Power, but not to see the world through that prism only. Be your own person. I suppose that is why I liked taking exams. It is one of the few places where it is difficult to be misjudged through others' perception about your ability as a black person. It's a much flatter playing field in many cases.

'Lavender is to Feminist as Purple is to Womanist' - Angela Davis

My favourite colour is purple. I have always liked it even as a young child. Maybe it has to do with growing up in the sixties, or maybe because it was my grand-mother's favourite colour as well, or maybe it is linked to what was going on around me at the time. I have vivid memories of the launch of UN International Women's year in 1975, the tune by Helen Reddy *'I am Woman'* and then later Chaka Khan *'I'm Every Woman'*. But even then, as now, I still feel more of a WOMANIST, that is, being able to assert my own abilities and needs in the context of a world in which there are men and women, sons and daughters, fathers and mothers, husbands and wives.

My sense of social justice comes from my father, who was a trade unionist. He always defined his job as a 'Chief Negotiator', and said that his main role was to keep people talking, that he was not leaving the discussion table until both sides had an agreement. I draw on that skill when I am fund-raising for a business or a community organisation or charity. I will write and redraft a proposal, and endure many a meeting until we have achieved the financial package.

I have never had a frivolous lifestyle. I travel in my profession, and many may think. "Wow what a life"! But they do not see that I am leaving my son for a few days and I am reviewing a report at 4.00am in the morning, or the overall uncertainty of income when you are running a business.

'Be careful what you wish for - you might get it.'

I spent a long time managing other people's expectations of me and the one freedom I have now is that I manage my own expectations. I am in control of where I go next, with lots of prayer and the grace of GOD.

My daily mantra:
Since what we choose is what we are
And what we Love, we yet shall be
The Goal may ever shine afar
The will to win, it makes us Free

Public Appointments

General Commissioner of Taxes, Manchester (appointed 1997)

This is an independent tribunal to hear appeals against charges or levy made by the Inland Revenue on an individual taxpayer or company. I feel strongly that, like any other situation, people have the right to be heard and to argue their case where they feel they have suffered some injustice. Sometimes we can uphold an appeal, other times we cannot.

Countryside Agency – Board member (appointed April 2000)

I now live in the countryside and with an urban background of life experiences I have come to appreciate what the countryside has to offer. I am also keen that all people, from every community and walk of life have access to and also appreciate the benefits of the countryside, not least as it is the place their food is grown.

Bruce Gill

Date of birth: 18 October 1953

Bruce Gill is Assistant Director of Personnel and Equalities in Birmingham's Education Department. He heads a division which includes a unit that looks at race, gender, disability and social inclusion. He has responsibility for ninety six officers and around five hundred teachers and classroom assistants.

I think it happens to a lot of black people that we have a personal empathy with race equality work and therefore, we're called to do it. So, even though there is the prospect of double work, we go to it willingly, as long as we can. But then it also brings with it its own pressures, our high expectations as we can be very hard on ourselves; we want the very best because of our personal commitment, and also there are community pressures. There are people out there looking who want to see things happening, who want to see things change, and they've looked and they've seen ten, twenty, thirty, fourty years have passed. These are decades, and things are moving very slowly.

Also, there's an acute sense of status in a way which I've never encountered before. So I have to be aware that it is significant; it has currency. And actually I can use it strategically for a variety of purposes.

I tend to think of success in terms of recognition of the contribution you make in any area of work. So success is not so much to do with the hierarchy, it's to do with the quality of what you've done as an individual being widely recognised.

My work is very well paid and there are very few people at this level so I enjoy a quality of life

'I tend to think of success in terms of recognition of the contribution you make in any area of work. So success is not so much to do with the hierarchy, it's to do with the quality of what you've done as an individual being widely recognised.'

that I couldn't if I wasn't on this path. My contributions are in the area of race, race equality, shifting thinking, moving people along together: helping race relations to improve, in a nutshell.

On another level though, once I'm out of the work mode walking in the street, I'm just another black face. So I will have people leaning out of the car and shouting at me "blackie" and feeling quite comfortable in doing so. They don't know I'm an assistant director. And the fact that those people feel they can do that tells me something else about what it means to be in this country. There's still a lot of work to be done so that superficial aspects like the colour of your skin or your size or your hair or your gender are not matters that will get you yelled at by someone from a passing car.

'A slightly open door is as much an opportunity as a wide open door.'

I came to England when I was four years old. I'm just about in the Windrush generation, and I remember coming across on a ship and going to live in a village outside Derby. I had my early primary education in a village school where we were the only black family. Growing up in a predominantly white environment helped me learn about how to relate to and manage white people at that age. You develop various skills, you can be extra charming, deflecting difficult situations. That's how I started to mould some of my skills which I think eventually led me into teaching. But I think they have also led me into the whole area of race relations and how you can project alternative ways which are less threatening to white people.

Because there was no way we could be construed as taking over the village, we were treated as though we were celebrities, novelties, exotic people: the process was kind of reversed, so the white people actually behaved differently to us because of how they felt about there just being one or two of us.

One of the first things that was said to me when I started my village school in Derby was, 'Eh-up – don't you talk posh!' I didn't know what 'posh' was – yeah! Being brought up on the World Service, as is often the case in the Caribbean, that's part of the culture. So I rapidly acquired a Derbyshire twang for the playground. Now, when I walk into an interview people have certain assumptions. I open my mouth and half the time they're listening to the sound of my voice, not to

*'The most influential
book that I have read
must be* The African
Origins of Civilisation
by Cheik Anta Diop.'

what I'm saying, thinking 'he sounds nice'. So I
realised there were things going for me which I
could tap into: having a sense of humour and
being witty.

Later when our family moved to London I met
many other black people for the first time who'd
had different experiences, different backgrounds
and had different presumptions about white
people and relationships that were much more
confrontational. There was a lot more 'attitude'
and resistance and I had to start learning the
place of those strategies and not be judgmental as
to why people were behaving that way. And I also
learnt that although you can't transform
somebody who may be out to do you down, the
way you handle them can actually make it difficult
for them and you can disarm them. There is a
whole set of stereotypes that black people are
aggressive and forthright and so on and people
can use those notions to dismiss what we are
saying.

The school I went to in London was a
secondary modern school. It was streamed and
there were only two black kids in that top stream.
And as you went down the streams, the streams
got progressively blacker so by the time you got
to the bottom stream which were all forms six and
seven all the classes were predominantly black so,
I was separated from my black peers by a
streaming system but also by my proximity to
academic success. If it wasn't for the church and
youth work, I don't think I would have had the
opportunity to meet socially with so many other
black youngsters.

My mother was amazing: active in the school
on the Parent Teacher Association, and she came
to all the functions. She was always there and it
was taken for granted that school work was taken
seriously.

I remember going to a classroom where there
was a huge pile of children at the front of the
class – I must have been about seventeen – and
telling them to go and sit down. I was absolutely
staggered that they listened to me! But they did
and at the bottom of this pile I found a teacher. So
that's when the seed of an idea of becoming a
teacher began.

I was doing music, I was doing my A levels, I
was doing sport, I did a lot for the church, I was

'I worked night and day.'

'One of the biggest differences is still the difficulty of defining who you are, and what it means to be black in Britain today and I think the important thing for the young people to understand is that the most important definition is their own, they define it.'

helping run the family. It was all happening at once.

I went to teacher training college to do English. In the meantime I'd won a Rotary Foundation scholarship to go to the States to study linguistics. So after my probationary teaching year I went to the States, and that's where I got my first degree. I worked night and day! It's a modular system so I studied from 8 o'clock in the morning till 8 o'clock at night piling up the credits.

After a year or so in teaching I became acting head of department. Then, at the age of twenty six, I became head of year in a large boys' comprehensive school. It was important for the black boys – 40% of the school population being Caribbean – to have somebody there as a role model, but also for the white kids, somebody black being even-handed and being committed to academic and pastoral development.

I have noticed that when I speak, people are very careful. It's not just what you say, but how you say it and they're on their guard. But then I've done training with the police in Birmingham. If you are articulate and persuasive, it's interesting how you get to be utilised.

When I first came to Birmingham there were seven of us in one team all of African-Caribbean background. To date, that's been the only time in my working experience that I've worked with a team of black colleagues and it was the most exciting, liberating and professionally developing experience I've ever had and I've been propelled by it ever since.

It's recognising what's an opportunity, and that opportunities aren't necessarily wide open doors. It's also part of the contribution. I would hope that certainly black people would recognize that we carry a kind of responsibility for others, I mean other generations who are following us, to make a positive mark in many ways, because that will ease the pathway for them, but also give them a higher platform from which they can make their contributions.

There is improvement. However, it's not uniform improvement across all spheres at the same rate. One of the biggest differences is still the difficulty of defining who you are, and what it means to be black in Britain today and I think the important thing for young people to understand is that the most important definition is their own, they define it. We are having new ethnicities being defined today. You've got many youngsters of dual heritage background, one white parent, one black parent. They are defining what it means for them to be black here, and we have to listen to them because their experience is their experience and I think that's one of the lessons that people of my generation have to come to terms with very quickly. Having come through the experience of migration, part of our difficulty was that we were not listened to; we can't carry on in the same vein with our young people today, we must be listening to them, even if what they are saying doesn't fit in with what we would like them to be saying, we actually need to have the grace and the understanding to accept that has to be part of the process.

'Don't underestimate what you can do.'

Don't underestimate what you can do. I cannot understand now why I never thought I was more academically able than I believed I was, because if I had had faith in myself I may actually have achieved more, and that's the irony. In life there are setbacks, but the beauty is how you overcome the setbacks so it's not to be daunted by setbacks, it's to recognise that they do happen, but it's how you pick yourself up and overcome them. One needs to recognise that all sorts of people are struggling and having battles of their own, it's to recognise the struggles that you do have in common with other people and to look out for those because sometimes other people may not even recognise them themselves. For black people there are issues which have their parallels with struggles that women generally have. For me, that's a very powerful message for black men to hear, to listen to what black women have to say to us as black men and women in general in this society. Then looking at people with disabilities and the struggles that they have, and the way they can be made invisible, and to recognise that. These are very powerful things to learn about society and what these different struggles show is that we're all human beings.

Eleanor Grant

Eleanor Grant was the Black Arts Development Officer at the Kuumba Project, an African Caribbean Arts and Resource Project in Bristol.

Date of birth: 14 September 1961
Place of birth: Bristol, UK

Kuumba has been going now for 24 years. It all began as a grassroots project, with people from the Rastafarian community coming together to celebrate their culture. Kuumba promotes the arts and culture of Africa and the Caribbean, primarily through two seasons of cultural arts activity, which includes theatre, dance, music, literature, film and video. I am responsible for bringing that programme of work together. This includes things like booking artists and performing companies, negotiating and issuing contracts but I also work with technicians to prepare for shows, rigging lighting and setting up the PA system and a lot of other general running around. My job is to ensure the event takes place, on time, and the visiting companies and performers are happy. The other part of my job is largely administrative, writing reports, applying for funding. I've just successfully applied for Arts for Everyone, National Lottery funding to support a three-year drama development programme, and lobbying and campaigning for black artistic development in the region. I am now focusing on completing a three year development plan, which looks at strategic long term developments for the project.

Working in the arts is hard work, it's poorly paid and African and Caribbean arts are marginalised. However, the work is varied, no two days are the same. You have to be familiar with the regional politics and the arts nationally. You can work extremely long hours with very little reward. Perhaps it's easier for me because I'm single but nonetheless it's very stressful. It's hard working for a black organisation, particularly when you have achieved success, since others then expect you to achieve it for them and want to burden you with more work.

I went to art college for three years and studied fine art and art history. I was always doing creative things at school, and art was my favourite subject. But even at art college I used to look at my paintings, and think that they didn't really say anything about who I was. It didn't reflect the person I was becoming, which was a more culturally aware black woman. All the way through college there was no attempt to understand my culture by my tutors or even to show me the work of other black artists. Everything as per usual was taught from a very Eurocentric perspective.

'I needed to go off, get a life and understand myself and the world.'

I thought I needed to go off and get a life and understand myself and the world, so I could begin to reflect this in my work, so I went travelling. In Israel I worked on a kibbutz picking apple and avocados. I also worked for a while in Jerusalem with Jews and Palestinians, then travelled home via Turkey, Cyprus and Italy. When I returned to England I worked for just over three years in the Post Office sorting mail, a job that didn't interest me greatly but provided me with the means to earn enough money so that I could go travelling again. This time I went away for a year, around the world on my own, through Thailand, Malaysia, Indonesia, spending six months in Australia hitch-hiking through the outback and New Zealand, to America, Mexico and Jamaica. The trip was a significant learning journey for me, opening my eyes to the world.

'Black people need to work much more collectively.'

I never thought I would earn my living working in the arts until this job came up. It has brought a degree of recognition. Because of what I have achieved within my field I have been asked to do more talks, travelled abroad and sit on several committees. I think I can influence certain things by my presence and by voicing my concerns. Nationally, I think there needs to be greater unity within the arts through something like a national black network. It's difficult to achieve change singly in this country – black people need to work much more collectively. I've become clear about the situation within the arts now and I feel very cynical about black artistic development in this country. Over the years funding to black arts organisations has slowly been chopped away – there is only one fully, revenue funded African

Caribbean touring theatre company in this country, and that's absurd. There has been a deliberate move to integrate work by black artists into mainstream white institutions that in itself is not a problem. However, what is problematic is that sometimes you will see new work and at other times it is invisible. It has not been promoted well in the black community, and so no one really knows it is happening. So that it then becomes a case of showing the work to the "converted". I know there is a common view that black work is difficult to programme and market, at some white venues, not all. There are many complex issues around marketing to black audiences, it is not simply a question of finding an instant fix.

'We've got a very long way to go.'

We haven't as black people in this country recognised the importance of networks. We have done very little to document and preserve our heritage in this country. We've just celebrated fifty years of the first large group of immigrants arriving in this country on the SS Empire Windrush. Without seeming pessimistic, I wonder what is it we've got to celebrate? The markers of success, a few high profile "famous" black people in areas namely sport, music and television. We're still dealing with the aftermath of the Stephen Lawrence case, and the McPherson report and still dealing with racism at an institutional level. I feel we've got a very long way to go, and should not become complacent.

I've been told I am impatient, that I want everything now but why shouldn't I? I do feel frustrated that there appears to be no radical changes initiated to combat racism. I went to the National Black Arts Festival in Atlanta in 1998, a very high profile celebration of arts from across the Diaspora, and I came back feeling very enthused by what I saw there. I was impressed by the unity and strength of African Americans and that a large group of professional people in the arts, in positions of power, are able to unite and initiate some serious changes. There were people present like leading playwright August Wilson, Nobel Laureate Wole Soyinke (Professor at Emory University), and writer Ntozake Shange, it was a very empowering experience. I know that there are articulate, intelligent black people working in this country who can initiate changes and many have done so. However, the major difference is that we

'Success to me means reaching the goals I set for myself.'

'My hard work paid off.'

do not in this country work together, the emphasis is too much on difference and not the common factors which bond us.

Success to me means reaching the goals I set for myself. I set very high standards. I feel I have a lot to contribute and a lot of energy. There are also lots of things I need to learn, and people I need to learn from. I can do this anywhere in the world. It is not about staying in Britain.

My mum came to this country from Jamaica in 1957; my father was already here. I went to an ordinary girls' comprehensive school in a white working class area in the north of Bristol. Our family moved there because of the availability of council housing. So having lived in a black area, sharing a house with other Caribbean migrants, we moved to this white area, and was one of a few black families living there. As black children we got used to the isolation and racism but it wasn't easy. As a first generation black British child navigating their way through the English school system in the 70s and 80s it was harsh. We were categorised and stereotyped – put into lower class streams, regardless of our intelligence. I was in the B stream, one from the top and wanted to do A levels. Already it became clear this would be difficult because I was not in the top class and so the feelings of inferiority and that you weren't really good enough were being impressed from that very critical age. I knew I would have to work twice as hard in order to overcome this and achieve my goal. Luckily for me there were a couple of teachers who encouraged me to look at further education. I did get my A levels and went on to college. So my hard work paid off in the end.

You do have to grow up with the belief that you're just as good as everybody else. My mum who raised us, taught me this lesson quite early. I remember her having to march up to the school to confront teachers about their racism. There was a sense of being alienated from both the black and white communities. The majority of the black girls from our school travelled in from St Paul's and Easton, predominantly black areas, whilst we lived in a white area, they spoke in patois, we didn't – so the differences were immediate. They would gang up and taunt both me and my sister. Accuse us of trying to be "white", simply because we had aspirations and believed we could achieve them. It was a cruel time, those girls used to hang out in large gangs and be constantly at you; they had power in numbers.

Racism is subtle in this country but it demonstrates itself very obviously in people's actions, overt and covert comments. I find the white middle classes are worse because they will say and do something really patronising, then pretend, "well I don't know what you mean" or flatly reject it as racist action.

'Everything I do is influenced by my history and the past.'

All the really clever creative people I know are working in isolation, in environments where they may be the only black person there. Quite a few of my friends now work abroad preferring to leave England altogether. I'm probably more attuned to the reality of the situation here now and by that I mean where we are as black people. I work in the arts and that's about being creative, changing people's perceptions and creating an understanding, appreciation and awareness of African and Caribbean culture. Some people would consider me to be black and middle class because I own my own home, car, have a fairly good job and appear to be fairly independent and well spoken. I am conscious of the way people perceive me but everything I do is influenced by my history and the past. I exist within the context of an historical and cultural time line, which is in essence our history as people of African descent. So the things I do now will have an impact. Others have walked that timeline, made sacrifices, enabling my path to be a smoother one. Being part of that makes me proud – and in acknowledging all of this I hope my achievements will do the same for others.

The whole education system in Britain, I believe has been geared towards failing black men. Every year I coordinate an educational programme of costume making and dance, as part of the St Paul's Carnival, I've been doing this for six years now. I work with a team in up to eight junior schools each summer with over 250 children from different ethnic backgrounds. It is work I enjoy and it enables me to build a rapport with children in my community, who have become part of my life. I see how some of the teachers, often in schools with no black teachers, treat some of the young black boys, labelling them as trouble makers, even at that early age. Many are bright intelligent boys who are not stimulated by what they are being taught and how it is taught. There are no role models for them to relate to, people who can influence them at what is a critical stage in their development. All of these things contribute to perpetuating the myths and stereotypes about black men, hence in cases like Stephen Lawrence, the initial poor reaction to his murder by the police, validated many black people's conviction that society holds a black mans life to be of little value.

I am fully aware of my own heritage and cultural heritage. I still feel like an outsider in Britain and a part of me will always feel that way. I am British born but that does not make me proud. I really believe everything is possible in life but it's up to the individual to make the choices which are best for them.

'Everything is possible in life – but the choice must be yours to begin'.

Eleanor Grant is now Director of Programming at The Drum, Britain's only African, Caribbean and Asian arts centre in Birmingham.

Martin Harding

Superintendent in charge of Operational Communications for the Greater Manchester Police

I am in charge of Operational Communications for the Greater Manchester Police, the largest provisional police service outside the capital. I am responsible largely for almost 800 staff. These staff answer and deal with all urgent and non-urgent telephone calls to the Greater Manchester Police. We also provide radio communications in the area. My department is the first point of contact for the majority of people who wish to or need to contact the police.

Date of birth: 10 October 1957
Place of birth: Manchester

'I would not be telling the truth if I said it was easy.'

I would not be telling the truth if I said it was easy. Because of the things we do, and the impact we have on people's lives, it's always a challenge because you can't afford to make too many wrong decisions. I was formerly an Operational Chief Inspector at Longsight, a tough inner city 'High Crime' area. There have been a lot of violent incidents: people being shot, a number of domestic burglaries, and so on.

I have previously served an attachment to the HMIC, Her Majesty's Inspectorate of Constabulary. The role of the Inspectorate is to make sure the service is performing in a manner that's expected in terms of community and race relations. I wouldn't mind continuing here, given the opportunity. Failing that I'll go back and try to attain the rank of superintendent.

'It's not so much overt racism, but there has been and still is a discriminatory practice.'

It's taken a lot of hard work for me to get to this position. It's not so much overt racism, but there has been and still is discriminatory practice. When I entered the system there were fourteen of us qualifying for promotion. In certain areas I was probably the most qualified person, yet I was passed over every time.

I lived in a place called Withenshawe, Greater Manchester: probably one of the most violent estates in the city. A lot of my friends went the other way and resorted to crime as a means of survival. I still speak to them and socialise with them. I've got no hang-ups about them: we go back a long way.

I went to primary school in Salford. Then, there were very few black people living in the Salford area. You normally had about four or five black kids in the school. There was never anything conscious made about the fact that my skin was different to theirs. In fact, I've got a lot of good memories of primary school.

The grammar school was about 99 per cent white, but I remember being well treated. I made some great friends at school. I don't remember any racism at school. I also don't remember there being any black role models while I was growing up.

At the local grammar school I did accountancy and technical drawing. But speaking to people I got the impression that the police service would suit me.

Originally, when leaving school at sixteen, I joined the cadets until I was eighteen.

The late sixties saw some situations in the States that crossed over here with the Civil Rights Movement. I had an idea of what was going on nationally. Role models tended to be musicians. Some of them had broken down barriers, whereas sportsmen and academics had not.

My dad's Nigerian and my mum is German; a strange mix of cultural influences – amazingly different! I've been to Germany a few times, but never to Nigeria.

I've got a comfortable house, a wife, two gorgeous girls: we're warm, we're comfortable. I do know how I want to live and I try and live that way. So, that's what success means to me.

' I wasn't ever in a position to challenge racism.'

Growing up, I never had the self confidence to challenge racism, so the coping mechanism I chose at that time was one of acquiescence. I think I worked on the basis that they're not being malicious, they just don't know what to say. So acquiescence prevailed, and it followed that there were no great tensions. Then again, I'm 6ft 4inches and weigh 17 stone, so there weren't going to be too many people who would call me something that was overtly stupid. So I've been fortunate that way, but I know black colleagues who don't weigh 17 stone and have had one or two problems.

Early on, I think there was a bit of suspicion of me. Obviously the relationship between the police and the black community meant that the police service was not regarded as a job to go into. But I've noticed that has changed a lot since the Stephen Lawrence tribunal because now it's okay to stand up and be counted, and be seen to be black in the service. I think they use the word 'coconut': black on the outside, but white on the inside. But you'll see me stand up and challenge issues of race.

'People have lost a lot more than I have, much more.'

My challenge to discrimination could have a high cost. That cost would be a personal one. You can see straight away the cost to yourself is a personal one. If I make no more progress in the job than I have today, people have lost a lot more than I have, much more.

I see that it's quite common that when somebody stands up and speaks up for themselves that in a very short time they are the subject of a performance review. Now that can be very damaging when you want to make progress. I had a personal setback for two years in that I was required to work to a personal development plan designed to remedy my alleged shortcomings.

'I'm not up there, up there, but I'm up there!'

But now, those coming through the grass roots can see that they're not on their own. There is somebody up there. I have been heavily involved in trying to ensure that minority ethnic staff achieve all that they are capable of.

Since 1911 we've had policewomen in the service, but there have only been three female Chief Officers. It speaks volumes about the fight women have had to get there. Black people have not been involved in the police service as long as females, so we're having the same fight, and making some progress.

'We've got a black middle-class.'

I'd never have imagined that we'd have a black head of state in South Africa before we had a black head of state in this country. We've got a black middle class who will, as far as I'm concerned, have got there on merit and hard work: these people really put their hours in.

'When there are set-backs there is no point in moaning.'

I don't think there is a black community: there are black communities. The only link seems to be the blackness, skin colour and nothing else. When there are set-backs there is no point in moaning. You've got to try and move on. If you stay in the past you're going to start to dwell on it. Go forward and take your experiences with you, and learn from those experiences.

I think one of the primary things young people should look for is what would make them happy, not financially but personally: to fulfil their potential and go with what they're good at. And, instead of going for the first thing, they should look around.

Also, it's a two-way thing. It's all right for the schools to help black youngsters, but black youngsters must help themselves as well.

'It's a two-way thing.'

The parents have got to get involved. The communities have got to get involved. We can't just blame the schools: the first and biggest forger of a child's abilities and perceptions is going to be the parents, so you've got to work with them.

Michael Hastings

Date of birth: 1958
Place of birth: UK

'I've always been intrigued by the media.'

'I don't like the word successful because the implication is that success equals material gains and status.'

Michael Hastings is Head of Public Affairs at the BBC.

As Head of Public Affairs for the BBC, I and my department are the conduit between the BBC and Parliament. We're interested in the BBC's long-term relationship with Parliament and that's because, uniquely, the BBC is constituted by Royal Charter and exists by the will of Parliament. We make sure that communication between the two is open and honest and we aim to secure the BBC's position in the long-term through awareness raising.

I've always been intrigued by the media, particularly television, and I've always been intrigued by politics. In this job, I combine the two. I got here by a series of circuitous routes, as usual. I came to the BBC first of all to be an education correspondent and the presenter of a politics programme. I'd been with ITV previously, doing a similar job because I happened to know somebody who was running a television company. So it was through personal connections.

But competition was pretty stiff for this job. Why me? I was here as Number Two for a couple of years and I built up a particularly fresh way of approaching things. I was able to help the BBC build a personal dynamic with Members of Parliament and to strengthen those relationships. We achieved great gains in legislation in 1996.

I was born in the UK, in the north west. My mother was a volunteer nurse but never worked again after she married. My father was a dental surgeon. We went to Jamaica as a family in 1966 when I was eight and returned to the UK when I

'My philosophy of life is absolutely guided by my strong personal commitment to Jesus Christ and that has been life-long.'

was 14. I went to boarding school in the north west. The education system in Jamaica was considerably more stringent and demanding than the state system here. I know that the results of the school I went to in Montego Bay were as strong as the best of the private system here.

I took the traditional route from school to university and then went into teaching. After that I did Government consultancy and then broadcasting.

I don't like the word 'successful' because the implication is that success equals material gain and status. This notion of success is misguided. I'm a husband and father, and I think that's more important than my role at the BBC. My philosophy of life is absolutely guided by my strong personal commitment to Jesus Christ, and that has been life-long.

A friend said to me long ago that the most important thing you can do for your children is to love their mother. Children hate rowing parents and insecurity. It doesn't matter a fig to the child what you're doing: titles and offices mean nothing. If I were to achieve the most glorified position possible in the media world but was about nothing of value to those closest to me and then to the poor, the marginalised, the unrepresented, then what have I achieved?

There is a black middle class within the Afro-Caribbean community in particular, where aspirations have always been high but achievements low and this mismatch between the two has got to be addressed. I would not say we want a black middle class in Britain. I would say we want as responsible and as committed, as mature and as able a people as we can. And if that means that some have money and others have learning, then that's great. Wisdom comes in many forms – character is the best outcome.

'The more educationally aware black people become, the more aware they are of the real power of injustice, the real place of discrimination.'

The more educationally aware black people become, the more aware they are of the real power of injustice, the real place of discrimination. I very firmly believe that economic, cultural and social advance for black people in Britain is not about their blackness. I think the emphasis on black history, black identity, is overplayed. What is important for a young black person is their ability to speak confidently, to be alert, to understand how the world works, to understand the economic and political and cultural systems, know where the power brokers are, understand the routes forward and not worry endlessly about background.

'I think the emphasis on black history, black identity is over played.'

If you say black men ought always to marry black women or black people ought to live in black areas, you're just creating a culture within a culture. There's no gain in that. There ought to be the widest diffusion of living styles and relationships so that people can rise to their potential and not be locked in by, 'You're black therefore you must ...'

The priority is to realise that certain educational and personal skills are far more important than background and culture. If you can't read and write, if you don't understand the world, and you can't articulate what you think, you can have every conceivable chip on your shoulder about being black, but you ain't going nowhere. Rather than stand on the sidelines and shout about how disgraceful they are, we need to join in with that great sense of national irritation that says this behaviour is unacceptable. But frankly, we must realise how important it is to honour norms. The more international our business culture becomes, the less room there is for the troublesome, awkward squad. So don't turn up at interviews with your Nikes undone and chewing gum: it doesn't work. It's not the way the world is and nobody owes you a living. We must be example setters and leaders – not just protesters and campaigners. We have to take our place as citizens too.

'Don't turn up at interviews with your Nikes undone and chewing gum: it doesn't work.'

'If you can't read and write... you ain't going nowhere.'

If more of our young men and women concentrated on sound, strong relationships, we'd have a better position in the life of the nation than if they became wealthy with grand titles. We want strong families, because the next generation don't need to spend their time being excluded from school and then going to prison. We have to set the framework of stability for them.

When I was in my late teens I met a very dear man, Major-General, Sir John Nelson. He became a mentor to me. He was as white as you could find – a traditional army General – and he took me under his wing. He introduced me into wider networks. If I'd stayed in my little Afro-Caribbean ghetto, I would have gone nowhere. You discover that people actually like you. The world isn't against you.

Mark Hendrick

Mark Hendrick was a member of the European Parliament for Lancashire Central and the Socialist Group's spokesperson on economic and monetary affairs in the European parliament.

The best part of this job is seeing a policy develop from its early stages, the policy then turning into legislation and that legislation being transformed into national legislation that has an impact on people's lives.

You're always subject to criticism but you wouldn't be doing anything worthwhile unless you were. The European Union as a body is misunderstood and talked down and it's difficult to get the message across, to be constructive at times when people are out to knock you.

I started off as an electronics engineer and then changed direction and became a scientist and thought I would have a life in a research institute or academia. I've always been very interested in political and social issues and in parallel with my professional career, was involved in local politics. I was a city councillor for eight years for Salford and Greater Manchester but I never really contemplated working full time in politics because I found my professional work very interesting as well. However, there came a point in my life where I couldn't really pursue two parallel paths and I had to choose one or the other. I found at the time, politics was interesting me more and therefore I chose a career in local government and in politics.

Like many people, I was politicised during my student days and I didn't join the Labour Party until I had graduated and finished my studies. I was very interested in politics and mixed with people who were active in politics during my student days. My entry into local politics was a reaction to Thatcherism, which I felt was very harsh and very aggressive. So although I had a very good job as a technologist, I felt that it was important to help the Labour Party because I believed they could offer the country a better deal. Little did I know that it would take eighteen years to shift the last government!

'There have been times when I have had to make difficult decisions and certain sacrifices.'

I spent four or five years just helping out at local level until somebody suggested that I stand for election in local government. So I did this as an aside rather than as a long-term future career.

After being elected to the local council in Salford in 1987, I served one term and then was elected for a second term. The build-up of responsibilities as a city councillor began to impinge on my other work and by 1993 I had to make a choice. I had originally thought that the House of Commons, Westminster would be the easier option although I had always preferred European politics. The European elections in 1994 were coming up and there was one vacancy in the whole of the North West, so I entered the contest to become a candidate. There were forty candidates so I wasn't really expecting to get elected. I was very fortunate to get into the European Parliament on my first attempt. The term of office is five years and I'm now in my second term after being re-elected in 1999. I'm the first black UK MEP.

I think nearly all MEPs spend the majority of the week in Brussels; there's committee work, meetings with political groups, meetings of the socialist group.

'I'm in my fourth job.'

I left school at sixteen to train as a technician and I was told to go back to study and do a degree. After doing that I went to work as an engineer. I returned to study again to do a masters and then postgraduate study as scientist. Finally, I trained as a teacher and taught for four years at technical college in Stockport. So now I'm in my fourth job!

The community I grew up in was predominately white and so I never really saw myself as Afro-Caribbean. Rather than make a big deal about my own ethnicity, I thought that the best way to deal with things was to get round them rather than tackle them head on.

*'I wanted to show what
black people can do...
rather than just
complain about how
bad things are.'*

If you want to do something in life then you
should pursue your objectives and use all
reasonable means at your disposal to achieve
them. People's experiences are different. My
experiences were probably different from other
black MPs because of my mixed cultural
upbringing. I tried to break down prejudice by
showing that I was a person who had ideas and
values to add to the society and community in
which I lived; by being diplomatic. I am criticised
now by one or two sections of the black
community for perhaps not being vehement or
vocal enough on issues of race, but I must
represent everybody's interests. I see myself as a
role model for black people, not necessarily
somebody who has campaigned on issues of race.
I want to show what black people can do if they
put their minds to it rather than just complain
about how bad things are. Mohammed Ali is a hero
of mine because he said what he thought and
worked to carry it through.

Other countries in the European Union aren't as
tolerant of Afro-Caribbean or Asian people as we
are in the UK; the laws in the UK reflect a much
fairer society than exists elsewhere.

I would say black people should pursue work in
other countries. I was fortunate to have
undertaken electrical engineering work in
Brussels. I was on a student placement there in
1981, so I had some experience of the place.
Things were difficult at first, but having picked up
the language and lived there for a while, I was at
an advantage when I was elected to the European
Parliament.

Most politicians come into politics for a
combination of reasons: they think the world's a
terrible place and they want to make it better for
everyone; they crave power and they like
membership of this organisation or club and the
publicity or fortune it brings. I'm much more
driven by the job and the work that I do and
probably the secret of my "success" has been that
single-mindedness.

Whilst I am in a middle class profession, I still
think of myself as working class. There is a black
middle class but I don't aspire to it in any sense.
Given the different countries that black people in
this country originate from, the different
experiences, the different cultures, no one person

can claim to speak for the black community. Anyone who does, I'm immediately suspicious of. There is a black community but it's not homogenous.

'The secret of my success has been my single-mindedness.'

I think it's difficult for any black kid if their parents don't feel that they have had opportunities or experiences to pass on. Without that, it's a bit like being given a map and not being told how to use it. After all, everyone needs guidance and support. My philosophy is about redistributing opportunity.

Lenny Henry

Lenny Henry is an actor and comedian who works in theatre, television and film and he sings with his own band. He is also involved in production and was awarded an Honorary BA by Warwick University in the early 90s.

'Success is having a dream and holding onto it.'

I've never felt that I've done enough: I've always wanted to be the best that I could be. I have a band, and we'll practise half a dozen times just to get it right. I continue to strive to be the best that I can. It's about having dreams and holding onto them, having faith in your abilities, having people around you who will encourage and support you.

It's important to achieve your fullest potential and not settle for second best. Set out to get what you want from life. See the goal and go for it. Kids need mentors: people who can give them support, someone they can look up to.

When I was at school, the teachers did not know what to do with me. I enjoyed some subjects but generally school was not the place that I wanted to be. I suppose allowing me to do my own thing at that point was their way of 'containing' me!

It's not easy for black people to get on TV and to do what I'm doing but it's getting better. It's a slow process but it's happening. We won't have fully achieved until there are more black and Asian people in the position of directors, deciding the programmes that we have on TV and radio. When we no longer see the usual faces on TV, then we'll know that we are moving on. It's important to me that my work appeals to a wide, multi-racial audience.

In this line of work you're automatically self employed. You are only employed for the contract

'It's important to have positive people around you, who wish you well.'

period and you need people around you to help organise you and arrange other contracts. Now I'm in a position where I'm employing others I feel that I have come full circle. Self employment has allowed me to be who I want to be and to do what I want to do.

I love my work but sometimes there is a feeling of isolation. You have to create a situation that allows you to survive the stresses of the job and this is where family and friends are important. It is a cut-throat business. Of course you're going to make mistakes but the important thing is to learn from them.

I think young people need to be prepared for life: how to fill out forms, write letters, carpentry, cooking as well as all the curriculum stuff. Young people do need their parents' love, help and support. They can't do this on their own.

I think that every kid has a talent. The teacher should be asking how can we help that kid utilize it for educational purposes. Every kid is waiting for a button to be pushed, it is the teachers' and parents' job to work in tandem to push that button.

The turning point was winning *New Faces* in 1975, getting public recognition and knowing that this is what I'm good at and other people agreeing.

A learning experience was me as part of *the Black and White Minstrel Show*, at the time not fully understanding why black people weren't coming to see me. I learnt the hard way about being conscious of the bigger picture. I think my work with Comic Relief has taught me a lot about compassion and resilience.

Jo Hodges

Date of birth: 5 June 1959
Place of birth: Leicester, UK

'Success for me (so far) hasn't meant having very much money.'

Jo Hodges is a screenwriter film maker and novelist. Her book The Girl with Brains in her Feet *was published by Virago in 1997. Her screenplay for the film (of the same name) was on general release at the same time.*

As a screenwriter, I spend most of my time writing scripts. This doesn't leave that much time left to write a second book which I would say in all honesty is my top priority, but staying alive is important too. Novels are a long time goal. To get just enough money to exist on is the short term one. Even with experience in screenwriting I still have to find temporary work in order to survive. Time recently has become even more precious as I have recently begun to direct films. This was always my intention as a natural extension from screenwriting, and seeing as a short film I've made has just won an award, I want to do more!

I find writing is at the core of everything. In the beginning I didn't dare write as I thought you had to be extremely clever and fantastically well educated to do it, but after years of denying my urge to be a writer, I eventually had a go and decided that maybe I wasn't so stupid after all.

A word of warning – success for me (so far) hasn't meant having very much money. In the past I had plenty. I used to have a very good job and I measured myself against how many expensive restaurants I would go to in a week or by the size of my company car. Since then I have found other things which mean more. Of course I'd like to be rich, but I don't consider being rich being well paid for something you don't really want to do. So now even though my bank manager would disagree with me, I would say I am richer than before.

I went to a primary school on a big council estate in Leicester where at that time there weren't any black people. I didn't know anybody black until I was thirteen or fourteen. My mum is white and my dad was a black American who left to go back to the USA before I was born. Being the only mixed race person, I think I was treated pretty well, but I do remember feeling that I always had to put on a good front to please people.

First I went to an o.k. comprehensive and then onto a bad one. I was lucky to find a few teachers who thought I was reasonably clever but I just played the idiot all the time. I'd found I had a good sense of humour and having lots of friends was more important to me than passing exams. I don't remember having worse behaviour than a lot of my friends, but I got expelled.

'I learned just how stupid I'd been.'

As a result of being expelled, I found myself put down from the A stream into the B stream in another school – which paradoxically was a good school. Here I learned just how stupid I'd been. To pass exams I realised takes hard work and revision which I hadn't bothered with at all before. I do remember though at the time how I'd been confused, that in class I was clever, but stupid when it came to exams. Eventually I worked out that I just hadn't worked out a method of memorizing facts and it wasn't until I'd left school that I managed to conquer this problem. Now I find exams easy.

'I've discovered that most people are ready to help you if you ask them.'

So after realising my mistakes, thanks to a couple of dedicated teachers who put in a good word for me, coupled with a lot of hard catching up, I was lucky enough to get a place at art school. My ideas had always been good but people were surprised when I told them that I thought about going into advertising afterwards. I do remember a tutor saying to me that I would shock most interviewers who I came across just by being able to speak properly because I was black. This I think, is the most negative thing anyone has said to me but this was an extreme. I've discovered that most people are ready to help you if you ask them. In addition to this I would also say that most people are prepared to like you if you like them back!

So, after a career in advertising I wound up winning a place on a writing course at Carlton Television where I was trained by leading professionals in the television and film business. At the end of it I got a good agent. Thereafter, I gained a place at the National Film and Television School.

'It's so much easier to give people the excuse to say you're a moaning minnie or accuse you of having a chip on your shoulder.'

Like most people (black or white) unpleasant things have happened and I could concentrate on those, but for my book I was much more interested in writing about a girl who makes it and doesn't end up being a victim. I do not consider myself a victim so why should I end up writing about one? It's so much easier to give people the excuse to say you're a moaning minnie or accuse you of having a chip on your shoulder – my advice is to sidestep all of that. Questions like, "Why is my stuff never picked? Is it because I'm black? Is it because I'm not as posh? Is it because"... Look – forget it. The best thing to realise is that nothing is going to happen unless you make it. But as I've said before, you do need friends to help you   – not friends like before who were happy to see me play the idiot but friends who are happy for me to do well and friends who are honest in their criticism. Another thing you eventually have to realise is people don't just say things to hurt you – they may be correct!

'The best thing to realise is that nothing is going to happen unless you make it.'

I remember being eighteen and very angry. Now I've worked a lot of that anger out by getting things done how I want them. I think a lot of black kids deliberately hold themselves back. They don't want to show their mates up by being cleverer than they are. But don't hold back. The idea of pleasing other people all the time is a mistake. That doesn't mean you have to go round being obnoxious either.

There is no need to be embarrassed if you're talented or clever at something. Go ahead and show people what you can do.

Claire Holder

Claire Holder is a barrister and chief executive of the Notting Hill Carnival Trust.

'I've been living as part of this community for well over 25 years and have a strong commitment to people here'.

I was in practice as a barrister for about 12 years but I scaled down my practice once I became involved in the Notting Hill Carnival. Now it's only occasionally that I will sit on a tribunal.

I organise the carnival: everything, from start to finish. It's a very complex job and a very rewarding one. It involves some serious administrative skills plus a good knowledge of finance. We do have a finance director who does all the accounting work, but I do most of the fundraising, organise the bands and generally look at all the operational issues. These include liaising with the local authority and the police, and making sure the streets are clean afterwards.

Too many people on the outside assume that carnival is simply about picking up a telephone. But you literally have to start from scratch each year. My legal background certainly gave me good discipline from which to work, and the carnival is now the bulk of my work.

I'd been living in Notting Hill since I was 12 and had been involved in carnival from the age of 16. Once I qualified as a barrister I used to help out at a local legal advice centre on Saturdays. It was a black people's information centre and from there I became involved in many community schemes. Carnival had a crisis in 1989: all the funders refused to continue funding unless there was a new committee. I was approached to become involved for three months initially. One of the things that made me stay around for so long was that I had to sign a number of personal guarantees as far as the funding was concerned. There was no way I was going to step away and allow other people to carry on the administration at a standard I would not approve of. I was here on a daily basis and the chambers I belonged to started withdrawing my work. But I wasn't earning anything in carnival because I was on the board and so not allowed to earn a wage.

This went on for nine years. Then last year carnival got some money so I resigned as chair and took the job of chief executive so that I'm literally doing the same thing but now being paid for it. My legal practice was kept going because I sit on a number of committees and tribunals. At least I'm keeping my finger in there; it would sadden me not to practise law. That's my talent; it's what I was trained for.

'Income is totally secondary. I make sure I get satisfaction out of whatever I do.'

When I left school I knew I didn't want to be a teacher or secretary, so I studied law and thoroughly enjoyed it. I'm a sole practitioner. I requalified to do Finance and Administration and I'm also a Chartered Secretary. I enjoy learning and I enjoy doing, not just for myself but for others. Income is totally secondary. I make sure I get satisfaction out of whatever I do.

If someone had said to me fifteen years ago that I'd be involved in carnival I wouldn't have believed them. I had a stereotyped view of the type of person who'd be involved. I didn't think I had the right personality, but I was wrong!

'There are some very positive black boys out there.'

In general, I think black girls are attentive in class; the black girl has career aspirations. But there are also some very positive black boys out there. What disturbs me is that too many are not positive. Many women fail to teach their sons how to respect women; they let them run wild and think arrogance will get them everywhere. I find that many black men are either afraid of black women who are their equal, or are hostile to them. The black men who are your intellectual equals put you down.

'Carnival represents a lot to black people.'

I do feel a strong sense of responsibility to the community from this particular organisation, more so than I did in legal practice. People in the community turn to this organisation for many

*'Carnival represents
our freedom from
slavery.'*

things: advice on education, legal advice. They
need this contact. Carnival represents a lot to
black people.

Certainly I'm part of the black community. People
say that carnival is a black event, but in fact this
isn't true. It has a 60% white following. Some black
people even say that they don't come along because
it's too much trouble. But carnival represents our
freedom from slavery. I feel emotional about it
because of my awareness of what it represents:
millions of people dying in slavery, and this one act
of freedom. Some people seem to think that if they
want to be seen to be achieving then they have to
leave things like carnival behind.

I was born here but did all my primary
schooling in Trinidad. We grew up with my
grandparents, then when I reached secondary age
I returned to my parents and went to school in
Notting Hill. I didn't have a particularly good time
at school. When I did A levels and all the girls
were getting careers advice and UCAS forms for
university entrance, I wasn't given one even
though I wanted to study law. I was told that I'd
need to go and work as a clerk with a solicitor and
work my way up from there. So I left school with A

*'Success is doing things
right and getting a
positive result.'*

levels not knowing where to go. Eventually I went
to the College of Law.

Success is doing things right and getting a
positive result. This isn't what I thought I wanted
to do but I'm achieving success in terms of the
day to day task.

When I was growing up in the Caribbean, my
teacher would write up on the blackboard every
morning, "The Will Does It". It took me a while to
understand what he meant, because he never
explained it. Your motivation is within yourself. If

*'If you want to get on in
life then you have to
put the work in
yourself.'*

you want to get on in life then you have got to put
the work in yourself.

Let's not expect too much from schools. They
are institutions of learning and what they are
doing should be complemented by what is
happening at home. It's too much to say that the
teachers' job is to motivate. Their job is to teach
their subject; to provide information. What
schools need to do is be fair and earn pupils'
respect. Schools don't have a duty to the
individual child in the way that parents do.

'The will does it'.

Paul Hull

Paul Hull is a professional rugby coach for Bristol Rugby Club. He retired from playing in January 2000 due to an achilles tendon injury.

Date of birth: 17 May 1968
Place of birth: London, UK

'Try to fulfil your dreams. Work hard and they will come true. Everyone started with dreams.'

Rugby as a sport only went professional a few years ago and before that we were all amateurs with full time jobs. We just played rugby as a very serious hobby and didn't get paid officially. Now that it's fully professional, we are accountable to the club in the same way as a professional footballer. We train twice a day, most days, and then we have games at the weekends.

Before this, I was in the Royal Air Force as a physical training instructor so I've always been involved in sport. I taught physical education and gave advice on diet and fitness. It was a good move to go from there into professional sport.

I grew up in London and I always wanted to be a professional footballer. It's funny that I've actually gone into rugby but I think the decision was made when I left school. I had trials for Southampton Football Club and I didn't make it, so I had to decide what sport I was going into. I chose rugby, played for England under 19s and never looked back.

When I was doing my training in the RAF rugby was my sport, so when I was due for my first posting they sent me to RAF Lyneham, near to Bath and Bristol rugby clubs. I joined Bristol then, and I've been with them ever since.

It's obviously great getting paid for something you love doing, but it does have its down side. You are fitness tested more frequently and the public demand a good standard of rugby. It's more business oriented and if you don't perform on the pitch you could lose your job. Winning is everything.

When I joined, there was another black player here: Ralph Knibbs. He'd played for Bristol at the age of 17, which was very young in those days, and he's only recently left the club. He was my mentor. He was playing rugby when there weren't many black players in the sport. Now we have a few black players at Bristol and if you look up and down the country there are quite a few black players coming into the sport.

'I was always in the minority.'

I was always in the minority. The good thing about being black and being a talented sports person is that it breaks down all the barriers. You're going to get digged as a kid, but if you can play a sport then you're seen as an equal straight away. Of course people should see you as an equal anyway, but if you do sport you're on a level playing field from the word go.

I made it into the England team and played out in South Africa. This was a great place to make a debut, especially as I met Nelson Mandela.

'I'm always striving to do better.'

I'm always striving to do better. I'm coaching the second team and under 21s but want to branch into promotion and also commercial activities in and around the city.

The school I went to was military based because my dad was in the RAF. I joined the RAF at 17 and had a really great time. When the RAF spotted that I could play rugby they looked after me very well as is the custom with most sportsmen and women in the services.

I was born in Balham, London, but I've lived in Cyprus and Hong Kong, and then in north London. From there I went to boarding school. One of the reasons dad sent me was because I was so possessed with sport: football, football, football! When it came to the decision whether to go to college or start work, I decided I'd go straight into the Air Force, start making a bit of money, and go from there.

I'm an outgoing character and a natural organiser of people. I'm not one to be picked on. I try to get on with whatever the job demands. When I started basic training I was like a leader amongst the other recruits because they'd never been away from home before and never ironed a shirt, so I found I was helping them out.

You can't be a great sportsman if you can't communicate, and to be a good instructor you need to be outgoing because it can be nervewracking teaching 30 or 40 people at once. I was quite nervous up to that point in my life but becoming a physical training instructor (PTI) changed that.

My PE teacher at school was very good. He put me forward for the Southampton trials and was always looking out for me. I still keep in touch with the school now. I think the PE teachers in schools have an important role to play.

My dad was a very good sportsman. He was a sprinter and also a cricketer. He joined the RAF at an early age and Worcestershire wanted to buy him out of the service to play as a professional cricketer. He had to make a big decision, and he chose to stay with the RAF and bring up his family. Dad knew I loved football but he also introduced me to a whole range of sports. As a kid you do go through phases and lots of parents say, "You're good at this so stick at it". When I coach kids now I see parents on the touchline wanting their kids to do well. But they forget it's all about fun at that age. My dad was great. He always gave me advice for whatever sport I wanted to play. He let me play! Now I have a wide experience in a number of sports, which helped me in my eventual career as a physical training instructor.

I originally joined the RAF as a movements operator but was able to change trades to a PTI. I finally left the RAF a few years ago because I wanted to pursue my rugby.

'I didn't set myself unrealistic goals. I can accept failure because I've been knocked back a few times, but you've got to pick yourself up, brush yourself down, and go on again.'

Every goal I've set myself since school I've achieved. Of course there have been lots of downs but I'm now in the latter stages of my career, so the next goal is to be a successful coach and also to develop some work outside rugby. I don't set myself unrealistic goals. I can accept failure because I've been knocked back a few times, but you've got to pick yourself up, brush yourself down, and go again.

Because I'm in my early thirties now I've got to set myself a new challenge and make sure I coach well. I'm also interested in the promotional side of things and I want to get into after dinner speaking, so the next two years are very important. There's always a challenge out there because I haven't got a trade to fall back on. Even though I have qualifications within the RAF framework, the only job I could really walk into

'Even though you want to do sport, it's good to have something else up your sleeve.'

'Everything I do I want to make a good go of it.'

would be working in a leisure centre, and I don't want to do that.

I want to go up the ladder as far as I can, and everything I do I want to make a good go of it. Because I didn't go to university I have to make sure whatever I do is one hundred per cent. Even though you want to do sport it's good to have something else up your sleeve. Do your studies so that whatever happens you have choices.

There are several black sportsmen who have not only made it, but are really positive role models, they include: John Barnes, Daly Thompson: they're the ones that have probably had the hardest time but their natural talents, hard work, charisma and character pulled them through. They are the ones who probably had hard starts, but paved the way for us entering the sporting professions. Now there's not one team in the country I can think of that hasn't got a black player. Even in Scotland now you're going to find black players. The boo chants from the stand are stopping.

You do need dedication and self-discipline. Your parents can push you and your teachers can push you and your coach can push you, but unless you have the desire within yourself you're not going to do it. If you've got a goal, even though people might mock you stick to your guns.

Jessica Huntley

Date of birth: 23 February 1927
Place of birth: Bagotstown/EBD,
Guyana (then British Guiana)

'My mother was a very positive person. She taught me that no one was better than I was.'

Jessica Huntley is a publisher, cultural and political activist. She founded and manages Bogle-L'Ouverture Publications Ltd.

My mother was a very positive person. She taught me that no one was better than I was. Some person would say, "Jessica would have been a nice girl if only her nose was straight". My mother would reply, "Her nose suits her face". So I grew up feeling very confident about myself'.

My husband Eric and I were both active in the political and trade union movement in Guyana, prior to our departure for England. During the colonial period Eric, along with many political activists, was imprisoned. He had been a civil servant but when he came out of prison employers was reluctant to employ him. I encouraged him to leave for England to study. In 1958 I joined him. We had two children then, and that's how we came to Britain.

My first job was at a shipping company. Within two weeks the manager told me that the bosses from the city did not want a coloured person in their office. I said ok. The manager was surprised how I took the news and said that he regretted it because I was a good worker.

One of the other jobs I had was at the Ministry of Pensions and National Insurance, Haringay Branch, London. At the interview, the manager told me that the post was temporary. (The Agency had already told me that temporary posts could be for two weeks to two years). The manager said it was not worth my accepting it. I said I would still take the job. When I reached home the manager who interviewed me was waiting at my door to see me. He said that the job was only for a week and it did not make sense for me to accept. I said if it were only for two days then I still would. He stood at the door trying to convince me that it was not worth taking up the post, I spent five years there and became an active member of the Union.

I got started as a publisher in 1968 after Dr Walter Rodney, a lecturer at the University of the West Indies, Mona Campus, Jamaica, attended a conference in Canada and was banned from returning by the Jamaican government. The people in Jamaica rioted, resulting in loss of life and damage to property. A group of friends in London decided to highlight what had happened to him. We held demonstrations and picketed the Jamaican Tourist Board in London. Walter was later offered a post at the University of Dar-Es-Salaam in Tanzania.

'We knew nothing about book publishing.'

En route to London he brought us copies of the lectures that he had given at the university and to the Rastafarians on Jamaica. We decided to publish those lectures. We knew nothing about book publishing but contacted friends for help with money and advice.

In 1972 we began to display books on shelves in the front room of our home and office space. John LaRose of New Beacon Books also sold us some of his books. At that time teachers were saying that there were no books for black children. We felt that it was important to have these books that could give our children the kind of confidence they so badly lacked, it would also help them to know their origins.

We were forced to seek public premises after a neighbour complained to the council and did so in 1974. In 1980 the Bogle-L'Ouverture Bookshop was renamed Walter Rodney Bookshop after he was murdered in Guyana. At the Bookshop we organized poetry readings, book launches, workshops at which the public and schools attended.

The Bookshop served as a focal point for our community. We found ourselves providing advice and counselling on a wide range of issues. The main one was on education.

'My generation made the sacrifices for the future generations.'

Some of the children who visited the Bookshop often complained that their teacher did not like them. My reply to those children was why should a teacher like you? You don't have to like your teacher: that's not the purpose for which you go to school. It would help both ways but it is not essential. 'You are going to school to obtain an education. The teacher has knowledge and you want and need that knowledge'. Education was seen by my generation as a means of social mobility: that is what our parents taught us. I was aware that some people with a good education still cannot find a suitable job, but one stood a much better chance if you have it, than if you don't. My generation made sacrifices for future generations and now they must move forward and take what is there.

Many of our young people are doing more than just surviving. Some are doing very well. Somehow we never seem to talk about those young people. It's the same as when we talk about Africa, the media can only show us how Africans are starving. We need to highlight all the positive things that young people are achieving, so that it helps those who are not.

In 1971 we published *Getting to know Ourselves* by Phyllis and Bernard Coard. This title was aimed at the nursery age group so as to give children a concept of where they came from and that black was beautiful. The one review which the book received, in the Times Educational Supplement, was negative.

We later published Rodney's seminal work *How Europe Underdeveloped Africa*.

'I see myself as making a pathway for others to follow.'

I see myself as making a pathway for others to follow. In the sixties we were assisting people to be more conscious and aware. We brought out posters and greetings cards by Errol Lloyd with black images, something that hadn't been done before.

With some modesty, we helped to make the concept that "black was indeed beautiful", acceptable.

Keith Kerr

Date of birth: 17 July 1955
Place of birth: Westmoreland, Jamaica

Keith Kerr is General Manager of Customer Services Development at British Airways. He manages 20,000 staff and a budget of £2.4bn. He is also involved in many voluntary activities.

There's a pressure that I bring on myself to achieve and to deliver to expectation. Then there's a secondary pressure from recognising that I'm in a fairly unique position corporately, being black, and so I'm carrying the cross or the banner for all minority groups. I'm breaking down a lot of barriers. There's a feeling that if I fail, I'll set the cause back ten or fifteen years.

Being the only black person in this position brings tensions because your friends think that you've changed. But the thing is that jobs like this bring a better quality of life. The fact that your children can go to a quality school, or go to the pony club or ballet classes is part of the rewards the job brings.

I've kept a lot of my friends, but I've done so deliberately. We still play dominoes and drink white rum once every month. But I think you've got to be schizophrenic in a sense and most people find that difficult to manage. You've got to be white when you're required to be white, and you've got to be black when you're required to be black and you've got to recognise that you're not being two faced, you're not being a hypocrite. It's recognising when your blackness needs to be in the fore, and when you need to tone it down and get on with what you need to do. When I spoke to the African Caribbean Finance Forum recently I deliberately wanted to be provocative, and talked about changing colours. This was a play on words because British Airways was changing its colours

'Being the only black person makes you incredibly strong and resourceful. You don't need anyone else's acknowledgement that you're okay because you know you've fought and you've got this far.'

at that time. I introduced the concept that we need to change our colour on occasion as well. We can't just be "in your face" all the time and expect to achieve. Some black people became very critical and accused me of becoming white. But, if you have that kind of attitude you'll never succeed at the upper level because white people can always marginalize you.

Being the only black person in this position makes you incredibly strong and resourceful. You don't need any one else's acknowledgement that you're okay because you know you've fought and you've got this far without anyone else.

I was born in Jamaica and came to the UK when I was seven. What I'd been doing at school was way in advance of what they were doing here. It made one relax, and suddenly you could cruise. There were so many other distractions. I benefited from having very strong parents with Victorian values! They stopped me going off the rails.

In the 60s there was a growing awareness of us being black, being alien, being immigrants and unwanted. To find strength, there was the desire to find your own. And the problem with finding your own at that time was that it meant we weren't taking opportunities or getting a good education. 'No compromise' was the situation. The Afro was there and if somebody looked at you, you stared them out, because you're bad, you know what I mean? I've learned since that you can get what you want without confrontation.

I think it is also important establishing yourself and establishing who you are. I'm firmly rooted psychologically in my community. I'm very aware that I'm black, I'm very aware that my children are black and my wife's black. And there's nothing more satisfying than to have my wife with me. When we go into a pub in Delhi or in Portsmouth, people look at us as a pair and we know what the other is feeling. It's very powerful and I'd like my children to have that.

I think I have a moral obligation to say to the rest of my society. "You too can do this, and if I can help in any way then let's see what we can do together". I think that if somebody ever said about me, "you see that boy there, him forget where him come from", it would hurt. The lifestyle I lead is that of the professional classes. We go skiing. We have three holidays a year. As you climb up the

'I think black men's salvation rests with black women.'

ladder your aspirations increase at the speed that you're rising.

Everything is done by network in this society. If people see you as part of a group, they project that group's values on you. When they see you out of context and performing really well,' all of a sudden it would seem that colour doesn't matter. People start to say, "Well you're not like..." and you want to say, "Well actually, I'm exactly like... it's just that you decided to take the time to get to know me, and you're looking at me as a person rather than the stereotype".

I think black men's salvation rests with black women. Black women achieve more than black men educationally, and there's a secondary element that women are not seen as a threat to the established order, men. A man is not very good at disguising that he wants to be top dog. A woman is more subtle and has more finesse. Black men have been emasculated, because we can't provide for our families, and we've retreated behind a wall of "they've all got it in for me". So we are not trying, we are not making an effort. We've ended up actually fitting the stereotype. When people say, "400 years under oppression, my time to take what I want now", I just say, "You're mad. You're a loser and it reinforces the stereotype". When I was campaigning in Brixton in the General Election, a lot of people told me they were not working and the state should pay. But getting £50 a week is not paying for you. Living in a council flat is not paying for you. You're missing out on a great deal. You're missing out on your independence. We've slipped the shackles of physical slavery, for social slavery, so we've got out of the fields and are free, but we are not free because we have now become dependent on the state to look after us.

'You've got to start with the belief that you can achieve something.'

Lots of people try and lots of people fail, black, white, yellow, green or whatever, But unless you start with a belief that you can achieve something you won't make any effort to do so. I see boys misbehaving in school. The more we make excuses for them, that it's the system to blame, the more we allow such behaviour to continue. Where somebody is being blatantly racist or unfair let's tackle it. But we must tell these kids that they are wasting their time. Until you get focused on what you are supposed to be doing, you will get nowhere. Stop blaming other people and take control.

'Respect yourself and abilities, don't wait for someone else to tell or approve of you.'

My parents came here to make our lives better. They made great sacrifices. They had long periods apart. They brought up a family, none of whom are delinquent. In fact, all of them are fairly successful in their own lives now. We never asked for handouts. We battled for what we achieved – that was pride. I think that's what we've lost now. We've lost our sense of pride and ownership of ourselves.

The significant individual for me has to be Marcus Garvey and reading his belief in *Doctrine of Self Reliance* made a big impact on me.

Everybody has the potential to make something of themselves. If you prepare yourself adequately, get your qualifications, get your training, then you will get lucky. If I hadn't done all the preparatory stuff no-one would have thought that I was capable and given me the chance.

That is my definition of luck "Preparation meeting opportunity".

Andrea Levy

Date Birth: 7 March 1956
Place of birth: London, UK

'I'm always looking to better myself.'

Andrea Levy is a graphic designer and a writer with three published novels, Every Light in the House Burnin, Never Far from Nowhere *and* Fruit of the Lemon. *She now travels widely to talk about her work.*

What I try to do is work for the graphic design business in the morning and write in the afternoon. I do the administration so it's all invoicing, estimating and keeping books; all that sort of stuff rather than actually getting involved in designing which takes too much of your brain. This leaves me space and time to write and I write in the afternoon, rumour has it.

I like having two different things to do. It's more stimulating. With books there is always pressure in that you have to keep up a standard. I want to grow within so I'm always looking to better myself. Then there is pressure because people expect things of you; people ring you up and ask you for things. Sometimes I feel I've had such good luck and it's all going to evaporate. I have a certain sense that I've got to keep, like those plate spinners, all my plates in the air at once.

My parents came from Jamaica in 1948. My dad in fact came on the Empire Windrush and my mum arrived six months later on a banana boat. Because it's a pigment-ocracy in Jamaica, no matter what anybody says, they had this sense of themselves being slightly better than all those "dark people" that came. So that was how they approached things when they came to this country. They were actually going to keep themselves apart. But they came and had exactly the same experiences as any black person. It was quite a shock to them I think, that they weren't treated in some way differently to the darker skinned people. So, my mum and dad lived for five years in one room in Earls Court, brought up three children there and eventually landed up in a council flat in Islington, which is where I was born. So I grew up as a working class girl, mostly with white people because my parents didn't want us to mix with black people. They thought if we mixed with whites we would be better off.

Coming from Jamaica, religion was important to them. So they chose a church school for us and there were two other black kids in the school. Mum was desperate for me to go to grammar school and I really, really didn't want to go. My sister was there and hated it. But she did put her foot down!

'I was the only black child in my class, but without a black sensibility.'

In the grammar school I was the only black child in my class but without a black sensibility, I have to say that. I was just trying to fit in and keep my hair straight! I just knew I was different, so I had to keep my head down a bit. I had really good teachers who were encouraging.

I was completely ashamed of myself. I was ashamed of who we were. So I was trying to hide it; trying to be as English as possible and to fit in. But I had this hair! I used to hate having to go to 'Nitty Nora', the school nurse when we all had to have our hair checked for lice. She used to take my hair out of its plait and it just sort of went for a walk. After she'd looked through it she could never get it back and would say "Ooh, I could pick you up and sweep the floor with you"! I'd have to spend the whole day showing my hair, everybody knowing that I had this thing that was completely different. So I didn't ever feel, "I am being discriminated against"! It was more, "Oh God, they'll know I'm like this". I was afraid the secret would get out. I never ever said that I was black, I hadn't grasped race.

In my early twenties I was working at the Grapevine Project, a sex education project in Islington. They were very strident times in the early eighties: a lot of "racism awareness". So everything had to come down to the white members of staff and the black members of staff. I was a black member of staff. I was politically left-wing and a feminist, but I hadn't grasped race. Then I went to some racism awareness workshops, just for black people. It was like the scales dropping from my eyes. From then on I became – black. And it was very hard... because all my friends were white. I just thought, "how am I gonna live now?" I've got to change the way I live. It was a really big deal.

'The problem is finding out what you want to do.'

When I was at school I had all sorts of ideas about what I wanted to do: choreographer, film director. There was this fantasy life – the person I would love to have been – and then the practical "Well, what am I actually going to do "? I had some really good teachers who were very encouraging. So, I went to art college after doing my A levels.

I actually got a job straight out of college working for a textile designer as a weaver. Later, I had six months unemployment which terrified me, so I got this job in a shop where I was meant to be an assistant buyer in the textiles department. It was working in a shop basically, with a few trips out to look at some fabrics. It was just dreadful. I always think that the problem is finding out what you want to do; doing it is the easy bit.

I wrote to the BBC and got a job in the costume department. I was slime on the wall. It was very low down, but everyone said "Get your foot in the door", so I got my foot in the door. The costume department at the BBC was actually one hell of a racist place at that time. I remember somebody telling me that they don't have black dressers because one of the managers thought that actors wouldn't like a black person dressing them. I was devastated. Eventually I did become a dresser and I did then become an assistant to the designer, but all on temporary contracts. I think because I was nervous because of my race, I was a bit feisty and I was into left wing politics as well. They didn't renew my contract after a while.

Then I went to the Royal Opera House. It was a very boring job, ironing crutch elastic for ballet dancers. And being treated like a servant. I felt really degraded by it. They actually stopped me from working with the dancers because I was rude to several of them, but I just had to stand my ground.

'I had to stand my ground.'

I'd never done any writing but somebody told me about the City Lit. I went there for six years, two hours a week. I wrote this novel and sent it to someone at Victor Gollanz, who said they liked it and would I like to meet up to discuss it. I was bowled over; on top of the world.

In the end I had to get an agent, which is as hard as getting a publisher. They were all saying really nice things about the book, but because I was one of the first black British born writers they thought there wasn't a market. Only black people would read it. Well, that was my first book and it's still selling!

Now it's not as hard and there are many black British writers being published. But with writing comes a lot of other things that you have to do, for example travelling and doing readings. There's something about being a writer in society; you get respect way beyond what is really due to you. Being successful has taken away the sense of embarrassment and made me feel that I'm not only contributing, I'm also shaping.

'Being successful makes me feel that I'm not only contributing; I'm also shaping.'

I'm not a great believer in progress but things change. I'm quite proud of myself to be honest. I was a judge on the Orange prize for fiction. We all sat round in this room and I felt that perhaps, everyone had been to Oxford and had all read English but I got grade E for my A Levels. I sat there thinking to myself, "My journey to this room was much longer than all of yours". I thought, I'm sitting here and I'm going to do it too – and I'm going to be listened to. If I could have changed anything then I would have had parents who accepted being black themselves. I had to go out to Jamaica and find out about myself.

'It is better to light one small candle than to rail against the dark'. Gandhi

Christopher B Lynch

Date of birth: 1 October 1947
Place of birth: West Africa

'It's the man that makes the place.'

'It is certainly harder to be recognised as a leading authority in a field that is predominantly white.'

'There is no point in aggression.'

Christopher B Lynch is a consultant obstetrician and gynaecological (O&G) surgeon for the Oxford region based at Milton Keynes General Hospital.

I was one of the three gynaecologists who founded Milton Keynes Hospital in April 1984. My father was instrumental in giving support, and said to me: It's the man that makes the place, not the place that makes the man. If you have an opportunity to start something, go and do it with all your might.

As well as my work for the NHS I do some private work and am also involved with O & G research and education. I have many publications to my name: over 27 in the last ten years. I've also been a District tutor for 14 years for the Oxford Region of the Royal College of Gynaecologists. But I do still have time for a social life! I've been President of the Milton Keynes Cricket League for a number of years, and I'm involved with the local Racial Equality Council.

The real aim of my job is the patients' satisfaction. Most of my patients come through a recommendation from someone else, and 80 per cent of them are white. It is certainly harder to be recognised as a leading authority in a field that is predominantly white. But it's the duty of the individual to break that barrier in a quiet and modest way. The more educated one is or becomes, the easier it is to cope with these problems. Obviously there are discriminatory situations; there's no doubt about that. When I was appointed as house surgeon to the Queen's Surgeon at Bart's – a most prestigious appointment - I could see they had difficulty in accepting that someone of my ethnic origin should be appointed to this position. As consultant in an area like the Oxford region, despite having good qualifications, white colleagues and patients alike continue to look for microscopic faults. The majority of the time, if you've got a balanced head, you can solve things by simple negotiation. I'm not saying it's easy but there's no point in aggression. It doesn't solve any problem.

'There is no point in being envious of someone else's achievements.'

When I was registrar at Bart's an opportunity arose to apply for a senior registrar post, which is the stepping stone to becoming a consultant, so that was a barrier I had to break. You have to stand your ground, but with politeness and with understanding. You need to do your homework beforehand otherwise you've only yourself to blame. My father used to say that there is no point in being envious of somebody else's achievements: try to understand his tactics. Then you will understand his route to success.

I went to school in West Africa, the oldest school in Sierra Leone. My father had the opportunity to go to Cambridge University, so we emigrated. I did a couple of years in a school in Canterbury. From there I won a place at Oxford, where I gained a first class degree. After graduation my father advised me to go into medicine. Because I was a graduate I had to pay for myself because I didn't have a scholarship to do medicine.

When I came to England I encountered many obstacles. I wasn't bullied, because I was a reasonable size. I was a sporty person and that helped a lot because you are always liked when you score the tries! If you have some sporting or social interests, whatever people do not like about you, they'll appreciate your talent. It does help to minimise the impact of discrimination. But it took me a while to feel comfortable at school. Canterbury is not an area with a large black population!

'It helps if you have a structured family background.'

My family is very religious. My granduncle was the first bishop and principal of the university in Sierra Leone. We were brought up in a very humble environment, but we were a respected family. I think it helps if you have a structured family background with two parents. If I came from a family which did not have any kind of guidance or identity I'm sure I would have lashed out and felt unjustly discriminated against. I felt secure and I knew if I didn't make a success of my surgical career I could always go back to the law and my family would accept me.

At Bart's there were many good white people who gave me support. Coming into a science faculty from arts was a huge step. When you are young it's very difficult deciding what you really want to do, but determination is the first essential.

'Determination is the first essential.'

My wife Julia is white and English, we have been married fourteen years and have four children. I think a stable family is the principle element of success: there are so many obstacles out there. It's true there are no friends among equals and, when your colleagues begin to praise you, you begin to worry; everyone is jockeying for position. But I try to aim for what I can achieve in a reasonable manner.

I've invented five leading surgical procedures in obstetrics and gynaecology. If success comes without arrogance you don't have to be hypocritically modest; you just have to be yourself. Most of my colleagues and friends are white. I don't confine myself to one community. Of course I feel extremely frustrated if I'm being obstructed because I'm black. In my student days I identified with the black community. When I was a houseman, people were curious about who I was and how I'd got there, almost as though I'd committed a criminal act.

My personal philosophy is never to upset anyone. You have to balance what you might gain from an episode with what you're likely to lose. If a black person gets upset it looks ten times worse than if it's a white person. And a white person has the solace of numbers and a common culture. The black person does not have that degree of flexibility or recourse to justice. The reason I say don't upset anyone is that it's not going to achieve anything, and if you haven't achieved anything, what's the point? You have to be modest, and a good appearance also helps. If a chap walks into the hospital with his tie and shirt undone, he's disrespected. If it's a black person, he's written off.

'You need to have discipline.'

Opportunities today are ample compared to when I was at school. But sometimes people who have the opportunity fritter it away because of bad company or lack of discipline. You need to have discipline, dress properly, look respectable. Employers will be thinking ahead: what effect is this person going to have on my business? So keep your head: look at the problem, find a solution and be disciplined enough to see it through. That's the basis of success.

This year I am a British surgeon trainer of the year finalist, through fierce competition. To win or lose, just to be nominated is an honour.

Dalton McConney

Date of birth: 13 July 1940
Place of birth: Barbados

'I'm concerned with 'black' issues. We sometimes forget that very many black people who came to this country have been living here 40 or 50 years and are the ones who are suffering disproportionately within our society.'

Dalton McConney is a chief inspector in the London metropolitan police service and is the borough liaison officer for Lambeth. He joined the police service at the age of 36.

In Lambeth we have three police divisions: Vauxhall, Streatham and Brixton. A chief superintendent has responsibility for those three divisions and obviously we do a lot of work for the community, the council and other agencies within the borough. Primarily, my responsibility is around community issues, crime reduction issues and building bridges within our community.

We start off as constables; even the commissioner started there. The next progression is sergeant and then you move to inspector, then to chief inspector and then to superintendent, so I'm somewhere in the middle management structure of the metropolitan police service.

I am a people's person. I believe in good order, that's why I'm a police officer, but I like the interaction with people. I'm blessed with a high degree of tolerance as an individual, the ability to soak up so much and still move forward. I believe that the area of work that I work in is very often misunderstood and it requires a lot of help and explanation to people within our communities. I believe that people should abide by the laws of the land and those who transgress should accept whatever punishment is meted out, providing it is done in accordance with the law.

There are frustrations in life, just as there are frustrations in my job. We do silly things from time to time, we don't always get it right. My biggest frustration is that sometimes our senior management do not listen to black officers within the job. We have built bridges of trust within our communities and they have talked to us. We have a pretty good understanding right across the various boroughs that we work in, of what is going on out there and I have great frustrations when our bosses tend not to consult with us, but go for the so-called 'experts'.

In the whole of the Metropolitan Police Service of about 27,000 police officers there are only just over six hundred black officers, so it's just a drop in the ocean. I'm concerned with black issues because we forget that many black people who came to this country have been living here for forty or fifty years and are the ones who are suffering disproportionately within our society.

'I never saw the police service as a career, but again it is about getting into this society, understanding this society.'

I came in 1960 which was at the peak of immigration into this country. Like most of my colleagues, we came here for economic reasons, not that we were fleeing any oppression but as colonials. There was a dire shortage of workers at that time and we came here to fill it, primarily in low status jobs. I gave up a job in the civil service to come and work for London Transport. Now for years I never told anyone at home what I was doing because to be a bus driver was a very low status job in Barbados. I think there is still something within the psyche of British society that perceives low status of everything as good enough for us. There is still some great discomfort in having Afro-Caribbean people sitting in an office.

I never had that burning ambition to be a police officer. I never saw the police service as a career. But it is about getting into society, understanding the society, seeing where the breaks are, what is acceptable and what isn't. I was at the ripe old age of 36, which is not the prime age to be a policeman, and I thought, well I'll give it a go. I thought I was too old to be studying, but as it turned out I wasn't. It shows you what dedication and commitment can do.

'We're British we're here.'

In the black community we don't support each other enough. We are still fragmented, there is no unifying force amongst us. We need to be an integral part of this society and we have got to accept that the only way that we are going to survive is if we put our roots down, because we aren't going back to the West Indies except for a holiday. We are going to die here, we have to take an interest in this society and be a part of it.

'We have to accept that this is our country.'

We're British, we're here. Whether or not the indigenous population would ever accept us as English is a different matter and I don't think we should even bother. What we have to accept is that this is our country. We have to start setting ourselves some goals, especially our young people. The support has got to come from our people, and from some of our black achievers, to start building confidence to become citizens of anywhere. Citizenship of a country doesn't mean that you've gone over to the other side and become 'white' because that is a nonsense. We are never ever going to become white, but we are an integral part of this society and our citizenship should be good citizenship. Why is it that after forty years, we are still associated with everything that is bad here? It is not only the police service; every walk of life in this country sees us as being the proverbial black sheep. What has given us this dastardly image? We have to start correcting that.

'Reward comes with effort.'

If you believe in yourself, if you believe you can make something of your life, you can. It's down to you. We've got to forget that society owes us a living, we've got to get away from this nonsense that we are going to start off as the managing director of a firm because we are not. Reward comes with effort.

'It is going to take a high degree of courage of any black person to join the police force if they are not to be seen as traitors to their cause.'

Black men have always been seen as a threat. What I find disconcerting is that the younger generation today have almost accepted this as a self-fulfilling prophecy. We should be working on the men, and saying "Let's get out from behind this barrier of racism, let us stop accepting that we are not going to get the job". Given the opportunity, anyone can achieve: it's a fact of life that our women are achieving. They're the ones with the qualifications, they're the ones who are putting in the effort.

I went to Hendon Police College at thirty six. I had guys in my class who were nineteen years old, guys who had just left school. I hadn't been in a classroom since 1958. When we left Hendon, we completed twenty-four months probationary period. Every month we had what we called continuation classes, where you had a section of the instruction book to study. It was about law and about procedure, and you were tested every

'I'm not as successful as I would want to be within this profession, but I will keep on trying.'

month. I did my final probation exam and came top of the group. I got my promotion to sergeant in 1981, after five years service, and I became an instructor at Hendon in 1983. I have faced a lot of obstacles but I have got there. Racism (and we've got to be very careful about how we use that word) becomes a blanket that covers everything that doesn't suit us. I'm not as successful as I would want to be within this profession but I will keep on trying.

However, we cannot sit on the fence. It takes a high degree of courage by any black person to join the police service and then not be seen as traitors to their cause. You have to understand the culture of this (and any) organization. I didn't get here without a struggle but I didn't join the police service to oppress my people, I didn't join a police service to oppress anyone! I think that if we want to see a police service of the future that is caring, that doesn't stereotype black people, doesn't see every person with a black skin as being a criminal, then black people need to be part of it. They have to be the ones who challenge bigotry, they have to be the ones who challenge racism. You can't do it from the outside. We have to do it from inside; if we go back to this idea of citizenship we have to get into every aspect of our community. We can't just say we want to be in the city but not the police service, we can't say we want to be consultants but we don't want to be a nurse, we can't say we want to be a head teacher but we aren't going to be the teacher at the bottom grade. We have to be part of every aspect of this society.

I remember Lord Pitt once saying "Don't aim for the mountain top, aim for the stars, and if you aim for the stars, you might just get up to the mountain top".

Since interviewing CI Dalton McConney, Lambeth has moved to a borough base policing system. There is now one Chief Superintendent in charge of the London Borough of Lambeth.

Penny MacDonald

'I loved my school years.'

'Academically I was useless.'

Penny MacDonald is currently the group editor-in-chief and head of press and publicity for Redwood.

At the age of five I went to a private convent school. Then, between the ages of 11and 17, I attended Bishop Thomas Grant, a comprehensive school in South London.

My careers teacher Mrs Muir played absolutely NO part in my decision to pursue a career in journalism. However, the Headteacher and the Head of the Fifth Year, singled me out as a special pupil and nurtured my final years at the school. I was given the lead part in *the Prime of Miss Jean Brodie*. I read aloud at school assemblies and ultimately ended up as Head Prefect and my leaving present from the school was an entire collection of Thomas Hardy's works. I loved my school years and made tremendous friendships with four people in particular, who to this day, are my closest friends, Nina, Sandra, Paul and John.

Academically, I was useless. I simply wasn't interested. I wasn't stupid, I did get 5 O levels and left with 2 A levels in English Literature and Sociology. I failed my Economics, but what I really wanted to do was pursue a career in photography or television. Why? To this day, I cannot tell you what the appeal was.

I was fortunate to become acquainted with Frances Cairncross, a friend of my mother's who worked on the *Guardian* at the time, and she informed me of a Communications and Media extra-mural course at London University. I applied and got the last place on the course. I also went to photography lessons twice a week at a local college.

Frances called me to tell me that she had heard of a vacancy at the *Daily Telegraph* which might appeal to me. It was as editorial assistant on the

TV and Arts desk. It was a glorified secretarial role, but it soon became clear to the *Telegraph* team that my talents were wasted and in my determination to get a real foot in the door, I offered to write assignments for the arts pages, using the byline PMcD. I was also asked by the then features editor, Morrison Halcrow, to write a feature on 'unusual weddings' - it was my first big break. It appeared - I was taken on staff as a TV sub editor by Lord Deedes.

The *Telegraph*'s fortunes changed and suddenly, Conrad Black acquired the newspaper, we were moved to the Isle of Dogs. My bosses were fired by the new editor, Max Hastings, and I was swiftly promoted to TV Editor for the *Daily* and *Sunday Telegraphs*. During my time with the *Telegraph*, I also contributed to *You and Your Family* as well as to *7 Days magazine*.

I was happy with my time at the Telegraph and to this day remain friends with a number of its current staff.

However, the prospect of being head-hunted is an appealing one, which is precisely what happened to me. Out of the blue, a call came through from a company called Redwood Publishing - they were looking for an editor for Rupert Murdoch's BSkyB publication, *SkyTVguide*. It was simply an offer I couldn't refuse - I could finally get my teeth back in to features, commissioning etc. The rest as they say is history!

'If you are nice to a colleague they reciprocate.'

Redwood won an award last year - Investors in People - that's precisely why I love working for this company. Everyone cares about one another here. If you are nice to a colleague, they reciprocate.

'Talented people are swiftly promoted, irrespective of what they look like or how they speak.'

The climate has changed. However, we do employ a minimum of six graduates each year into our company irrespective of race, gender or class. I consider myself to be a professional and look for professionalism in anyone I meet, employ or work with. It gets the desired results. There are so many talented people around, however, they may not have received a lucky break in their lives - I'm here - and other people are here at Redwood - to rectify that. We spot talent and talented people are swiftly promoted, irrespective of what they look like or how they speak. We have a policy of work hard – play hard!

I have never shied away from hard work, which I think is the secret of my success. If you

'If you want to get on in this world you can't be work-shy, you can't be a clock watcher, you have to be a team player.'

'I don't believe in ghetto-ising your self worth.'

want to get on in this world you can't be work-shy, you can't be a clock-watcher, you have to be a team player, you have to have drive. Consider this: "What have you achieved today?" If you can honestly put hand on heart and say, I've changed somebody's life, I've made a difference, I've challenged convention, you'll feel as though you can conquer the earth. I sleep well at night and have a bounce in my step, because I enjoy what I do and every day is a challenge to see what I can do to make it better.

I don't belong to any affiliated group. I consider myself to be middle class. I don't believe in ghetto-ising your self. I won't be pigeon-holed into a group of any description. I'm a female. I'm an executive. I'm black. I love standing out in a crowd. My parents taught me to be proud in everything I do. Being the youngest of five girls – I've always had a competitive spirit. It came with my birth - who knows if I'd been an only child things might have been different. As a child, all I remember is warmth, love - fabulous Christmases, birthday cakes from Harrods in the shape of my age. I was spoilt and so were my sisters - and I simply loved every moment of it, which is why I'm secure in myself.

Britain today is breeding a new generation of 'wannabees'. Everyone wants to be a millionaire, a pop star, a movie star, a success - but some people are born to succeed - others expect it to fall in their laps - others have to work hard for a living to survive - so inevitably, they cling to the 'community spirit' for comfort - when realistically, the love you get from your family and your own self respect and appreciation of your history and past generations should be the things to cherish.

Parents need to return to parenting. Both my parents worked, my mother was a midwife and my father was an engineer by trade - yet, we always woke up and went to sleep in the comfort of knowing that they followed our every step, they took an active part in our education and were utterly disappointed if we failed to get the grades we were expected to achieve. To this day, our parents keep an active interest in each of our professional careers and well-being.

A school can, and will, only be able to do its job, if and when parents do theirs. Provide love and care and support; the school will then nurture and nourish the brain to formulate ideas which

'Be wise, be knowledgeable.'

grow in an individual. On its own, however, a child will resent this intrusion.

The media has a responsibility to remind parents - and indeed, schools, of their respective responsibilities. It should not be judgemental, unless, there is a fundamental flaw to report, which needs to be brought to the public's attention. Irresponsible journalism can and does ruin lives.

This is what I would say to any young person, especially those from an ethnic background. Study hard. Learn a skill. Be an expert - everyone can do general things in life - but experts can command jobs, pay, a way of life - wherever they are raised. Be culturally savvy, be wise, be knowledgeable. Fit in, do not allow yourself to be dictated to, or bullied, but always hold your head to the sky. I was told this once and it may aid others: "we're all in the gutter, but some our looking up to the sky"... or something to that effect.

'Study hard, learn a skill, be an expert.'

I would like this to be written as my epitaph: "Always remember her sunny days, let others talk of their storms and showers - she's a typical Leo!"

Enjoy!

Penny MacDonald is Group Editor in Chief and Head of Press & Publicity for Redwood - the UK's largest customer magazine publishing house. Part of the AMV/BBDO/Omnicom group.

The idea behind customer magazines is simple: "communicating with customers". The company has grown in the last four years to include: a magazine division:

Redwood publishing - including: *Sky* for BSkyB; *Marks and Spencer Magazine* for M&S; *Health & Beauty* for Boots; *HN* for Harvey Nichols and numerous others.

an internet division:

Redwood New Media - including Boots, Swarovski, Hasbro, ActionMan, Prince's Trust and numerous others.

a catalogue division:

RedCat - including *New Look, Molton Brown, Designers Guild* and *Morel Brothers* and others

an international division:

Redwood International - including: *Mandarin Oriental Hotel Group, Kraft* and numerous others.

Squadron Leader Sidney McFarlane MBE

Squadron Leader Sidney McFarlane, MBE, has been involved in personnel management throughout his working life. In his present appointment, he provides counselling and advice to the young men and women who attend the selection boards at the RAF Officers and Aircrew Selection Centre at RAF College Cranwell. He was awarded the MBE in June 1999.

Date of birth: 13 April 1935
Place of birth: St. Catherine, Jamaica

"Heights that great men reached and kept were not attained by sudden flight, but they, while their companions slept, kept toiling onward through the night."

The major part of my work now is careers advice and counselling. All unsuccessful candidates attending the selection boards are debriefed individually before they leave the Centre. Our selection standards are high, and many very good quality candidates are not selected. They find it very difficult to come to terms with failure. My task is to provide them with counselling and advice on alternative options (which, inter alia, may include maintaining their aim and ambition), so that they leave, if not cheerfully, then at least in a positive frame of mind.

'I've always had a feeling that you should devote some of your life to helping others.'

I've always had a feeling that you should devote some of your life to helping others. I was always very politically conscious and socially aware from about the age of fifteen. Most of my schooling was in Jamaica. My first job was as a cost account clerk with a firm of civil engineers. I worked there until I left Jamaica, when I was about twenty.

'In 1955 I came to the mother country.'

In 1955, myself and three close friends all left our jobs to come to the 'mother country'. We expected to work, save a fortune, and return home. I really had imagined I'd be able to get work that reflected my ability and experience I had had in Jamaica. I had some very good references. But after a number of unsuccessful interviews it became obvious to me that 'colonials' no matter how well qualified or experienced, weren't going to be accepted in certain types of employment. Indeed, I came to that conclusion following an unsuccessful interview at the British Oxygen Company in Edmonton, London, when a very honest and open Personnel Manager actually told me, "I would love to recommend your our employment, but not in the office, as I don't think other staff are ready or willing to accept West Indians, but if you wish you could start in Factory". Hospitals, public transport, the railways and other jobs with inherent unsociable hours, all of which were of little or no interest to the indigenous population, were readily available. So I joined London Transport as a bus conductor, albeit I considered myself over qualified. It was a cleaner job then a factory job, my money that I brought with me was running out, and I did not want the indignity of having to accept help from 'the National Assistance Board'.

'Essentially, good jobs weren't open to us.'

I was lucky operating from Hackney Depot where I was initially accepted although not really welcomed with open arms! A fellow Jamaican who was on my bus conductor's training course at main Chiswick Depot, in West London, did not fare as well as I did. Fellow employees did not readily accept him, and this was demonstrated by a 'lightening (24 hours) strike' on his first day at Camberwell Green Depot! Essentially, good jobs weren't open to us, no matter how well qualified! But, as someone who was born in a British colony, once I had lived in the UK for two years, I became eligible for national service, under the Armed Forces (National Service Act) at that time. Indeed, the medical and other registration procedures were started at the eighteen months point.

When I received my 'call-up' papers for service I wasn't keen at all, as the military was the furthest occupation from my mind at that time. I tried desperately without success to find enough money to return home. In the end, I chose the RAF rather than the Army, and eventually signed from national service to regular service. There were many incentives on offer for national servicemen to transfer to regular service For example, annual leave increased from fourteen days to three weeks, rail warrants were increased from two to three and more importantly pay was doubled from £2.50 per week (old money). My service career then progressed from aircraftman to commissioned rank.

'I took every opportunity to further develop my education.'

I had had to leave school when I was sixteen, as my parents could not afford to pay for secondary education. Although the secondary education was free in the UK under the 1944 Education Act, this was not extended to the Colonies. However, I was able to undertake further correspondence course and part time studies at evening classes. So when I came here, I took every opportunity to further develop my education. I did some A level studies during national service. The forces are always keen in encouraging the individual to further their education, and I took full advantage throughout my service career. When the Open University came on stream, I started a social science degree course, then switched to psychology and finally achieved an Honours degree. The degree discipline in psychology has certainly complemented my employment in the field of recruiting, personnel selection, and careers counselling and in other areas concerned with the management of human resources.

'Apparent challenges were in fact racism.'

When I joined the RAF there were many challenges to face in the early days, particularly in the junior ranks. I called 'apparent problems' challenges at the time, but looking back I realise it was racism, because the forms that they often took were inherently inequitable or unfair, which was always prejudicial to career progression. During those early days, I took the view that I was an ambassador for Jamaica, so I must try and conform the best I can. I would bend over backwards to make sure that I came across in the right way, and it was a struggle in many respects. Every time I arrived at a new RAF station, 'I would lay my cards on the table' by explaining to my bosses that I wanted to be treated like everyone else - if I made a mistake for example, I wanted to be told about it there and then, rather than being

'No blacks, no Irish, no dogs.'

informed at the end of the appraisal reporting year that I hadn't been given any testing or challenging tasks, because they didn't think that I was up to the job. Some officers and senior NCO's were often overheard saying, 'most of these West Indian chaps tend to carry chips on their shoulders, they are easily offended and we just can't get through to them'. This was often a precursor for a mediocre or uncompetitive annual appraisal report. So I was always rather robust in my attitude and approach, not only for myself, but also for my contemporaries! The Redress and Complaints procedures that prevailed in the Services were inadequate, essentially because they were the final arbiters.

Today, the Service Disciplinary procedures have been much improved, but there are systems in place such as, Equal Opportunity and Race Relations Acts, through which one can get redress. These new systems were not available in the '50s and 60s' when people could openly say or publish advertisements, "No blacks, no Irish, no dogs". Everything was a challenge in those days. Not only were you struggling within your job within the Service, but also with the entire civilian population.

'I try not to rush to judgement very quickly.'

I've always confronted people's prejudices head on at all levels. If I perceive that a person should know better, then I will clamp down very quickly. I don't give things time to fester. But also I try not to rush to judgement very quickly either; I rather like to wait a little bit for the evidence to emerge.

Although I've been here now since the 1950s, my roots are still very much West Indian. Several years ago I volunteered and was selected to join the Air Attaches' staff in Venezuela. The MOD as my employer was quite sure that I was the right and suitable man for the job, having pre-selected me. However the Foreign Office would not issue me with a diplomatic passport because I was 'not UK born'! Although not UK born, I was in my 19th year of RAF service at that time. The assignment was subsequently cancelled. Was this not what we would describe as 'institutional racism'? Was it the case that Foreign Office policy deliberately did not allow for black faces to be representing the UK abroad?

I guess people would categorize me as middle class now, being a RAF officer, but I have worked

'I have worked my way up.'

'Young blacks have got to work hard and get an education, despite all the obstacles.'

'You've got to get involved....'

my way up from being the lowest of the low when I first joined as a National Serviceman. It all had to be earned; no one did me any special favours. In one of my appointments, I was on the personal staff of the Commander-in-Chief for over two years, and you don't get selected for these appointments unless you are good at your job, are credible and can command respect at every level of the service hierarchical structure.

I see myself as a West Indian who's integrated into British society to a certain extent, and I would like to help others as much as I can. But I wouldn't say I am solely part of a black community. I prefer to think of myself as mainstream within the whole community, so I am happy to live anywhere.

Young blacks have got to work hard and get an education, despite all the obstacles. Once you are well qualified it is much easier to fight your battle on the employment front. You don't want to give employers the excuse that you're unqualified. You want them to say something different, which you can challenge successfully.

During the early days in the service, when I was progressing through the ranks, I invariably had to do much more than my white counterparts to achieve similar rewards. But that hasn't been the case once I had become a commissioned officer. That said, there were positive spin-offs, because my hard work was recognised and it enhanced my promotion prospects.

I have always involved myself in numerous spare time activities, embracing social and sporting pursuits. On one station in Germany, with a committee of three, I was instrumental in starting up an all ranks social club with a loan of DM500 from the Station Wives Club. Two and a half years later we had an operating turnover in excess of DM10,000. We organised various family trips throughout Germany, held social functions and children's Christmas parties within the Club. My current activities include: Chairman of the Board of Visitors for a local prison, Chairman of Voluntary marriage support and counselling service, a cricket umpire and a member of an all male voice choir where we do concerts for charity. These and similar activities make one's life more fulfilling and complete.

'Parents must encourage their kids.'

The award of the MBE gives me great satisfaction. My wife and I have had to make many personal and financial sacrifices, but our three sons all went to university. I would say to all parents, that no matter what else is happening, you have got to encourage your kids and get them a reasonable education. Get them into a position where an employer cannot use the lack of qualifications as an excuse. A scenario where one is considered to be overqualified has got to be better than one where the reverse applies. When parents neglect their children's education, they are denying them any reasonable chances in life, and they and their offspring are in real trouble!

Reverend Bazil Meade

Date of birth: 4 May 1951

Place of birth: Montserrat,
West Indies

Revd. Bazil Meade runs 'Choir Connexion', a music management company, and is the founder of The London Community Gospel Choir (LCGC).

'If you behave all the time as if your bag's packed, then you're not going to achieve anything'.

I write, compose and arrange most of LCGC's choir music, but I'm completely self-taught as a musician. I've now been involved with the development of gospel music in the UK for over twenty five years, eighteen of them with the London Community Gospel Choir. I also perform solo as well as being front man for the choir on and off stage. We now have an international reputation.

I came to England from rural Montserrat when I was nine. My mother had had no real education and couldn't read, so she wasn't able to take advantage of things on offer in the UK.

I went to school in East London. Primary school was fine but at secondary school I remember having to fight a lot because of the racism there. Teachers just didn't know how to integrate us. It was a whole new ball-game for the authorities: they didn't know how to handle all these foreigners coming in.

'The history of slavery must be taught, but sensitively.'

At that time there was nothing in the school that acknowledged different cultures. It's essential to address diversity. For example, the history of slavery must be taught, but sensitively, so that it doesn't cause hatred and prevent progress. It's no good if it just teaches black kids to hate every white person.

'The fear of the Lord teaches a man wisdom.'

Expectations of me were certainly low. Like so many others I was put in low-ability classes, became frustrated and misbehaved. Then things really changed for me in my mid-teens because I decided to pursue a Christian way of life. This gave me a sense of purpose and direction.

I left school at fifteen without any qualifications. But my church pastor took me under her wing, encouraging me to read and educate myself. She took time to work with me on developing my vocabulary, doing crosswords and learning music. She became my mentor in all areas of my life.

'Christianity has given me a sense of purpose and direction.'

We started the LCGC after the Brixton and Toxteth riots in the 80s. At that time, there were so many negative images of young blacks, and here was a large group of black kids creating uplifting song. Our philosophy was love and respect for people of all colours and creeds. We were a black community choir, uniting a number of black-led churches, but we soon received many invitations from white churches. By not staying in their homes, meeting each other face to face, we established relationships and made friends.

Over the years we've done five Royal Variety Shows. We've performed for Prince Charles at Highgrove and also at the Queen's 60th birthday celebration at the Opera House. But the choir's ministry of befriending ex-offenders is as important as our performing.

'All of us encounter difficulties in our lives but we should see them as a means to enrichment.'

I think the situation is much easier now for young people. But sometimes they give up too easily. They need to learn how to get established in the culture earlier on. All of us encounter difficulties in our lives but we should see them as a means to enrichment. If you behave all the time as if your bag's packed, then you're not going to achieve anything. The thing is to get educated, learn how the system works, and work within it. The system can work against young black males, but the key is not to accept other people's expectations.

'The key is not to accept other people's expectations.'

I've certainly made plenty of mistakes and looking back I'm sure there's a lot I'd do differently. But I've no regrets. You need to take risks in order to achieve anything.

Errol Murray

Date of birth: 23 October 1963

Place of birth: Stafford, West
Midlands

'It was an opportunity.'

'It's pleasing to know
that you can still make
it.'

*Errol Murray is currently a
producer at BBC London Live
on-line.*

I started working at GLR in 1995 as
a freelance reporter. I began
working two or three days a week
and within about nine months I
was working five days a week. The
Community Affairs Unit, which is
the BBC's flagship unit for black
news, was launched in 1996, and
I've been on it ever since.

GLR has expanded into multi-
media work and I'm now producing
web pages for BBC London Live on-
line.

As a youngster I was always
interested in science and medicine
and I wanted to be a doctor. But
when we moved town and changed
schools I lost all interest and went
into engineering communications.
My careers officer told me I had no
other choice. I became a telecommunications
engineer and then a computer engineer, but in
1991 I was made redundant.

I was out of work for about nine months. At
that time we were in the midst of the Gulf War and
I was totally blitzed by the amount of coverage it
received. I always had an interest in journalism,
always thought I'd love to get into it, but I didn't
know how. So as I was out of work, I decided to go
and train to be a journalist. It was an opportunity.

I studied on a course for black journalists at
the Central London Polytechnic. If it wasn't for
that course I would have found it next to
impossible to get into journalism. It opened a hell
of a lot of doors. Journalism does seem to be a
privileged occupation.

The majority of people who work in the media are middle class. They probably went to a top university and possibly also a private school. I didn't take any of these routes and it's pleasing to know that you can still make it.

I'm currently on an attachment working on general news, but I normally produce a programme called *Up Front*. It's a black news programme and I cover stories about the lives of people like me, black people in London and the things to which we relate directly.

Every night is a challenge. Every night you've got to be able to get the right stories and the right people to talk about them.

'People don't always see the big picture.'

I don't think people see how important a programme like this is going to be. Within the next five years one in three people in London will be from an ethnic minority. Black people are becoming businessmen, and bankers. Very soon that's not going to be seen as anything new because black people will be everywhere. A lot of organisations are failing to recognise that society, and London specifically, is going to change drastically and they're missing out on how to tap into this new style. People don't always see the big picture.

We need black people in the boardroom. Until then it's going to be very hard for the mainstream to relate to black people as a whole, and black people will become even more independent and detached from mainstream society.

'Life is about having opportunities.'

Life is about having opportunities. There are so many areas that I'm being made aware of through the BBC every day and I think it's sad that people don't get to see all the opportunities that are out there. Maybe it's down to education and training or who you know. I wouldn't say it's pure racism. That's too simplistic.

School up to the age of about 14 was fantastic. I loved it. I had lots of very good friends and I enjoyed studying. I was studying two languages. I was the head boy. It was great. But then I moved from Stafford in the Midlands to Milton Keynes in Buckinghamshire, where there were more opportunities and greater scope for me to do more. But I did less; I got into trouble; everything went wrong. I took seven O levels and came out with only two.

It was good to go through this because I remember being 16 and having my exam result slip and thinking that what I had in my hand was just what I deserved for the work that I did.

It's important for parents to be around, not just pushing you but talking to you and instilling confidence and the work ethic. That's important, but I didn't have enough of it. I guess when you're working class you concentrate on keeping yourself afloat and everything is very short term. The work ethic was there, but life was very hand to mouth.

'Racism is much more sophisticated than just being called a nigger.'

My mum told me of an experience she had at a local church, being told by the vicar not to come back because being black she was scaring his congregation away. You realise that racism is very real. It's not just being called 'nigger' and fighting skinheads; it's much more sophisticated than that.

I left school with next to no qualifications so I went to college and gained a B.Tech. in telecommunications. My white friends went to jobs and apprenticeships, working in offices. I went to college because I couldn't get a job. All my black friends were stuck without work.

There were white kids who didn't work at school but they were in an environment where they were still pushed and opened up to opportunities. We were not pushed to succeed.

'I turned the situation round to my advantage.'

We were failed partly by the school and poor careers advice, partly by our families and, yes, partly we failed ourselves. At sixteen, I think most kids don't know what they want to do: I think society should acknowledge its responsibility to keep kids on the straight and narrow. I managed to turn the situation round to my advantage.

I think one thing that has helped me to get where I am today is that I was always interested in literature. But going back to study aged twenty seven as a mature student was one of the toughest things I've ever had to do. It's hard to sit down and apply yourself to books after ten years away from them.

Being part of a black community doesn't always mean being black. It's a set of values more than anything. First of all it's an awareness of what is happening to black people; a recognition of the importance of black people sticking together. Not every black person has that. Some white people have more awareness than black people.

'Being part of the black community doesn't always mean being black.'

People will look at you and see your colour first, rather than look at a person. When you have a black face there's still an element within society that thinks that if you are different maybe they should treat you differently. I don't think people are always conscious of how they treat you but I feel it. It's the same on hearing a voice. The voice could be crystal clear and speak the Queen's English, but be black. You don't know where they're coming from and that should be fine.

'You get nothing less than you put in.'

There was a report in the *New Nation* a little while back that showed that the pulses of white men went up when a black man entered the room. Black men are perceived as aggressive; there are all sorts of stereotypes around the black man. The end result is that someone is judged and boxed before they step through the door. Society is not perfect, but it must try to be inclusive.

Youngsters need to know that they can be sergeants in the army; they can be editors of newspapers. A greater emphasis should be placed on the importance of universities. No, I don't have a degree; but I wish I did.

Chris Nasah

Chris Nasah trained as an architect and is currently an urban development consultant responsible for all aspects of the provision of the built environment. He and his partner run their own practice, Knak Design.

Date of Birth: 22 April 1964
Place of Birth: Ibadan, Nigeria

'There was a certain amount of pre-judgement.'

I am Cameroonian. I spent the first three years of my life in Nigeria then went back to Cameroon and lived there until the age of sixteen. I then came to the UK.

In Cameroon there was a better sense of discipline in the school. Something that struck me when I got here was that my level of understanding of science subjects was higher than the British equivalent. I took my A level mathematics after one year of studying and the teacher was quite astounded that someone coming from West Africa should have such an in-depth knowledge of the subject.

I think there was a certain amount of pre-judgement of what they expected me to do, but once you come out of the mould within which you are supposed to fit then you can immediately become a threat. It is an image that's accentuated by the popular media. I have been here for eighteen years and I've seen certain changes: stereotypes still prevail in certain cases and I suppose it is a lack of understanding of what someone else could contribute to the wellbeing of this country.

Sometimes it seems that if you try to contribute it's as though what you have to say is insignificant. It must be very difficult for kids who are born here. I see myself as a citizen of the world so I can go anywhere, but for others there is that sense of being trapped and it manifests itself as rejection of the society.

'Look for possible solutions... it's okay to make mistakes.'

I feel quite privileged. I am happy that I took this route. It's made me realise that there is a lot that you can achieve if you are a free thinker. You can always question the circumstances that you are in, look for possible solutions and then try to apply them. I feel quite happy that I chose the route of self-employment. The fact that I am in practice has allowed me to address my other interests, such as education and mentoring and also to begin to look at policy issues for a good environment.

It is not easy to be reflective. It has to come from developing a vision and also being willing to make a sacrifice. It's being in a position where you tell yourself that it's okay to make mistakes and that what you come across are not obstacles but challenges. It is not to do with hitting your head against a brick wall all the time but with looking for alternatives. It's engaging with society in order to understand the mechanisms that shape it. When you understand those mechanisms then, you can manoeuvre yourself through the path of least resistance.

'Spirituality is very important.'

My father always told us that a man admits when he has done something wrong, apologises, and then proposes a solution. So from that point of view, in everything that we did we always tried to get a sense of balance, a sense of fairness, a sense of good governance. Architecture balances, quite delicately, the arts and the science of creating the built environment. It is not just about quantity, but also the quality of the environment.

For me, spirituality is very important. I feel that it can act as a fulcrum, balancing one's moral attitude towards life. I am in the process of rediscovering it in my architecture, in the things that I like, in the drawing that I do and in the way in which I try to engage with society.

At school I was good at both arts and sciences. I enjoyed making things, I enjoyed sports, I was very interested in nature and how it designed the environment. I had an uncle who was an architect so I used to go on to building sites with him and I took to it naturally. By the time I was thirteen I had already made up my mind that was what I wanted to do.

It was after losing my first job due to the economic recession in the late eighties that I decided to work for myself.

Self-employment has allowed me to develop a different kind of strength, spiritual strength, to reach somewhere deep to be able to cope. You get to the point where you may decide to wear a tie, but it is not the tie that gets you where you want to - you wear it when you need to.

I did my first degree, then worked at the Greater London Council for fourteen months. After that, I went back to university to do something completely different: a master's degree in Building Design for Developing Countries (BDDC).

'We all have the ability to turn dust into gold.'

My dad would never tell us that this is absolutely right, or this is absolutely wrong, he would contextualise it. It is more to do with giving children the tools or the formulae for them to be able to craft their survival. People act out of ignorance and I call this the matador effect. You realise that someone else may be controlling a situation but you have got to be able to define who is behind this, who is the matador. Children have to be encouraged to feel comfortable about their heritage.

As a teenager, I tended to do a lot of research. I used the local libraries; all the resources and information that were available. The sky truly is the limit; it is more to do with making children believe in themselves and value themselves because if you don't value yourself you engage in activities that are divisive. It is the difference between saying, "Ah, I told you so" every time you make a mistake instead of saying, "Okay, that may be a mistake but it is possible to correct it." We should also recognise the importance of the education that takes place outside the school.

'Children have to be encouraged to feel comfortable about their heritage.'

If you go outside of the mainstream you may then have the opportunity to plant that seed and begin to redefine your sense of who you are. We are advocating self-employment within the mainstream.

Social skills are very important because being black in this community means you receive a lot of hostility which is based on ignorance and sometimes stupidity. We can help people understand and respect other cultures by exposing them to as many qualified professionals as possible.

Success is to do with passing on to the next generation: engaging with the younger generation and opening up a path for them to discover their own destiny. I think this would have been difficult for me to do as an employee.

Reverend Ronald Nathan

Date of birth: 26 April 1957

Place of birth: Northampton, England

'Some habits die hard.'

Reverend Ronald Nathan is an international consultant on community development, involved in management consultancy for black religious groups seeking to develop social, economic, cultural and political programmes.

' Every human being has a right to fulfil their God-given potential. Helping them do it is a divine enterprise.'

I was ordained by the West Indies Pentecostal Assemblies but I no longer have church responsibilities. Technically it's a misnomer to be using 'Reverend' when you don't have a parish, but some habits die hard.

In my consultancy work I have noticed, especially within the context of the black religious scene, that many churches either do not have a developed sense of their responsibility to the community or they do not know how to go about it. I go in and assess the strengths and weaknesses of the particular religious body. I look at the community which they are trying to serve and then help them to develop a strategy on what they can best do.

The job is international, so I travel and have friends all over the world. There is a great sense of job satisfaction in seeing people empowered to help themselves.

When I graduated from the theological seminary and went into pastoral work, I recognised that the needs of my parishioners extended beyond my theological know-how. I needed to address certain issues: the health of my members, and the reasons why they were unemployed or not getting the necessary benefits.

That broad sphere of responsibility has meant I've become a bit more political than most black ministers.

'The drive our teachers had in getting us to learn.'

I'm British born but grew up in the Caribbean and experienced the Black Power Movement. Having grown up in an area which was socio-economically deprived and under-developed, I've wanted to help my community. From that experience came the preparation for the 'call' that would come later. I went back to Trinidad at the age of five and returned to the UK when I was nineteen. The most memorable thing about primary education was the drive our teachers had in getting us to learn. But education doesn't only come through school. I found the calypsonians in Trinidad had a great impact on me. There was one particular calypso by the famous Mighty Sparrow, who said, 'Children go to school and do well, otherwise here in life you will catch real hell.'

'History became a great part of my life.'

At secondary school you begin to lose sight of the goal. My history teacher stimulated my aspirations, especially as this was the first year we were doing black history and finding out about the Black Power Movement. History became a great part of my life. It gave me a consciousness of who I was and where I came from. I felt a great sense of injustice at the way black people were treated, through my reading of James Baldwin and Alex Hailey's *Roots*.

I used to listen to my grandfather's political conversations while I was doing my chores. This was how I came to understand that there were people who were 'white' who seemed to have greater opportunities than ourselves.

It was when I found something I was good at, something that I loved, that I gained a sense of who I am and that I was as good as anyone else. It wasn't so much wanting to achieve to show other people that I was good but wanting to please my extended family and fulfil the aspirations they had for me.

'I felt a great sense of loss in coming back to the UK.'

I felt a great sense of loss in coming back to the UK. I missed my grandmother in particular, I missed the familiar surroundings, and especially the church, which was lively. Here, people just come to church privately and then go back home.

I went to theological seminary where I was one of only three blacks. That was such a shock to me, coming from a majority black community. I

'I needed to keep my head down.'

'Just accusing institutions of racism may not be the most helpful way forward.'

'It's a rather schizophrenic identity we have in the UK.'

'We are here to stay, and are committed to making a worthy contribution.'

suppressed my own sense of identity trying to survive within that academic framework. So, although I always questioned the Christian ideal that colour doesn't matter, I recognised that even within that institution, it did.

I knew that if I wanted to come out with the qualifications, I needed to keep my head down. After that I went into pastoral work in a multi-racial community in South London. I decided to get a little more involved in things like the youth service, and providing opportunities for young people to come into church. I realised that some people were more concerned with the infra-structure of the buildings than with the services the church offered to the community. When things got broken, there were great tensions.

Whilst at college I'd given priority to the fact that I could not afford to fail and therefore it was not in my best interest to agitate. I was one of the youngest students and trying to come to grips with a new environment, a new culture, and people who thought differently.

Just accusing institutions of racism may not be the most helpful way forward. Some people might say that this is 'sucking up' to the institution, but in fact it's about finding yourself, gaining confidence. Later I began to ask certain questions, because then I knew what the questions were. I knew how to frame them rather than just giving vent to my anger.

It was a difficult time at the college. The only way I maintained my stability was to focus on the subject at hand. I don't find learning easy, so I had to study and revise from day one, reciting and writing over and over the things I wanted to know.

I think it's a rather schizophrenic identity we have in the UK. On the one hand, as you look at the development of the British Isles, you cannot help but think of the tremendous contribution people of colour have made to this society, in every field. It hurts, then, when you see that people's sense of belonging is undermined by racism, prejudice and discrimination - and a type of nationalism that would exclude us.

What is our place? It would seem, on the one hand, that our place is here; we are here to stay, and are committed to making a worthy contribution. Yet at the back of our minds we feel that we don't belong. There's the feeling that somehow we have to do a little more than everyone else and still we're not secure. Everybody wants to be accepted: that's part of the process of socialisation. Because we want to be considered part of society, we will always make these trade-offs.

'Be true to yourself and the truth will set you free.'

I believe that as black people, even though we may have grown up in the UK, we have a different world view from the majority population. It is shaped by the historical experiences of our forefathers. We're not as individualistic or as secular as the majority society. We must not surrender the facility we have of drinking from our own wells. We have certain resources that help us to cope, as individuals and as a community.

If we are to live in a truly multicultural society, certain values and norms must inform policy development and strategic planning. But I cannot wait for other people to define me or affirm me before I do something. I have just as much to offer as anyone else. I can offer it at the highest level in order to make an input back. We're not fulfilling our purpose in life if we do not.

'I appeal to you, in your success, not to forget where you've come from.'

We all have a responsibility. 'Be true to yourself and the truth will set you free.' There is a future for people of African origin. But I appeal to you in your success not to forget where you've come from.

Lloyd Newton

Date of birth: 7 November 1956
Place of birth: St Catherine, Jamaica

'Black faces should be a feature all the time because they are part of the community.'

Lloyd Newton is the artistic director and founder of the Pegasus Opera Company and was a nominee for the Creative Britons Award 1998 (through ABSA).

We tend to do one production and tour this work to medium scale theatres usually accompanied by educational workshops. We are taking opera to areas where it is regarded as elitist. We're trying to de-mystify opera, make it more accessible.

There is a lot of pressure; there is no doubt about it. Pegasus cares about the lack of opportunities for ethnic minorities to work within this supposedly elitist art form which is white orientated. Pegasus is not a black company, it's a multi-racial company and that is one of our main objectives. All our productions have multi-racial casting. It is a platform to allow singers to develop and prepare them for national and international houses. So it is a stepping stone. We insist on having very high standards so we don't just take singers because they are black. We also run an understudy cover programme where we take singers who are not ready and let them cover roles within the opera production to gain experience in order to prepare themselves for future work.

Most companies want them to wait until they are very good before they take them on. But how do you get good? It's a catch 22 situation. So one of our aims is to nurture and to develop singers' talents. I'm doing this job because I think it's necessary for our community. I'm also a professional singer and I've sung at most of the opera houses in this country. On occasions when there has been type casting and they need black singers for a particular production we are used and when it's finished we are discarded with little follow up or opportunity to expand further. But black people should feature all the time because they are part of the community.

I spend the morning working on my voice. During afternoons and evenings, I'm working in the office, so it's very demanding. Often I'm alone, but when we are doing a production, then there are other people involved in the company. During the last production there were about forty people on the books to be paid. But in the planning process you have to have the vision and know where you want to go.

We've just had some funding from the Arts Council for an administrator to work three days per week. That will enable me to work on a development and funding strategy for the next three years.

I came from Jamaica when I was fourteen and it was a wrench. Imagine coming from a totally different environment into the school system and feeling completely lost. It was an absolute shock.

'If you don't get educated you're kaput.'

I can only thank my parents who believed in me, and pushed me. If you don't get educated, you're kaput. I left school with CSE's, then went and worked as an assistant lab technician. I was studying O levels at evening classes and it was hard for quite a while studying and working full time. I worked for two and a half years at the London Hospital as an assistant lab technician and was able to combine work and study in order to achieve further qualifications. I returned to full time education and did my A levels, and a degree plus postgraduate certificate in education. I taught in secondary schools for fourteen years. I thought what else am I going to do with a music degree? I had no idea about all the things I could do but I felt this was not it. I really wanted to sing. I knew teaching was not what I wanted to do for the rest of my life.

Piano was my main subject when I was at college. But I was always singing. Someone said to me one day that I should go and get my voice trained. So I only started to take up singing seriously after I left college. I never seemed to stop studying. I went back to college to do a second postgraduate course in opera studies at the Welsh College of Music and Drama (part of Cardiff University).

I've always sung in church choirs. Music has been my life. In the classroom I was basically policing most of the time; I wasn't really able to deal with music at the level I wanted to. I decided to leave full time teaching in order to set up Pegasus and to pursue my singing. With additional funding from the Arts Council of England, Pegasus has a wonderful future and much potential. I would like it to become self-financing, over the next few years, so that I can take a back seat and pursue my singing career.

'At school, I was picked on a lot.'

At school I was picked on a lot. I used to wear these black framed glasses and they called me 'Joe 90'. I don't remember fun experiences in school in England. I loved school back home. I always wanted to go to school and when I came here it was quite different. I was starting again and feeling vulnerable. It was very hard. But I think what gave me the strength was my Christian upbringing. It's still strong even though I don't go to church regularly. I think it has become more internal. It's about being thoughtful, being kind.

I remember the first time I went to see an opera – *Carmen* by the English National Opera where I have subsequently made my debut. I knew then that this was the world I wanted to be in because I was overwhelmed after hearing a live orchestra and the singing, it was wonderful.

A turning point for me was singing in *Porgy and Bess* at Glyndebourne Festival Opera in 1986. It was a wonderful experience seeing all these other black singers and it spurred me on. Pegasus came about just after the production at The Royal Opera House at Covent Garden in 1992. You had all these black singers coming together for this wonderful production and then disappearing at the end of the production. There was nothing for them to do, there was zilch. It was like crawling back into the woodwork and so I started making plans to form a multi-racial opera company and that experience gave birth to Pegasus in 1992.

'To a large extent you have to create your own opportunities.'

To a large extent you have to create your own opportunities. You can't sit back on your rear and expect things to happen. You have to get up and make things happen. You have to work hard. It has taught me how to deal with human beings. That is one of the hardest things, to make sure everybody is taken care of because people are diverse and

'I'm still learning.'

'Education isn't a white or black thing, it's a thing for mankind.'

different. I've always prayed to know how to deal with human beings and I'm still learning.

On reflection, I recall that in one of the last schools I taught in, there appeared to be a low expectation of the pupils, so they delivered very little and they became a problem. They used to say to me, "Oh you are a Bounty Bar", because I had achieved and they thought I was sucking up. Many saw education as a white thing.

Education is a tool for mankind. All human beings should be educated, it doesn't matter what colour they are. Some pupils saw this as a black person sucking up to a white system. Many do not have the structure to work within, and it is sad because the black community is losing out in a big way. Many of our black men will sadly grow up to face a future where they will fail to achieve the great things they are capable of. As a black or white individual you need to believe in yourself, pursue your dreams, face the difficulties and never give up.

Dele Ogun

Date of birth: 9 February 1962
Place of birth: Lagos, Nigeria

'You have to start from scratch, from the ground up.'

'When you are playing away from home, don't expect the supporters of the home team to applaud you; but don't let that stop you from playing to the best of your ability.'

Dele Ogun is a solicitor and the founder of the first black full service commercial law firm in the City.

Having spent ten years in the city as a tax lawyer, I knew I still had not utilised all my skills. I was very keen to bring those skills together and, in particular, to marry my original qualification, as an advocate (barrister), with my more recent experience, as a solicitor, so as to have the best of both worlds. I started from home in my spare bedroom and the business just grew until we moved to the city.

We are now a three partner operation and we've come a long way. We won the New Business of the Year Award for 1997 from the North London Training and Enterprise Council. The award suggests that the formula we've got is promising for the future. You have to start from scratch, from the ground up.

The thing that I like most about my job is the freedom and the ability to shape the vehicle, and to drive it in your own style. I like making the decisions, from recruitment to marketing to financial controls: it's all down to you and that's fun. It's nice to blend legal skills with the business management side. Law is really a business and you need business skills to make a go of it. The least satisfying thing is not having the money to move as quickly as you would like to do at this stage.

We are a minority law firm trying to sell our services in a majority community. Law is very much an inter-personal thing and it's a real challenge to package yourself attractively in a society that is riddled with suspicions and mistrust. It can frustrate you if you've got the technical capability and the organisational

'The harder the obstacles the more focused I become on my strategy.'

'It was hard to convince those on the inside to let me in.'

'I don't think the world would be a pretty place if all the flowers were one shape and colour.'

competence, but you can't get close enough to make the deal. It's also a challenge when, small as you are, you tender for work from bigger corporations, and your lack of critical mass is against you. But this is what makes it fun. I think the harder the obstacles the more focused I become on my strategy.

I came to this country at the age of seven. I was the first child in the family and the first graduate. My father aspired to be a lawyer, but as a mature student with children and working full-time, it was impossible. So my being a lawyer is a fulfilment for him as well as for myself. I did have tremendous difficulty getting into practice in the first instance. Realising that I had an ability for commercial subjects, rather than the conventional areas of crime and immigration (which a lot of minority law firms have to settle for), I made up my mind that this was the area I was going to go in for. However, if you go for the juicier apples, there's a danger that because they're further up the tree, you could fall down and so there were times when I really was staring unemployment in the face. Notwithstanding a good CV and doing extra studies, it was hard to convince those on the inside to let me in. I know my surname was a factor in that. Ogun is the shortened form of my surname which is Oguntimoju and my first name is Akindele. Well, they know I'm not exactly from Surrey and in the bin it goes. The legal profession is very difficult to get into and not being able to secure a position as a pupil barrister, I went to the accountants Coopers and Lybrand, and got a toe in the door to the City that way. It was not until the age of twenty nine that I finally arrived in a law firm, even though I'd done a degree in the normal way like everybody else. It was a late start in terms of getting into the legal profession.

I was now in a major city law firm. However, the key to partnership in the major law firms is your ability to bring something to the partnership, rather than just doing the work. I realised that I did not have the connections to bring the work in at the City level and so my mind was set on running my own firm. As far as I am concerned the City is just there to give you the experience, and a credibility to demonstrate to the outside world that you can perform at the very top level, but then you've got to strategise beyond that. I'm pleased that I'm now in the situation where I can help other students get work experience which they can put on their CV because if you can demonstrate that you've done some of the basics then you're more marketable.

'The key is to find the unique quality that you have.'

When we had meetings in the City and I was the tax lawyer on the transaction there was always an initial look of surprise. You've got to demonstrate that you're capable and we need to be ready for that. There's no point in carping about it because if the roles were reversed it would be exactly the same. You always do have to prove yourself whenever you tender for work. All firms have to do that. It feels like you're back in the interview room whenever I go and tender for work, but that's life.

Once you understand who you are, your capabilities, your strengths and your weaknesses, then you will feel equipped and composed when dealing with the rest of the world. For example, my voice projection and the way that I conduct meetings very quickly indicate that this person is not intimidated. I deliberately went for tax law just to give myself a competitive advantage and I think the key is to find that unique quality that you have inside yourself and try to put that to the fore. City law is made up of the Oxford and Cambridge crew, and seeing the extent of their ability, I have been able to match them in fundamental respects. There will always be something that makes you special, that gives you that competitive edge. Then it's just a question of using that special quality to redress the balance in your favour on that first contact, at that first meeting.

'...that's life.'

At fifteen or sixteen I think I was still a bit muddled. I fantasised. I liked being popular, I liked being the leader as it were, quietly. I admired those ones who were at the front. I was still suffering from a degree of insecurity then, stemming from the fact my parents couldn't really give me practical guidance. I used to get butterflies in my stomach at the thought of speaking in public and couldn't imagine myself being a lawyer.

Sometimes the expectations that I had of myself were lower than the expectations my teachers had of me. At secondary school I did good work. I was well liked and I used to participate. So I had none of the negative experiences. My parents' expectations were also high. As a family we would almost move forward as a unit because of the values instilled in us by my parents. I was really on a voyage of discovery, of self-discovery a discovery of life as a whole.

The kind of interaction that my white colleagues had with the tutors, I didn't have. Not because of discrimination but because of my cultural background. The idea of talking to a senior or an elder so informally does not happen in our culture and so you really just respond to questions, you do not really engage in conversation. I used to look at my white colleagues and think, "how do they do that"? That was a factor that ran through the whole of my education.

'Sometimes, the expectations that I had of myself were lower than the expectations my teachers had of me.'

The real measure of success for me is inner peace. I'm stress free! Success is discovering the skills that I have and getting myself into a position where the gifts that I have been endowed with, can be used to the fullest. I don't really measure it in monetary terms. You've got to draw on your inner qualities so that they can blossom like a flower.

'The real measure of success...is inner peace.'

The life that I was living in the City was a dual life. I was there because of my technical capability, but my relationship with my colleagues was very much on the surface. We never went to each others' homes. I led two lives and there was a dichotomy. I was living a compromise, because I realised that I was playing away from home. But I knew I had to acquire the skills that I needed to get to the promised land.

I don't believe your identity changes simply because of the place of your birth. If you asked the majority of my community why they are British they'd say because they were born here. But you can be Nigerian and still be part of the British community.

We all have gifts and we all have this gift of life. My first duty is to myself. For me to sell myself short on the basis that I look different from somebody – that just doesn't cut with me. I'll push to the best of my ability. The starting point is to be truthful to myself. If you go through that self analysis and self criticism then you can move forward.

'I'll push to the best of my ability.'

I celebrate differences in the communities. The danger is when you resent them. I don't think the world would be a pretty place if all the flowers were one shape and one colour. There's no need to hide our differences and pretend that we are one.

My community is the source of my strength, and I think those who try and become white make a mistake. Respect comes when an individual likes himself, not through trying to be what they are not. If you value who you are and what you have, that gives you confidence and assurance. You have to have your own style and find your own unique approach. The black community here have to work towards being in a position to influence what goes on back home to get the house in order there, and then we can talk as equal partners with respect.

'Respect comes when an individual likes himself.'

Bruce Oldfield

Bruce Oldfield is a fashion designer, and owner and chairman of his own company. He also works as a design consultant to a range of other organisations.

Date of birth: 14 July 1950
Place of birth: London

'I had to employ myself because I wasn't employable.'

'Success is being able to do more or less what you want to do and being able to call the tune.'

I design couture dresses and suits and try to maintain a standard that I think is lacking in the business generally.

The main challenge is just keeping enough customers coming through the door to pay for the amount of people that I employ, and also to keep me in the lifestyle I've become accustomed to!

When I was a child, I was brought up by a dressmaker so I suppose the seeds were sown a long time ago. But I went through the usual things: get a qualification, fashion is not for boys. So I didn't really do anything about it until I was 21. I was quite a late starter.

I did my O levels, and my A levels and teacher training, but I knew that I couldn't teach because I just wasn't very good at it. You have to have enthusiasm for the subjects you are teaching. So from there I went to art school, to Ravensborne and then to St. Martins. After that I went to New York and did a collection for a big store. I was there for about two months but wasn't that successful at it. I came back to London, then went to Paris, Milan and just moved around. I finally started my own business in 1975.

I had to employ myself because I wasn't employable. I wasn't offered a job. I had so much publicity when I left St. Martins, because I was seen as a kind of fly stream boy. But they don't offer jobs to people who are fly streamers. It was premature adulation.

'It's learning by your mistakes, learning by other people's mistakes always thinking positive.'

'People think if they don't get it right the first time, they should give up.'

I do a lot of consultancies. This is mainly how I earn my money, and its fun. It's expanding what I do, not just fitting expensive frocks. I'd like to do men's wear. And I'd like to maintain 'small is better'. I think if you can do it, you should always try and maintain your independence. Which is not easy.

I'm relatively successful, I suppose, but financially I'm not that successful. Success is being able to do more or less what you want to do, and being able to call the tune. I'm supposed to be quite a good business man. It's learning by your mistakes, learning by other people's mistakes, and always thinking positive. You need to take a little step half way up, then do it again. I think people think if they don't get it right the first time, they should give up.

I didn't enjoy my first school. I hated it. Then I moved down to Ripon in 1963 and went to Ripon Grammar School, a liberal grammar school, and I loved it. My whole background was quite odd: I belong to every minority going practically! But I think I'm classless, colourless, everything-less really, because I'm in limbo as far as belonging is concerned. And it's quite a nice place to be.

I think people have got to be realistic and have realistic expectations. Being brought up by Barnardos, you had a very low threshold of expectation. I certainly was one of a tiny number of children to attend grammar school. I guess at school I was probably given more of a feeling of what I could achieve, than was reflected in my home surroundings. I think that also in my earlier years, my foster mother had higher expectations for us children than other parents in the region. We were looked upon as being rather cute. Of course there was racism at that time, but I think we were always looked on as cute little novelties. I still am!

My philosophy is don't set your sights too low – judgements along the way will show you where and when you should make adjustments to your goals.

Sir Herman Ouseley

Sir Herman Ouseley is a former Chairman and Chief Executive of the Commission for Racial Equality. Previously he was the chief executive of the Inner London Education Authority and then of the London Borough of Lambeth. He is also the original creator of KICK IT OUT, the campaign against racism in football, which he now chairs. He also chairs the Prince's Trust's Ethnic Minority Advisory Committee, the Policy Research Institute on Ageing and Ethnicity at the University of Bradford and the PRESET Education and Training Trust.

Date of birth: 24 March 1945
Place of birth: Guyana

'You can never satisfy all the people, yet you have to work for all the people.'

The role of the CRE is prescribed by the Race Relations Act. In a nutshell, it is work for the elimination of unlawful racial discrimination and the promotion on equality of opportunity and good relations between people of different racial groups. They do so by helping individual complainants and carrying out further investigations into areas and patterns of discrimination. They also do a lot of promotional activity to spread good practice. In addition, they support a network of nearly 100 Racial Equality Councils across the country.

I got much personal satisfaction from what I did at CRE. It was a very responsible job and carried a high profile. I gave as much as I could to help make British society better for everyone who lives here. You feel satisfied knowing that you have helped someone. Most of the time it was not an enjoyable job because it was very pressurised and many people are critical of the organisation's 'failure' to end racism in Britain.

"It is difficult to achieve your goals within a situation that is often beyond your control.'

The main challenge always was how to position CRE so that it had some credibility. But however well you think you are doing, there are people who are suffering and never see that what you are doing is making a difference to their lives. We tried to get the best out of people so that they endeavoured to contribute as much as they could to the organisations work.

You had to deliver as much as you could with fixed resources. We had four successive years of cuts in our budget. When I came in 1993 there were 247 staff and when I left there were only 190. Expectations were raised but we were not always capable of meeting them. It was difficult to achieve your goals within a situation that was often beyond your control.

Originally, I was appointed for a five year term and I was asked to extend it for another five, but I always intended to go in January 2000. Progress in race relations depends on a lot of people, not just the CRE. My major task was to get out of people's heads the idea that the CRE was going to solve the problems of discrimination and racism. It can't by itself. It's makes a specific contribution but it also relies on many people doing the right thing and there is a huge amount to be done.

'Racism comes in different shapes, disguises and sophistications and you've got to be ready for it. You've got to be one step ahead of it.'

The pressure is self-generating: the more you build the profile, the more you raise expectations and the more people want a piece of you. The more you are not able to fulfil those demands, the more complaints come to you. I reorganised CRE about six times in five years. The reason was always driven by the need to do things differently and to do them better. Racism comes in different shapes, forms, subtleties, disguises and sophistications and you've got to be ready for it. You've got to be one step ahead of it.

'When I got turned down for jobs I told myself it wasn't the job for me.'

I didn't have a plan when I left school. I wanted to go into local government and I ended up in local government, but I didn't really know what it had in store for me. Luck and fate play a part in destiny in my view. Things happen when they happen. I was in the right place at the right time.

When I got turned down for jobs I told myself it wasn't the job for me. Even jobs I really wanted that people said I should have got, I just shrugged my shoulders and thought well, maybe that's not the one. I think you've got to see things that happen as your destiny, because things happen to us in our lives that are tragic, and we can't explain why. Equally, I didn't sit down and make a plan. I certainly didn't expect to do what I ended up doing. I always hoped to have the experience of a job of public service at national level. I do know for certain that my current new role of running my own business is not going to consume my life 24 hours a day!

I went to school at William Penn in Dulwich, South London. I arrived in this country and went straight there when I was 12. Everything was so new, so different. The whole experience was one that had me in shock for a while. There wasn't anything I could locate myself in or have control over. I think the school itself was pretty good. I know I behaved badly at times, like many other boys in that school. I was pretty average, both in terms of my work and my contribution. It was only towards the end of school that I realised it was time to work hard and get something out of it. I had romantic ambitions of becoming a professional footballer. I didn't think of becoming a doctor or lawyer because it appeared then to be outside my reach. Maybe it wasn't, but I knew I'd really have to go for it and I wasn't quite ready. But I also realised that it was no good pretending you were going to go for something if you were not prepared to give it everything. I realised that you're not going to get anything without hard work. I committed myself to working hard at the time. I did correspondence courses, attended Further Education and developed a professional base to run alongside the practical experience.

My mother and certain other people around me had a strong influence. They had a work ethic and they were decent people. They believed it was right to work in order to succeed and to do the best for the people they cared for. A lot of that rubbed off on me, even though I didn't know it at the time.

As for school, there were teachers you thought were incompetent merely because everyone thought that they were useless. But when you look

'I think the school itself was pretty good I know I behaved badly.'

'It was only towards the end of school that I realised it was time to work hard and get something out of it.'

'You're not going to get anything without hard work.'

'Success is part of a continuum; being able to maintain your own personal integrity alongside measurable results.'

'If you're going to be part of this society you've got to contribute to it, and that means you've got to develop yourself.'

back on them, you realise they weren't that bad, and many were dedicated and committed.

You're always walking a line between success and failure. It's a very thin dividing line and I suppose I nearly crossed it many times. Once again, I can only reflect that there is something in your home life that keeps pulling you back. I was on the brink on many occasions. It was more mischievousness and stupidity than anything malicious. It was always playing to the gallery. But there are certain values: respecting other people, respecting yourself, not inflicting violence, not violating other people's space, that you must never breach in my view. There is no compromise on these values.

Some people expect you to fail because of who you are, and some people have huge expectations that you can't deliver. You have to try to balance both of these. Success is part of a continuum; being able to maintain your own personal integrity alongside measurable results. It certainly isn't about having everything going your way. Like other people I've had bad experiences, but you've got to hold on to yourself and realise that you can still move on.

I came here British, I'm still British and I'll die British. I am proud of who I am and what I am. You've got to take some responsibility for your life and the things going on around you, not just leave it to others. There are black communities in Britain but there isn't a coherent black community. Black people have been here for hundreds of years and many of them have made a huge contribution. Young black people have got to understand what other black people have done before. They've struggled. There's been racism but they've survived. They fought in the great World Wars. They have been doctors, lawyers, scientists. If you are going to be part of this society you've got to contribute to it, and that means you've got to develop yourself continuously, have respect for yourself and be self critical for survival and success.

The trick is always to take the good and leave the bad alone. When people come to me asking what I'm going to do for them I say, "What are you going to do for yourself?" The people who are going to make it in this country are those who have done things for themselves or for someone

'*You only cheat on yourself.*'

else. I know there are obstacles; but no-one else can educate you continuously as much as you yourself. The opportunities are there and it's down to individual determination, commitment and perseverance.

My mum was a nurse but also had to do other jobs as well to pay the rent and keep the family. Other people too were slaving away, working hard to make it better for us. We repay their commitment by working continuously to succeed for ourselves and others that we have responsibilities for, who may be less able to help themselves – children, elderly, sick and disabled.

Herman Ouseley stepped down as chairman of CRE at the end of January 2000. He has since taken up the chair of the Caribbean Advisory Group (foreign and commonwealth office), is a director of Focus Consultancy Ltd and is managing director of the Different Realities Partnership Ltd. He is also chair of several other organisations and carries a large charitable and voluntary portfolio serving the minority ethnic communities.

Elsie Owusu

Date of birth: 1953
Place of birth: Ghana

'At primary school I was always top of the class but at senior school I realised this didn't get you admired.'

Elsie Owusu is an architect and runs her own practice in London.

I was born in Ghana and came to England in 1962 when I was nine. My sister and I were the only two black girls in the school and my main memory was that we got away with a hell of a lot. I think I was a good girl when we first arrived but within a year I was the naughtiest.

At primary school I was always top of the class but at senior school I realised this didn't get you admired. Everybody called you a 'goody two shoes' and all the glamorous people were being very naughty. However, I did leave school with six O levels.

At seventeen I started living with my daughter's father and my daughter was born when I was eighteen. This put a hold on my education for a while but my mother said I should do A levels and get a decent profession, so I went back to study when my daughter was five months old. That took a couple of years; then I applied to various schools of architecture.

I think I decided to become an architect when I was about eleven. My parents had always been involved in building projects; I often remember them talking about buying land and building things... After my baby was born, the health visitor asked me what I planned to do and she said with my educational history and having a baby she didn't think that anyone would take me. But it didn't occur to me that I shouldn't do what I'd decided on.

In the event, I was offered places at all three institutions I'd applied to but I chose the Architectural Association. During my time there I found myself involved in a number of political activities. I managed to get myself excluded at one point and I didn't find it easy. Eventually I finished as an external student, so it took me eight or nine years rather than seven.

My first job once I'd qualified in 1981 was with Solon Housing Association. I'd been working for them for free whilst I was a student and I stayed with them for four years. It was great at the beginning but in the end I had a big bust up with them. At that point I went to a GLC organisation called The Woman's Design Service and out of that I started my own practice in 1985.

'I'd been working for them for free whilst I was a student.'

I'm interested in working on things that will benefit the community. We set up the practice with the aim of working for black organisations and women's organisations because we felt they were being badly served by the architectural profession.

'I was the first chair of the Society of Black Architects.'

I was the first chair of the Society of Black Architects. Two per cent of the profession at the last count was black and a good fifty per cent of these are women.

Over the years I did a lot of work with Bernie Grant. For example, I've been involved with the International Centre for the Performing Arts based in Tottenham. The scheme was a mixture of education and music, putting money from the industry back into the black community.

'It's choosing to live a certain kind of life and taking the consequences.'

I'm forty six now and I once thought I'd have retired by the time I was forty. I've always wanted to have a farm in Ghana, so I think I might try and make some money so that can happen. But what I do doesn't give you time; it's choosing to live a certain kind of life and taking the consequences. It's not easy but who does have an easy life?

I'd define success as an architect in terms of having some decent buildings there to be looked at. I do feel that I haven't yet done what I wanted to do, which is to make the world a better place.

It wasn't ambition that drove me, it just seemed to be what I did. My father was of an evangelical turn of mind, thinking that the world would always need changing. He'd been at Cambridge University during the war and his sense of what this country was about was conditioned by the people he met there. He then returned to Africa after independence to play his part in this new country. He wasn't a political person but he was doggedly sure of what was right and what was wrong. So that's the background I've come from.

'I think you need to work within the system.'

I think you need to work within the system. Architecture is a profession based on rules: fire regulations, building regulations and means of escape. When I was much younger I was always wanting to be outside the system but now I realise that being at peace in this kind of society is about managing the system. My great complaint about politicians is that they always want to make changes. But if it ain't broke don't fix it!

It seems to me that our society is very fragmented, and I do tend to identify with individuals rather than groups. But if I align myself with any groups it's with the black female middle aged architects who live in the West End.

'I think the idea of the black community is a great myth myself.'

I think the idea of the black community is a great myth myself. When it is convenient people hold up the flag and say, "Speaking as a member of the black community" but in private you hear how much sectarianism there is. People in the 'black community' refer to 'bloody Africans...' for example.

Part of the problem with black kids is that they can see what's wrong with society, and they can see a system which is stacked against them. But no one says what they need to hear; how to change that system. They only talk about how to be a cog within the wheel. What child in their right mind wouldn't be disaffected?

Carl Palmer

Carl Palmer is the editor of the diary page on the Manchester Evening News. *He joined the paper as a general news reporter twelve years ago.*

As diary editor I have to make something happen on that page every day, six days a week. I have to find other writers to bring in stuff I can't do for myself, but at the end of the day if something is wrong it's down to me. If we sell one of my stories to another newspaper for a lot of money, it pleases me because it means that I'm doing all they're going to expect of me.

This is my fifth year as diary editor. Before that I was in the newsroom, but after eight years I was getting a bit tired of doorstepping people and chasing up stories. Then one day the editor called me in and said, "Carl, how do you fancy the diary?" It was very different then because the kind of thing we did was chasing old soldiers, talking about their days in the Somme. But it became very trendy, doing stories about pop stars and Manchester United Footballers, out to clubs that were opening. I was able to create something new from it.

In my case something very peculiar happened and it seems to have happened all through my life: I went to college to take a one year pre-entry journalism course because that was the quickest way to do what I wanted – to be a journalist. But after college everybody was getting jobs and I wasn't. Yes, I would say that there was a degree of racism out there, but not enough for me to throw my hands in the air and say, "Oh, this is hopeless, I'm not going to do this". It sounds an odd thing to say, but it was very entertaining to have people reveal themselves in that way, sometimes without them realising what they were saying and doing to

'Success to me has always meant doing a job well, whether that means playing ninety minutes of football or doing a story from start to finish, not only to your boss's satisfaction but more importantly to your own satisfaction.'

you. I went along to a newspaper in Nottingham, and I was sitting outside the editor's desk, waiting to be called in. He came out, and the only person that was there was me. Then he turns to his secretary and said, "When Mr Palmer comes for his interview, could you show him through". And she said "But he's here". And he turned and looked at me, and even though there was only me there, it was as if it just couldn't possibly be true.

'If this is what you want for yourself, then yeah, you go to school and mess about!'

I was the second black student to study journalism at Preston Poly. There were over 200 students applying for thirty six places. When I went for my interview, I was so well drilled I knew the members of the entire Cabinet; I knew all sorts of bits and pieces that I thought would impress them, but they didn't ask me any of that. They spent half the time telling me about the first black student that they'd had and the rest of the time wanting to know what my hobbies were. I was thinking, "This can't be right it can't be this simple". After half an hour, they said, "Carl, as long as you get through your A levels there's a place here for you". I'm sure that most of the others who were interviewed were not told that. It was all happening in my favour. What could I complain about?

My dad's idea of encouraging me was to say, "If this is what you want for yourself then yeah, you go to school and mess about". That really was the full extent of his encouragement. My mother was different in that when we were swotting for our O levels and A levels she would be the one that would be up at night, making us the bacon sandwiches. She'd be the one who worried if we were worried. She had a much closer contact with what was happening in our lives.

As a kid I played football for Manchester Boys, which really is the first step on the ladder to a professional career. Growing up in the Moss Side, I was the only black player in the team, so of course straight away your peers think, "A few seasons and then Manchester City, England, who knows what". My name and picture appeared in the paper a few times. For an eleven year old to have that degree of respect from their peers really is something. And I have to say that has carried me through to my late teens because I played basketball and played for Manchester Boys, played for North of England, went for England trials and in all of this time I was developing this reputation as somebody who did something, who was somebody, and no-one could take that away from me. Because of the sport, when I went to secondary school I was put in the top stream. Not because I was bright academically but because I had this reputation that went before me. They thought there must be something special about this boy they had heard so much about. And somehow I managed to cling on in that top stream and do fairly well at school.

At primary school I would say it was 80% black. Growing up in Moss Side, there were many second generation children of immigrant parents, and you have that comfort of being able to relate to people of your own colour, your own background. Secondary school was a bit of a shock for a lot of people. Not a great shock to me, because by then I'd got used to being the sole black face in so many different areas, and I think that did make a difference. In my class I was the only black child.

'Journalism wasn't my first career choice.'

I enjoyed writing but journalism wasn't my first career choice At the age of eight or nine I wanted to be a barrister, but someone said to me I'd have to learn Latin. I thought, "No, I can't do that", and dismissed the idea from my mind. I think I was probably sixteen when I realised I wasn't going to be a professional footballer or basketball player because I had stopped growing.

'It's not because you're black that you have to work for things; everybody has to do that.'

My family moved from Moss Side to Stretford. It was very nice, very quiet and very clean but I wasn't happy there because it didn't have that cohesive feel about it. Everybody was living their own lives and nobody seemed to care about you. I think all of that had a very strong impact on me. In Moss Side we cared about each other and we care about each other now. What happened later comes as a bit of a shock, when you realised that life isn't really like that, that it's quite harsh out there. But I refuse to believe that whatever problems I have come down to the fact that I was black. Of course some of them were, but I'm not one of these people who say I would have done better had I been white. I can't ever use that because white people have the same problems. It's not because you're black that you have to work for things: everybody has to do that.

I didn't get a newspaper job to start with. I went straight to a news agency. Now a news agency does not have the time and even less so,

'Success means doing the job well.'

the inclination to teach you anything. On my very first day I went in very nice and neat, crisp and shiny, and the phone was ringing. My boss tuned round, swore at me and said "Don't just sit there, answer the phone". It was somebody from Greater Manchester Police Press Office. They didn't say hello or anything, they just bombarded me with details from the weekend crime sheet. I think I got down maybe a third of what they said to me, and spent the rest of the day trying to sort out the story. My boss didn't say anything, just left me, and at the end of the day I actually didn't produce anything; the same thing happened the next day, and the day after that. I thought about giving up, but couldn't because that's what I wanted to do. Slowly it did get better, and my confidence grew. I was doing bits that were appearing on TV, in the *Daily Telegraph*, in the *Mail*, the *Daily Mirror*, and that really did lift me.

Success to me has always meant doing the job well, whether that means playing ninety minutes of football or doing a story from start to finish not only to your boss's satisfaction but more importantly to your own satisfaction.

Having been born here of West Indian parents I still to this day feel totally stateless. I don't and never have felt that I belong here. I think of it as my home, but deep down in my heart of hearts I don't see myself as English. By the same token I can't go to the West Indies and just slot in and be accepted.

I have been inspired by many people and events: parents, teachers and school 'events' which resulted in me winning prizes. I am also inspired by books such as *Catcher in the Rye*, Sidney Poitier in the film *In the Heat of the Night*, James Baldwin and the Vietnam War.

Geoff Palmer

Date of birth: 9 April 1940
Place of birth: Jamaica

Geoff Palmer is Research Professor at the International Centre for Brewing and Distilling in the Dept of Biological Sciences at Heriot-Watt University in Edinburgh. He is an international expert on barley and sorghum.

I got into this area of work by chance. I came to this country, to London, in 1955, when I was nearly 15. As with many kids in my situation at that time, my mother had left Jamaica in 1948 to come to England. My aunts looked after me, which meant making sure I was fed and watered. They couldn't control my school attendance so it was fairly erratic. The only thing that was consistent was going to church on a Sunday.

They got me ready for my journey to England by wrapping me in newspaper, *The Gleaner*, because they obviously thought it would be cold. I was put on a plane and when I reached Miami I was sweltering in all this newspaper! In New York we weren't even allowed in the airport lounge. This was during the MacCarthy era, and we Jamaicans had to stay outside in the cold: it was February. The questions I had to answer at 14 years and 11 months were, "Are you a communist?" and, "Have you any communist friends?"

'I have succeeded because no-one who could have influenced my life negatively had the opportunity or power to do so. The best protection against those who dislike you is to be ready.'

We came across the Atlantic by boat, which was a hell of a journey. We were in the hole, in the basement of the boat, while people coming back from Canada after the Christmas holidays were on the top. But in an odd way I enjoyed it. It was a great experience for me.

I hadn't seen my mum for about seven years, so when she met me at Victoria Station I didn't know her. She took me to a place on the Caledonian Road, a large house with about ten families in it. Everybody had their own separate room but there were no kitchens. One room was used for everything and the stove was on the landing. We were on the top floor.

Next thing I knew, she was up in the morning at six. I'd never heard of anyone actually getting up in the dark! She was going to send me out to work, but at that time it was illegal for anyone under 15 to work, so instead I went to the local school. I would rather have gone to work because I hadn't been to school much in Jamaica. I was the only black kid in the school and the headmaster got me some money to buy the uniform. I went to Shelbourne Road Secondary Modern School and it changed my life. The games master saw me playing cricket in the playground one day and took me for a trial. Before long I was playing against Eton, Harrow and Winchester. I hadn't a clue who they were. They weren't like the people from London! My mum had no idea what I was doing. I was transferred to Highbury County – a grammar school – and she went "bananas": she couldn't afford it. But again we were given money to help with the uniform.

I left school with a few O levels, but had no idea what I was going to do. I used to spend my time in Islington Public Library. The trick was to stay in the reference library without falling asleep, because if you fell asleep you were thrown out. There I saw an advertisement for a job at London University and I applied. Professor Garth Chapman was the Professor of Zoology at the time, and I remember at the interview he asked my name. When I said 'Godfrey Palmer' he said he'd give me a job provided he could call me Geoff. So that was it! I started work as a junior technician, basically doing the cleaning up.

'We were just surviving in a very hostile environment.'

I wasn't really aware of the race issue until the 60s. For example, black people had to pay higher mortgages and higher car insurance policies, because they said black people carried greater risks. We had an inkling that this was wrong, but you had to survive: you couldn't afford to dwell on it. Jamaican immigrants didn't understand the concept of racism. We were just surviving in a very hostile environment.

Professor Chapman gave me a day off a week to study. So I did more O levels, then A levels, and applied to university. The great fiasco was that everybody turned me down. They didn't take immigrants. When I told Chapman he went

'Institutional racism it's not illegal, that's what makes it more pernicious.'

'Real life opportunities are about accidents, trying to cope with difficult situations and succeeding most of the time - and sometimes only just.'

"bananas" and half an hour later he'd got me a place at Leicester University in 1961.

If you are in a society that is relatively hostile and you don't know the rules, you depend on the goodwill of those around you. If you have people in institutions who are prepared to use the rules against you, then you have a problem. And that would be my definition of institutional racism: using those rules to the limit. It's often not illegal, and that's what makes it more pernicious.

After university I went back to London and tried to get a job with a degree but it was difficult. I didn't realise the implications of having a degree. When I went to the labour exchange I was given two choices: a restaurant, or the Mecca bookmakers. So I went to Beals to peel potatoes, was promoted to vegetable cook, then fish cook and then I was doing the Rotary dinners. At this point I spotted an advert to do a PhD in grain at Edinburgh University and I applied. I hadn't planned to do a PhD, but I got it.

My doctorate was on barley and it seemed that some of the work I did was considered useful. I then joined the Brewing Research Foundation in Surrey. It was tough because I had not worked like that before in a competitive environment. I did barley research there and developed what was called the abrasion process which accelerated the production process of malt. By the 70s most of the beers in the UK were made using that process. In 1977 I joined Heriot-Watt as a junior lecturer, was made a fellow of the Institute of Brewing, and was given a professorship in 1989. It's a personal chair, in recognition of research and an international reputation. The Americans have just given me the Distinguished Award for Research. Apparently I'm the first "European" to have won it. I am also a Fellow of the Royal Society of Arts, a Fellow of the Institute of Biology and a Doctor of Science.

I work as a consultant for most of the big brewers world wide, including the USA, China, South Africa and other parts of Africa. I'm in what I call the mainstream because I'm regarded as a world expert in this area. To those who want the best person available, my colour is irrelevant. Unless you are in the mainstream, you tend to be seen as some sort of novelty.

Power is the management of a society, it's about decision making. If you are going to live in

*'Blacks have a
responsibility too...'*

a society you must have a distribution of people in those key positions. No matter how well they say the blacks are doing, we are not in those positions, yet other minority groups are; whose "Britishness" does not extend to 1655.

Society needs to understand that black people are part of its history and culture and that race hate is idiotic and unjust. I think teachers would then be more sympathetic and understand that we are all one people. Blacks have a responsibility too, because for their own self interest they will try to say they don't give a damn. Some of these blacks are from a middle class background and are using the system for their own benefit. I want black road sweepers, but I also want black men and women in the power structures of society, and that will only happen when we have an education system that is equitable. I try to promote this in my professional and my community work.

Once kids get up to A level or whatever, they should do subjects other than the ones black people usually do, so that when a white person goes to collect the dole it could be a black person giving it out; when a white person goes for an operation the chances are a black person will be doing it; when a plane is taking off, a black person might be flying it. We don't only sing and dance and compere programmes on the box. I want us to spread from Channels 2 and 4 to Channels 1 and 3.

I have got a responsibility to try and show other people that my achievement is no big deal. Nothing changes perception more than what people see to be true. As it's turned out, it's the black girls who are the better achievers. It's not surprising because ultimately a black woman has to fend for herself. It's in the nature of the culture, let's be honest about it. If you keep on projecting a lie, it won't work. We are living a lie because we don't want certain things to be known. We are conspiring against ourselves.

*'Society is about
understanding
ourselves so that we
can do something about
it. Despite the disparity
in our looks, I always
say we're genetically
99% alike, all human
beings, everywhere.'*

My background is British and I live in Britain. I'm not an outsider so I work hard for the country I live in. I will do everything I can to improve its status. Society is about understanding ourselves so that we can do something about it. Despite the disparity in our looks, I always say we're genetically ninety nine per cent alike, all human beings, everywhere. We've made a hell of a lot of play over one per cent difference. It's time we started addressing the ninety nine per cent of similarity.

Alex Pascall OBE

Date of birth: Classified
Place of birth: Grenada,
Southern Caribbean

Alex Pascall is a freelance broadcaster, educationalist and cultural strategist.

My pioneering work in broadcasting, education and culture has affected significant structural changes in these fields. I continue to lecture and consult across the breadth of Britain as well as conduct music cultural residencies from elementary school to university level. I serve as a member of the National Executive Committee and Chairman of the Black Members Council, the National Union of Journalists (NUJ) as well as being a representative of IMRAX (International Media for Race and Xenophobia of the International Federation of Journalists).

It is extremely difficult to catalogue the breadth and depth of the influence people have had on my work because it cuts across so many fields and disciplines and has involved so many people. Most central however has been my wife, Joyce Rennie-Pascall who has forged with me much of the work I have done throughout the many strands of my career, including the running of the company Good Vibes Records and Music Ltd. Then there is my immediate family, the lives of legends and personalities that I have met and many unsung heroes and heroines who have played a part in my life's journey in fulfilling my aspirations.

I guess what I enjoy today is working with children along with documenting the history of the black presence in Britain and memories of the elders in England, Ireland and Wales. Wherever I travel I investigate aspects of life, which reflect the ancestral roots of deeply retained values and allow me to nurture my keen interest in an oral tradition from which much of our history is preserved. This is especially relevant as we look at the fast-changing multicultural society that Britain is today.

My tools are simply my drum, poetry, stories, historical data, fabric and experiences gained from my multifaceted professional experiences. These tools I crafted from cultural knowledge back home in Grenada before coming to England and of course the wealth of experience afforded me during the 1970s and 1980s while presenting and producing *Black Londoners*, Britain's first daily black radio magazine programme of fourteen years; one of the flagships of my career.

Numerous influences have helped to shape my life, both back home and externally. My family believed in education. Some became nurses, teachers, and police officers. The elders of my community (who did not have the privilege of higher education), insisted upon making the economic sacrifices necessary to afford the youth of my period the opportunity to climb the upper ladder of the educational system. In my opinion this system needed change and needed to be released from its colonial grip in order to allow us to think as a Caribbean nation and reflect on the political aspirations that "The West Indies must be West Indian". These words of TA Marryshow, the "Father of the Federation of the West Indies" I have never forgotten. I was exposed to the works of Shakespeare well before the works of West Indian historians like CLR James and other black writers like WB Dubois. Although Shakespeare's *Merchant of Venice* and *Julius Caesar* are prized among my collection of books, CLR James highlighted for me a direction for Caribbeanness and of nationhood in his *Beyond A Boundary*.

'I had come to Britain to forge forward not to regress.'

As a result of my family commitment to education, I became a student of the prestigious Grenada Boys Secondary School, one of the leading schools of the Caribbean at that period. When I left school, my first and only job in Grenada was as assistant manager to an all-purpose department store. By comparison, after writing sixty applications for comparable jobs upon my arrival in Britain, the only response I received was from Saxa Salt, offering me a job interview for a packer's job. That for me was totally disheartening, because I had come to Britain to forge forward not to regress.

I arrived in England in 1959, looking for opportunities. I had a specific aim, to leave the island of Grenada for five years to study Modern Communication in Britain, and to visit Africa to study African Rhythms.

My departure was loaded with mixed emotions, the voyage was a thrilling experience but my arrival proved to be a daunting culture shock to say the least. Even forty winters on, it can be summed up thus.

'I came like an explorer - I came looking to find my goal!'

As we say back home, "Come see me and come live with me" proved to be two different realities. Having read so much English history at school in addition to watching the Pathe newsreels in the cinema, the realities of that baptismal period were disappointing, considering that I came like an explorer – I came looking to find my goal.

Shock number one was the way people in England spoke. Some of their accents and the slang such as, "that Bloke" or, "that Geezer" seemed so lower-class. When I saw the sign, "Bookmaker", I thought that was a place where books were made but it happened to mean a "betting shop". Additionally, there were the continual questions surrounding our presence, which took me a while to digest, and gave rise to a picture of life in London, more dismal than I had imagined.

Just picture the situation. Here I am, from a sunny climate, having to adjust quickly to the bitter wintry conditions and a totally different way of life from that which I was accustomed to back home. Bangers and mash sounded like cannons on a battlefield. However, it was just a nickname for sausages and mashed potatoes. steak and kidney pie! What's that? I finally ate it, but in my mind it was, "Steak and kill me pie" because the meat was mushy and watery and came with "two veg", cabbage and carrots - a real test for my constitution.

The houses seemed cold and strangely huddled together with smoking chimney tops looking like tall Englishmen with big cigars. This reminded me of the smoking coke burners, which we called "coal pits", at home. That was the nearest comparison I could draw while others viewed them as numberless factories.

'London Underground afforded me many opportunities.'

Employment for many newcomers was the London Underground tube trains and the last job I ever wanted to do was to work on the London Underground as a station man. I viewed this as a menial entry-level job which involved cleaning the toilets and the Underground in order to progress to better positions. Well guess what? I eventually found myself working on the Underground as a station man having to do just that. I progressed to guard, and then trainee motorman (train driver) and then wondered what was I doing all this for. I had no trains to return to back home and I did not come for that!

Nevertheless, working on the London Underground afforded me many opportunities to gain insight into the social fabric of war-torn Britain. Eventually, as people came and went through my station and in and out of the trains I guarded, I could discern who they were and where they came from. The job became a study of people for me and as it happens, many years later I returned to London Transport to serve as a member of their London Regional Committee.

For sure, London Transport even afforded me my entry into a show-biz career. My work schedule enabled me to take music lessons, write songs, poetry and to develop my first musical band, The Magnets.

By August 1964 I said goodbye to London Transport, bound for the West End's nightclubs, restaurants and dancehalls. This was a chapter of my life where I uncovered the superficiality of meaning in the words "show business". In between the glitter and romance I often blushed – best I leave you guessing.

A far cry from the London Underground and the world of entertainment, my fourteen years with the BBC was the greatest university of all. As presenter/producer of the first Black daily radio magazine programme in Britain, *Black Londoners*, on BBC Radio London which began in 1974, I had the world of communication at my fingertips. *Black Londoners* answered one of the dreams I came to fulfill – to be in the centre of the world of communication and later on in my career an executive membership of the journalistic trade union the (NUJ) the hub of journalism in Britain.

People of all sorts came and went through *Black Londoners* from every level of the black diaspora and from diverse cultural backgrounds it featured politicians like Sir Leon Britton, Home Secretary of Britain, Prime Minister Maurice Bishop of Grenada and Prime Minister of Jamaica, Michael Manley to name a few. Academics included Professor Ivan Van Sertimer, CLR James, Ngugi Watiango, and Angela Davis. There were also performers like Michael Jackson, Marvin Gaye and Miriam Mekaba. Among the numerous visiting writers were Louise Bennett, Alex Haley and Maya Angelou. Favourites of mine include the messengers of song, The Mighty Sparrow (Slinger Francisco), Bob Marley and Calypso Rose not to mention sports personalities who were featured on the show including, Clive Lloyd, Arthur Ashe, Muhammed Ali and McDonald Bailey.

Black Londoners also supported and helped to stimulate the rise in the black theatre scene in London and for many British stars who were rising at the time, provided a platform for promoting themselves on radio which was not available to them before then. These included artists such as Linton Qwesi-Johnson, Eddy Grant, Aswad, Steel Pulse, Musical Youth and some of the well-known gospel choirs familiar to audiences today.

These are but a few of the many personalities and categories that spanned the breadth of people and topics within my domain, through *Black Londoners*, in the world of global information and communication.

'Black Londoners *revolutionised neccessary changes in the British media.'*

In media terms, what was deemed only local radio began to challenge attitudes nationally and aroused interest and discussion in relation to black presence globally. Along the way, one had to contend with outlooks similar to the following: a white newsroom producer aiming to create a programme on mugging, felt it natural to approach me in order to assist in finding a few 'black muggers' to interview, thus perpetuating the stereotypical view that all blacks are muggers, the highest form of disrespect. This was one in a catalogue of examples. In short, *Black Londoners* revolutionised necessary changes in the British media that was devoid of black representation at that time except for newscaster Trevor MacDonald and *Black Londoners'* eventually predominantly black staff. This led to black presenters in mainstream British Broadcasting as it is today.

It was during my entertainment chapter prior to *Black Londoners* that I dabbled as a standup comedian, which was a horrible experience, but my working schedule allowed me time to be a visiting folklorist in schools, supplementing the schools' curriculum for the young black population that was having horrendous times within the education system. Until that time, black pupils had been denied any educational input that related to their cultural background. Most black supplementary teachers going into schools were focusing on culture and by so doing, were focusing on history. The British educational infrastructure failed to see culture's relevance to teaching history as it pertained to these young children. During that period also, fearing the Black Power movement that was making its impact in the sixties, the authorities trivialised our input into "Black Studies", as these classes were entitled. However many of these young people in a very real sense have benefited from these classes of cultural awareness. Speaking to some who are successful adults, on reflection they express the difference the classes made to their view of themselves.

As a Caribbean national, I feel language and culture equals identity always; except in our case.

My life's work continues due to determination, the support of Joyce, my wife and a reservoir of valued people along this journey. Britain is a country filled with opportunities, though an ungrateful "Mother Country", to those of us who came as invited guests our wealth and energy, along with our ancestors, have helped to make Britain what is today a diverse and progressive multicultural society with enormous wealth.

'Britain is a country filled with opportunities though an ungrateful Mother Country.'

We pay expensively for any privileges offered and to be still thought of as immigrants can be disheartening. The children of Caribbean and or African parentage remain sub-classified in my views, except when they forge their way into stardom and international success. Only at this time, like Linford Christie, are they openly heralded with the recent classification, "Black Brits". The issue of black identity within Britain is still on course for change in my view. Our presence here, along with contributions we have made in the pursuit of a better life, have undoubtedly changed the fabric of this society and the ailing economy of the post-war period.

Racism continues to be a scourge to contend with, even though the people of the Commonwealth in Britain are one of its greatests assets. "The cuckoo has come home to nest", and it would seem that Caribbeans themselves should build institutions within this society that will impart and share our heritage, for the younger generation.

'Not only have we warmed the atmosphere, chased away the fog, added colour throughout the nation and within the Houses that govern it, we have expanded its musical palette to include reggae, toasting, soca, calypso and soul.'

Not only have we warmed the atmosphere, chased away the fog, added colour throughout the nation and within the Houses that govern it, we have expanded its musical palette to include reggae, toasting, soca, calypso and soul. Caribbeans have introduced the steel pan and revolutionised fashion, food and culture. We have changed many of the old norms including the frozen smiles encountered upon our arrival, created, nurtured and managed up until recently Europe's largest street festival, *The Notting Hill Carnival (NHC),* of which I was Chairman for four years. NHC engendered the formation of the Foundation for European Carnival Cities. As one of the founder Vice Presidents of this organization arts and music came under my jurisdiction.

The success of Caribbean Focus '86, a one year national festival to promote Caribbean arts and culture hosted by the Commonwealth Institute in consort with the Caribbean Caricom governments, helped Joyce and myself determine that a Caribbean heritage centre was needed. It would promote and preserve the heritage and culture of those who came prior to the Second World War but in particular those that followed in the fifties; a centre for global development: for the rest of Britain to experience who we are and what achievements we have made. Our community would have little positive future for the 21st century and beyond without this. We would have come and gone leaving no footprints for future generations.

Many came believing
That the streets are paved with gold,
'Cos that's what the story told:
"Come to the Motherland,
Land of opportunity, hope and prosperity
That's what the story told
The streets are paved with gold".

The Streets are Paved with Gold! by Alex Pascall, 1981.

I knew Britain was a land of opportunity before I arrived. I came with hope. Now I want our children to share the glory and wealth in Britain's prosperity.

Trevor Phillips

Date of birth: 31 December 1953
Place of birth: London

'Up to a point you make your own luck.'

'I took the opportunities that were offered to me, even though sometimes they didn't look so attractive and though other people might have scorned them.'

Trevor Phillips is a broadcaster and journalist who writes for several newspapers and magazines and presented Radio 4's weekly science programme, Material World. *He runs Pepper Productions - a company specialising in programmes about the black British experience and in May 2000 was elected to the Greater London Assembly.*

Running Pepper basically consists of having an idea, recruiting and managing people and making some profit. The first two are not easy but they're do-able, the third is quite difficult. It's to do with planning, making sure that you respond to eventualities, motivate people, and give them ownership of all the projects that you are doing. The thing I find most interesting at the moment is writing, whether it's for newspaper, radio or television.

I trained as a chemist at Imperial College and then went into student politics for about 4 or 5 years. Then I thought I would go into industry. That was my first desire but it turned out not to be practicable. I'd been a student firebrand, and was told that everybody would be suspicious of me. So I looked in the papers and I saw a job that involved current affairs, which I was interested in, and research, which I'd done a bit of as a chemist. I had no idea that they were quite different kinds of research. I was interviewed, and they gave me a job as researcher at London Weekend Television. I was 26.

I worked as a staff member for LWT altogether for about 17 years, first as a researcher on a very fine production called *Skin*. Then I became a producer, making a whole series of programmes. Later I became the editor and presenter of the

'You have to work very hard!'

London Programme which was my television vehicle for 12 years. I was first editor, then executive producer, and then I became Head of Current Affairs. I was an executive; the only black programme executive in the ITV system, a big system with tens of thousands of people. But I found it unsatisfactory for a variety of reasons. For one thing, being an executive in this business doesn't give you that much time or flexibility for your family. Also, I had the opportunity to be in front of the camera more, so over the last 5 years I've tapered off my working relationship with LWT. I now have my own company so we co-operate and do co-productions. I've been very lucky that at various stages of my career, where I've felt I wanted to go in a different direction, an opportunity opened up for me.

Up to a point you make your own luck. And you have to work very hard! I learnt when I first became a producer that you had to give up your life. You were responsible for the programme and this meant that for 40 weeks of the year between 1982 and 1985 I virtually had no days off. I worked weekends and all of the night, but by the end of that time I could make almost any kind of television programme. I took the opportunities that were offered me, even though sometimes they didn't look so attractive and though other people might have scorned them as mundane and unglamorous.

'If you want to be successful you do have to take risks. You've got to take decisions and you have to stick to those decisions. People don't float into positions. They stride or fly or scramble into them. You have to make a positive commitment to jump. It means also that you don't weep when it goes wrong because it sometimes does.'

If you want to be successful you do have to take risks. You've got to take decisions and you have to stick to those decisions. People don't float into positions. They stride or fly or scramble into them. You have to make a positive commitment to jump. It means also that you don't weep when it goes wrong because it sometimes does.

You sacrifice some things but you have to decide what's important to you. I have a growing family and elderly relatives for whom I am responsible. That's very important to me. Much of what I have tried to do with my career has been to fit my life so that I can sustain those relationships. Many black families allow themselves to be weakened and atomised and I think all members of those families lose out. In a society that is basically hostile you have to ensure that you've got a base that's completely loyal and isn't going to run away from you. There's no better protective place than the clan.

As the only black person in a certain position you do feel different kinds of pressures. One is that you know that people have to be persuaded. You're always marking out territory. Anybody who comes after you will be judged more for what they do but if you're the first you're always being judged through a particular filter, "How does a black person cope with this?" There's a different kind of pressure on you to succeed, do it well, do whatever it is that you are doing competently or better. There is always a temptation to pretend to everybody that actually you are not different: you will behave in exactly the same way as a white person. I learnt quite early on in my career that this was a route to disaster. We are different and we should celebrate the fact. Indeed, in my business it can become an asset.

I personally believe that almost whatever level you are in society, things are structured in such a way that had you been white you would have been at a higher level. We are all individuals, we like different things. The term 'black community' is simply used as a way of forcing us to conform to someone else's idea of what we should be like. As for there being a black middle class, this would presuppose some generations of wealth and property and stability, and very few black people are in that position. We may have black professionals but that is a different thing from belonging to the middle class.

'There is always a temptation to persuade everybody that actually you are not different: you will behave in exactly the same way as a white person. I learnt early on in my career that this was a route to disaster.'

I think that for those of us in this position there is a responsibility to make things better for other people in our community. The Lawrence case has changed the climate dramatically for all of us. There's an appetite for change, and an opportunity. We know now that there is a big job to be done and we can't leave it to the other guys to do it.

My father was a very remarkable man, very dominant in our family and rather Edwardian in style. Any West Indian will know that there are good things and bad things about that. He was an inspiring example but also massively rigid. We were poor, but my mother and father had high expectations of themselves and of their children. It was not, therefore, surprising that my parents would be amongst those who wanted to come to

*'Once you've chosen
the thing that you're
going to do with your
life, you have to believe
that you can do it,
maybe, that you can
even be the best at it.'*

England. I was born in North London and we lived like most Caribbean families in a tenement. The social space was the stairs in between floors. I was the last of seven children and there were too many of us, so my parents sent some of us back to the Caribbean. So that's why I feel that I belong to a clan. The strength of attachment of black families is often underestimated.

For a young person the challenge is really to be part of the community. There is a real danger that as the world gets bigger and there are more commercial and other forces on young people, they abandon the things that give them strength; the basic values of integrity and trust. Without those things we are all like corks on the ocean of change and we become blown hither and thither. Even though you get irritated and your parents may seem unfair - you have to believe that they want the best thing for you and you have to work with them. For many of us Afro-Caribbean people we grow up with a history of being told by other people that we are not that good. I think we can start to believe in ourselves, and have high but realistic expectations.

*'Education can be as
important as inheriting
money.'*

The schools' principal role is to make people capable and competitive. School is not always a happy place, like the world, it is tough and demanding. What will make a real difference to black children is being able to compete. Leave comfort and niceness to the families, it's actually the parent's job to teach you about your culture.

Maybe schools need to lean on parents to do more. No matter how many white teachers tell them they should be proud of being black if the message they get from their parents is something different that's what they are going to listen to. They are going to be worried, anxious, feel insecure about their identity. Education can be as important as inheriting money. If you are well educated, you're bright, you're lively, you're flexible, somebody will employ you to do the things you want to do.

Sybil Phoenix

Sybil Phoenix is the first black woman living in Britain to have received the MBE and started the Southwark Diocese Race Relations Group in the early 1960s. She is founder and director of the Marsha Phoenix Memorial Trust, caring for young women in difficulty by offering accommodation, education and support. She was an acting mayoress of Lewisham in 1998.

'*Success is contentment, happiness. It would mean the Marsha Phoenix Trust having a 'life' long after me.*'

We started the house as a home plus education, with classes in maths and English, art, pottery, photography, sewing, cooking and also a computer room. We take in girls who are battered by society and try to help them go back to school or college and to become useful adults, to be better citizens, to contribute to society. Over the twenty five or thirty years that we have been here we have had eleven young women who have gone to university. I feel that is a credit to the black community, that we've been able to do this work right across the spectrum of ethnic groups. You can say I'm the director of the project, but I do more than the director's job: I will sleep in, I will do the cleaning when the cleaner is away and I'm the dog's body for the project.

The most positive thing is to see the girls progress. Some have become solicitors, social workers, secretaries, all kinds of things. I get a lot of pleasure out of my preaching as well. I'm a methodist local preacher. I take services everywhere, and the work I do in the church helps

'I was born a member of the British Empire. I'm nothing but British.'

to fund the project. I get a lot of pleasure out of doing it, but I'm tired and there's only so much one person can do.

The most challenging aspect is the counselling work that I do with the girls and their parents and with the council. It makes you weep and it makes you happy. It's difficult but rewarding. I've become a professional beggar to raise the funds. In another sense the counselling work that I do enables young women to live again and to have a second bite of society. I wouldn't change that for the world.

I see myself as an enabler, that is my personal achievement. Getting them out of bed and so on and screaming and shouting for them to press their clothes – it can be tough!

I'm was a milliner by profession. Now I'm a youth and community worker. I did my training at Avery Hill College. I am also a professional counsellor and have a counselling certificate. I have done lots of other work.

'Young black people need to get as much education as they can. Because it's only by educating yourself and understanding a bit of your history that you can survive in this society.'

I was born in (British) Guyana. My mother died when I was ten and I went to live in the big house of my grandfather, my aunt and uncle-in-law. I never lacked for food or clothing, but the love wasn't there, and I used to adopt all my friend's mothers because I never really had anyone to love me. I always used to say to my husband, if I ever have any money I will take in girls that haven't got any mothers, just to love them and look after them. A social worker said she couldn't help overhearing that and Lewisham had literally hundreds of girls who would like a foster mother and would I like to do it. In 1971 when I was awarded the MBE I had already fostered over one hundred young people.

I became a church secretary when the minister's secretary was ill one day and I went over and helped him out after school. Then I was trained by the British Council of Churches and later had a placement at the Citizens Advice Bureau. I thought I'd be in England for two or three years and then go home but then I got married, had children and all kinds of things happened. One of my children died. I was running a youth club and took thirty eight young people away for a week's holiday. While on that holiday I was involved in a car accident that killed my daughter Marsha.

But I've done many different things in my life. I joined the Bedford Methodist Church Choir and the Philharmonic Choir. I started running a club at Shepherd's Bush Methodist Church and also the youth club in Lewisham Church. I started the Southwark Diocese Race Relations Group in the early 60s.

I was born a member of the British Empire. I'm nothing but British! But there has been a cost. The National Front used to come and throw stuff. At one stage we had to block up the letterbox. The police took it seriously when they threatened to burn us out. I've paid a price.

People speak about racial equality but they don't do anything about it, they don't live up to it. Society has learned how to act in a covert way. There's a hymn that goes "I cannot tell how I will win the Nation, but this I know", - equality must come.

'Equality must come!'

Young black people need to get as much education as they can. Because it's only by educating yourself and understanding a bit of your history that you can survive in this society. And history needs to be rewritten in an honest way.

Bob Purkiss

Date of birth: 11 November 1945
Place of birth: Winchester, UK

Bob Purkiss is a former National Secretary for Equality at the Transport and General Workers Union(TGWU) and a senior commissioner at the Commission for Racial Equality(CRE). He is currently Vice-Chair of the European Monitoring Centre on racism and xenophobia.

'Learn where you come from, and respect yourself.'

Since I left school I have always been a trade unionist. In my former job I was responsible at national level for race and sexuality issues. At the age of 15, I became a member of the National Union of Seamen when I joined the Merchant Navy. In 1965/66 after a major strike, I became a convenor for the National Union of Seamen and at the same time started to study. Later on, when I went to work for the Red Funnel, Isle of Wight ferries, I had an opportunity to further my studies in industrial relations at Southampton University while still a shop steward within the Transport & General Workers' Union. In 1973 I joined the Industrial Society as a lecturer working on trade union and industrial relations issues. In 1975, I went to Jamaica as a national research officer for the National Workers' Union. At that time the head of the union was Michael Manley, who became Prime Minister. When I came back to this country, I joined the TGWU as education and research officer. I also worked as a district officer and then a regional officer, all over the south of England.

In 1988, the Union decided that positive action needed to be taken to develop work on race issues, I was asked to head up a team of people to advance this. This led to me becoming the national officer and I sat on the general council of the TUC and chaired the TUC race committee. I am now the UK Representative and Vice Chair of the European Monitoring Centre on Racism and Xenophobia based in Vienna.

The highs of the job are the satisfaction you get from doing something for other people that they can't do for themselves. It's having the ability to influence change; knowing that people are listening.

'You can't overcome the barriers instantly. It's a long-term process.'

Because I was born in Winchester I have a very 'Hampshire' accent, so that often when I contact people by phone they don't realise I'm black. However, they often have a different attitude when I meet them.

There are tremendous frustrations that go with the job because no matter how good you are there are still many barriers which you can't overcome. Many people are suffering injustice, and though you see it you often can't do anything about it, no matter how hard you try. You can't overcome the barriers instantly: it's a long-term process.

'I've never had a career path; it just developed.'

I've never had a career path; it just developed. This job didn't exist before I came along. I'm one of those lucky people who's managed to turn a hobby into a job. As a shop steward I spent a lot of my time at weekend schools and going to meetings after work. Now I actually get paid for the things I used to do for nothing. Few people are given that opportunity.

'I'm successful because I've survived.'

If money's the driver, forget this job. But I think I get more satisfaction than people who are just chasing money because they have to worry about tomorrow. I'm successful because I've survived, and achieved a great degree of happiness in my job. I'm lucky to have Bill Morris as my boss; he's allowed me to develop.

I liked school, though it was never really challenging. I did enough to keep in the top stream all the way through but I wanted to leave because my only ambition was to join the navy. I came from a little village near Southampton. My mum's brothers were in the navy and I joined the Sea Cadets when I was eleven. Career choices were limited anyway, so I made my own career choice.

My mother's white English, my father was a black American soldier from Arizona and my wife is Jamaican. When I joined the merchant navy I went to South Africa for three years, in 1961. Then I went to the southern states of America in 1964, from both of these experiences I learnt a lot about being black. It wasn't until I went to South Africa that I actually understood about my colour. There were two of us black kids on the ship out of six hundred crew. The captain pulled us up one day and asked if we knew about apartheid. He tried to explain that because of our colour we couldn't go where the rest of the crew could go. The other guy was black, and as a half-caste I could go where he couldn't, because I was classified in the category 'Cape coloured' and he was classified as 'black'. He lasted one trip, but I stayed for three years. I only went ashore with white people once and it was a disaster. We played football, but afterwards when they went for a drink in a bar I wasn't allowed in and had to sit outside. I was there when Mandela was arrested. The experience stood me in good stead because now I can understand when people talk about institutionalised racism.

I fight all discrimination, whether it's through class, age or sexual orientation. No-one taught me black history so I had to pick it up for myself. It's part and parcel of how you develop. We are 'black British'. We're not going anywhere; there's nowhere else to go. This is our home. We have to get over the idea, though, that being British means 'English'. Young people need to know their identity but be proud of being black, and make a contribution to breaking down barriers. There are mental barriers, but black people have the tenacity to break them. We don't always appreciate the extent of our mental strength.

People should not feel defensive because they're black. I have heard some successful people almost deny their blackness. We have to challenge in a positive way. The endemic racism in our society means that individuals cannot challenge alone. You need support; from your parents, from your school and from the curriculum, which needs to teach the total history of Britain. You need support from the government and also from industry, so that you can find your niche in society.

When you're out and you see another black person you always acknowledge them, because you know what they're going through. They're part

'I fight all discrimination, whether it's through class, age or sexual orientation.'

'Young people need to feel that identity but be proud of being black, and make a contribution to breaking down barriers.'

'That middle passage gave us a lot of strength. We don't always appreciate the extent of our mental strength.'

of something you understand. So there is that community thing, but it's not an identifiable group of people living together. You don't have to live in Brixton to be part of the black community.

There is a very macho image of some black men, but the woman is the mainstay of the family. This fact has never been respected because there's institutionalised sexism in some societies, and macho men can't admit it. There are many young black boys looking for role models in the wrong way, whereas a young black woman will say, "I want to be respected for what I am".

'What is it that black people want?'

What is it that black people want? Exactly the same as white people; decent schools, decent houses, decent jobs. All that stops us achieving these needs are peoples' perception and prejudices. That is what has to be challenged through education, raising the level of awareness and by being honest with ourselves as to the type of society we are living in.

We have to challenge in a positive way.

Heather Rabbatts

Heather Rabbatts was chief Executive of the London Borough of Lambeth with responsibility for housing, social services and education. The borough has a £750m annual turnover and employs 6500 people. She is now a consultant with her own company called Empire Ltd.

'Invariably I'm the only black person and only woman in the room.'

As Chief Executive I'm ultimately responsible and accountable for what we do, and I'm charged with the task of leading the management of the organisation. My job ranges across a variety of areas; I've just been talking about some housing issues because we have a block of flats that exploded. Earlier, I was trying to ensure that we have a clean audit on our superannuation fund. Later, I'll be talking about young offenders. You're constantly ranging across a very broad area which on one level is very interesting, but sometimes you feel like you never quite get to grips with anything. It's a very visible job: if things go wrong, you're the one who's lined up. It's the little things, actually, that make you feel good about it.

Yesterday I visited a project that we run in Brixton for people with mental health needs and learning difficulties. It was clearly making fundamental difference to the quality of their lives. It is enormously rewarding and satisfying, and that far outweighs the stresses and pressures, though they are significant.

I'm very well paid so that obviously gives me economic status. The private sector doesn't really understand local government so you're not really in their ball park. I'm invariably the only black person, and the only woman in the room, and as far as they're concerned I'm not a big hitter; just the reserve player on the bench. The title doesn't guarantee you acceptance, and there would have been a time when I felt very intimidated. Now I feel much more able to say that if you can't handle this,then it's your problem, not mine. You're not one of them, and they know that you're not. I don't think you can be until you've got other black people, other women there.

'The title doesn't guarantee your acceptance.'

I failed my eleven plus and left school when I was 16. My school told me that if I was lucky I'd get a job in an office. I want to go back to those teachers and say, You shouldn't have written me off. Never, ever let anyone write you off. I came out of a system that said I was going nowhere and ended up qualifying as a barrister.

My first black teacher was when I came to London. I came to work as a waitress and it was evening work so I needed something to do in the day. Max Johnson taught sociology at Kingsway and he persuaded me to sign up for English and history as well. It was the turning point for me, him saying, You can do this, it is not beyond your grasp.

'Never let anyone write you off.'

I did my A levels in a year then travelled in Europe doing lots of different jobs. Then I went to the LSE to study history. There I discovered that academically I was very bright: I got an upper second, and then a Masters with distinction. But I wanted to have a skill that would mean I would always have some choices in my life. My mum had brought me up never to rely on a man. I wanted to do something that would make a difference, which is why I studied law and became a barrister. I hated being in chambers; it was like a permanent boardroom meeting, so when I had my son I decided to go freelance. I worked as a lawyer in childcare, housing and employment and then came into local government on a six month temporary contract. So, I'm comparatively new to the local government scene. I had a permanent post with Hammersmith and Fulham for about five years, was recruited to be the Chief Executive of Merton, and from there was headhunted for Lambeth.

I think there's a ceiling of concrete if you're black, let alone glass. As a black person you especially need to network, make alliances, build up contacts. There's the black public managers forum, and I know some people disapprove of it

'*You've got to understand how the game is played.*'

because it seems to be replicating the old boys' network. But all you're trying to do is get on. You've got to understand how the game is played and what's going down in your organisation. You only get to know that by talking to people.

I'm a mentor to a number of black managers in other organisations. The important thing is to be able to go into a room and not feel like your guts are being torn apart. It's about trying to have resilience and also deal with people. It can help to share those experiences.

'*For black people there is the issue of identity.*'

For us as black people, there is the issue of identity. Some people say, You've betrayed us, you've sold out, and others say they're really proud of you. I'm always feeling that I mustn't let people down, but there has to be a space in your life where you can just be you. If you're a white manager, nobody sees you as representing your race. To a certain extent it happens with white women around gender. But you don't need that additional pressure. Get out, have fun, and don't work Friday nights.

It's not that things are difficult that we do not dare, but that we do not dare.

Trevor Robinson

Date of birth: 20 March 1964
Place of birth: London, England

'It's a gamble that you take.'

Trevor Robinson is a commercials director and owner of the company Quiet Storm. He also writes film scripts.

Quiet Storm is a creative company producing its own work, but also directing for other agencies. What's good about that is working alongside different creators and learning how other people do things. Pitching for work as an agency is a bit of a lottery: sometimes people like you, sometimes they don't.

I didn't want to be pigeonholed as a commercial director, so I decided to branch out and form my own company. This has given me creative freedom and time to write feature films. I would not have been able to do this if I'd stayed working for other people. It's a gamble that you take, but I'm at the right age and have the right experience.

'Everything is a challenge to anyone from my background. But I wouldn't have it any other way'.

I started off as a freelance illustrator, doing courtroom impressions and some work for magazines. The only thing I'd ever been good at was art: I enjoyed the attention I got from drawing people and coming up with ideas.

But I felt pretty isolated working like this, and it wasn't paying the bills! So I took a job as a visualiser with a small advertising agency. I started out with the naïve idea that creative people are all enlightened and intelligent, but of course I discovered that wasn't true. I was depressed working there: it was hard to get out of bed in the mornings. That made me think about what I really wanted, and at that point I decided to try and achieve my goals.

When I left school I didn't know what I wanted. I went to a boys' comprehensive in south London.

As usual, they tried to push most black kids towards sports, or to be bus drivers. I used to bunk off and I hated the teachers. But when I got to the third year I decided I needed to do something with my life. I was going to have to play the game, and in the end I did get enough O and A levels to go to college.

'Find something that you want to do and go for it.'

I've never liked the institutional mentality and I found it very difficult at college to stay put. But it was important to me to know I could compete. I've always known I wanted to be in the creative field. I need people to like what I do, and to get something from it.

'You're constantly trying to do something that's going to stand out.'

When I was growing up I didn't know anyone who was doing what I wanted to do. Then I discovered that there were actually two black guys who'd been in advertising. When I first got into it, I was expecting the door to be kicked off the hinges at any moment and people to say, 'Hey you're black, get out'. But that fear can work positively, too. It means you're constantly trying to do something that is going to stand out. So I'm always striving to find new things rather than sit back and keep doing what I've always been doing.

'It's not good to be angry all the time.'

People do take me a bit more seriously now. I know when I was at college and used to walk into a bank...well, people looked at you as if you were going to rob the place. You feel unwanted, as if you can't be a part of the whole thing. Nowadays I feel confident, but you can't afford to get too cocky about the way you are. Be smart, and don't become bitter. That's just self-destructive. It's not good to be angry all the time because you just end up being as stupid as the people who are against you. They see you as part of a mass and not as an individual. It's ironic: there are lots of us around, but when you walk in that door they still act as if you're the first black person they've ever seen!

It might feel as if there's no change, but I think society is progressing. We're here and we're in their face. And it's not just one person who's managed to get through the net, there are a lot of us. People's perceptions of us are starting to change, at one stage there were only white clients and now some of them are black.

When I'm walking down the street and see another black guy, he'll look at me and nod. It's just a thing that we do. I feel a comradeship, but I wouldn't say we have a group culture, like Indians do, for example. We haven't developed in that way.

'English people are uptight about success but I think black people are worse.'

English people are uptight about success but I think black people are worse. There's a lack of tolerance, and if you don't go to Night Moves every weekend then they think you've sold out. But I can't play that game. I can only be me.

You've got to do what you get drawn towards. When I was growing up I only lived for reggae: nothing else but dub! But now I've experienced too much from other cultures for me to want to stay in one little area. It's good to treat life as an experiment: take it all in and don't try to condition your mind only to enjoy the world through a certain space.

Everybody's got their own vibe. You've got to find out what motivates you, what you want out of life. I do think it's important to treat people as I myself want to be treated. Sometimes, when I'm working, I'm nasty! I don't like it. I'm rude, and I can't abide people who are rude to me, so I'm always checking myself.

'Try and put yourself in other people's shoes, even the ones that you hate.'

Try and put yourself in other people's shoes, even the ones that you hate. It's really helpful, even if it's only about understanding how to deal with them. Intelligent people, no matter where they're from, have a style about them. They could be from the slums, but they have a certain aura. I've discovered what it is: they're looking you in the eye, and they're listening to what you're saying.

Rt Rev John Sentamu

Date of birth: 10 June 1949
Place of birth: Uganda

'There's an element of pride beginning to develop in young black people who know their roots and their inheritance.'

John Sentamu is Bishop of Stepney in the East End of London.

'Success is being at peace with yourself: being at home in the wider community.'

I come from Uganda originally; the sixth of 13 children. My father was headmaster of a primary school and my mother was a domestic science teacher. I went to my father's school. In Uganda you had to pay your own school fees for primary, and secondary school.

Our home was about 12 miles away from the secondary school so I had to get up very early to walk there. Before I sat for my O levels a missionary helped me acquire a bicycle to do the journey. Uganda's education system was not unlike the English public school model.

When the money for my fees eventually ran out, one of the missionaries paid them for me. So I did my O levels and A levels and wanted to read medicine. At that time the country was pushing everyone to go and study sciences, particularly engineering, because not many people there had these qualifications. But in the end I decided to read law.

I got a good degree, became a barrister then practised for a while and became a member of the judiciary of Uganda. At that time Amin came to power and it was pretty difficult. I was one of those who protested against the government for expelling Ugandan Asians who were citizens. Amin was making no distinction between those who were citizens and those who were not. It got me into a lot of trouble, so I left in '74 and went to Cambridge to do two years of theology. I was a lay preacher but at that point I wanted to continue

'...other minorities have arrived since and the word 'black' was not a term they would use to define themselves.'

to sit on the bench of the courts of Uganda and do my law, and to preach at weekends.

Because my A levels and degree were recognised by Cambridge, I was able to come in as a mature student and complete my theology degree in two years. Then the university offered me a scholarship to do a doctorate in theology. After that I wanted to return to Uganda, but Amin had murdered the archbishop of Uganda, Janani Luwum, so I couldn't go back. I had previously been the archbishop's adviser on Sudanese refugees and he was a close friend of mine. I was ordained then, and became assistant chaplain at Selwyn College. Later, I was a prison chaplain at the remand centre for young offenders at Latchmere House and then became a vicar in Tulse Hill, south London. During that time I was also on the General Synod of the Church of England, and the first black person to be elected to the standing committee of the General Synod, which is like an inner cabinet.

From 1991 I've been chair of a sub-committee of the standing committee of the General Synod of the Church of England, a sub-committee then known as the Committee for Black Anglican Concerns. It was renamed the Committee for Minority Ethnic Anglican Concerns because we felt that the word 'black' no longer represented the remit, which was to monitor that racism did not persist within the structures of the Church. Many people had experienced being frozen out when they arrived from the Caribbean: the Church of England owned up to that. But other minorities have arrived since and the word 'black' was not a term they would use to define themselves.

I was consecrated Bishop in the September of '96 and then in the July of '97 was asked to sit on the Stephen Lawrence inquiry. The first black bishop was Wilfred Wood from Barbados, who is now Bishop of Croydon. I was the first African bishop to be appointed.

When I was a parish priest I was involved with housing matters and people's rights. Now I have been involved in one of the most high profile cases ever to take place in this country; the Stephen Lawrence inquiry. My law background helped me to understand the evidence. Someone once said to me that law and grace are two sides of the same coin!

'No one is an island.'

I still look forward to going back to Uganda but it is no good longing to return unless there is something specific to do. Amin was in power for a long time and then there were other regimes as brutal as his. I have two children, and must consider their education. I'm no longer a free agent taking risks just for myself. One of the greatest lessons I learned from my home is that no-one is an island. We have to care for one another and now that I have my own family I must show the same amount of commitment and care to them. There is a strong African view that you continue your life through your children so the future of whoever I am is only guaranteed through my kids. Whatever time and energy I invest in them, I'm also investing in myself.

My children hold British passports and see themselves as British but I have continued to travel on a Ugandan passport. When Amin was there, we couldn't get our passports renewed, so we travelled on British travel documents. Now with the EEC, it's becoming more problematic. Whenever I go to any EEC country I have to apply for a visa and it's becoming very expensive.

'I think the greatest mistake people make... is to have a half-hearted attitude.'

I think the greatest mistake people make in situations like mine, is to have a half-hearted attitude, as if the grass in Uganda was greener, instead of giving their energy and effort to where they are now. It's no good thinking that when it comes to Britain I'm not going to contribute. I think that's wrong. We must be willing to become loyal citizens and assist in the proper treatment of people. I want to try and ensure that I play my part in making society more - just, more kind, more caring, and making the church of Jesus Christ more as he intended it to be.

I have been very heartened by the number of incredibly talented black people out there who are not going to let what happened to their parents and grandparents, happen to them. They're not going to play the ostrich, head in the sand, bottom in the air: a very ugly sight! There's an element of pride beginning to develop in young black people who know their roots and their inheritance. A fine African proverb is, "We are people through other people: I am because I belong to a community". It is community belonging that is being destroyed in this country. People live in their blocks of flats and they've got their immediate circle but seem not to be bothered about the wider community or their neighbourhood. But in fact, that's not a typically African or black thing at all.

'I have discovered for myself that my true identity is not the things that I've achieved.'

As a boy, I did all sorts of things to get money to go to school. I was determined, but it did not come easy. Success is being at peace with yourself: being at home in the wider community. My Christian faith is one great success story. I have discovered for myself that my true identity is not in the things that I've achieved; it is in God and in other human beings.

The report on the racist murder of Stephen Lawrence called for a change in culture, in the police in particular and in society in general. Institutional racism is not a police matter alone; it is in all our institutions. For some time it was overt, but now it is mostly covert. It happens without people realising they're being racist, and this needs to be tackled. There is a wonderful Swahili word: *harambe,* and it simply means, 'Let us pull together'.

'Let us pull together.'

Ideally young people should stay on at school and go to university. One of the challenges that faces the black community is the large number of fathers whose dignity and self-respect in terms of fatherhood was robbed by the effects of the colonial and slavery experience, as a result of which they appear to be leaving the parenting of their children to their partners. Urgent answers must be found to the vitally important question of the role of black men as fathers and spouses in the perpetuation of poverty and other social ills among their own children. Otherwise we will ever be watching other ethnic groups advance from the injustice of social, economic and political disadvantage to a position of collective emancipation. There is a challenge to our black community to take greater responsibility for investing in our children.

However, quite a lot of black families have been disadvantaged for a long time. Some affirmative action has got to happen, but it's got to be in tandem with community responsibility.

Wilben Short

Date of birth: 15 August 1951
Place of birth: Croydon, Surrey

'...black people do make a significant contribution.'

Wilben Short was General Manager of the Northern Line on London Underground, responsible for 2000 employees and an operating budget of £90m. He oversaw an extensive modernisation programme of the line.

My job was a classic leadership role, encouraging all the various functions to work together. I tried to represent the customer to my staff. I was also the voice of the Northern Line to the rest of the company and to the public. I was often involved with local authorities, MPs, ministers. It was very interesting and varied.

I did this job for five years. When I started, some of the press made a play on my name and said that I'd drawn the "short" straw, describing it as the toughest transport job in London. But I am a positive person and I took this as a challenge. It became my personal ambition to bury the 'misery line' tag, but I knew that it couldn't be done overnight. Five years later one of our strongest critics, the *London Evening Standard*, has described the line as "once described as the misery line".

This is an important job: it does something for London. My background is in the tobacco industry and I used to be the Operations Director of one of the BAT subsidiaries in West Africa. The social status of the job was extremely high. Although I led a very good lifestyle, in terms of personal satisfaction I didn't fancy manufacturing cigarettes for the rest of my life. I liked the fact that I was doing something that was of good value. I am still proud of the fact that I can demonstrate that black people do make a

*'Being black is a fact
and I am proud of it.'*

significant contribution, but I am not a crusader
in that regard. I just aim to be the best person I
can be. To me, being black is a fact and I am
proud of it.

I am passionate about leading a balanced life. I
lead a church congregation of about 80 people. My
identity comes much more out of the fact that I
am a committed Christian, not because I am black
or that I am a General Manager.

Although I was born in Croydon, I had all my
primary education in Ghana and then moved to
Sierra Leone where I did all my secondary
education. Then I came to university in England.

At university, the students that I lived with
found it difficult coping with a black African
whose expectations were very different from what
they thought it should be! A few of the British
students got drunk every weekend and indulged
in hosepipe fights. That, to me, was something
you did when you were 13 not 18! I did not
encounter much direct racism from the other
students and a few were very friendly.

The first time I experienced overt racism was
when I started applying for holiday jobs. Some of
my less qualified British colleagues seemed to
find it much easier to get placements. I did not
allow this to get me down.

After university I went back to Sierra Leone and
taught in my old school for a year. I hadn't really
been thinking about a career in engineering. I
wanted to teach at the university and pursue an
academic career. But I met the manager of the BAT
Tobacco Company who offered me a job as their
Technical Training Manager. He felt he could use
my combination of a technical background and
teaching experience to begin to train local
technical staff. So that's how I got in. Three years
later I was asked to take over and run two
departments; so overnight I moved from being
responsible for training a few technicians to fix
machines to being responsible for about 120
people. Looking back the shift from engineering to
management was the first defining moment in my
career.

*'I was certainly
apprehensive at first.'*

I was certainly apprehensive at first, but I had
support from senior management. Later I had a
British factory manager who coached me, and
taught me the value of patience and tolerance in
the process. I used to get angry when he would

ask that I do work that I felt was really the responsibility of some of my colleagues, but I now realise that it broadened my experience immensely and in the end I took over from this manager.

My leaving the tobacco company was an ethical decision. I became a committed Christian about four years after I joined the tobacco industry, and I began to question the value of spending my life making cigarettes, an addictive substance. But the company treated me royally when I left. I couldn't have asked for more and still cherish my time there. I decided to move to the UK in 1988 and went straight to Cranfield Business School where I did a full time MBA. I would select this as another defining moment in my career.

I came to London Underground in 1989, initially working on a series of projects on the Central Line. Later I led a team that put in various efficiency improvements that radically changed the working practices on stations and across the Underground. I was appointed to my current job after two days of assessments with eleven other shortlisted candidates.

In the long term my desire is to go back to the developing world, probably to Africa. I'm basically a leader of change who likes to lead by persuasion and example. It is very easy to think that you can change people and organisations by relying on authority, but that is seldom true. You might create change in the short term if you have power over their immediate circumstances, but it's not going to last for long. You create lasting change by changing values and the best way to do that is by example, so that over a period of time people see values being worked out.

'Certain things may be stacked against you in a society, but the more you dwell on it the more it becomes self defeating.'

I have been a mentor to a few young black people who have talked to me about "the system" and how they're going to change it; how things are very different somewhere else where they've never been. One said, "This is not the way it happens in Africa". But they're not talking out of real experience. Certain things may be stacked against you in a society, but the more you dwell on it the more it becomes self-defeating. We can all take something and turn it into the reason that's stopping us from doing what we want. The person you've got to fight the most is yourself.

'Associate with people from whom you can learn.'

I encourage young people to associate with people from whom they can learn; you cannot achieve change single-handedly. It is difficult trying to reprogramme society but you can refuse to accept the negatives that society tries to programme into you and it helps if there are other people feeding you the same positive messages. Don't allow yourself to be put in a mould by others. You owe it to yourself to reject the mould and build your own!

Elaine Sihera

Date of birth: 18 April 1948
Place of birth: Kingston,
Jamaica

'Believe in yourself, acknowledge your strengths and weaknesses, learn from your mistakes. Know who you are and be proud of yourself.'

Elaine Sihera is managing director of AnSer House of Marlow UK (Publishing), the editor of the New Impact *journal, and the founder of the British Diversity Awards and Windrush Achievement Awards. She was the first black graduate of the Open University. She is also a writer and training consultant.*

New Impact journal is a bi-monthly publication that deals with diversity in all its forms: age, gender, race, disability. But it also deals with professional training, and above all promoting minorities positively. We hear a lot of negative things about black people in the mainstream press and this magazine is a forum to enhance society. Around that, we have the British Diversity Awards, which give accolades and recognition to companies which are showing true commitment not just paying lipservice to the equality ideal. There is also the Windrush Achievement Awards on the other hand which are for outstanding minority performers to boost recruitment in under represented fields.

My role in all this is as head cook and bottlewasher! One day I could be stuffing envelopes to send out to the public, and the next dealing with the Prime Minister's Office. The job can be demanding and, at times, I may not get to bed till four in the morning as I want to make sure that everything goes well and I have only a small team. Yes, I do find it terribly stressful at times, but I also get an enormous amount of pleasure and a great sense of achievement.

The magazine has been running for seven years now, and for the first three it made a loss. But I am a woman obsessed with a vision, to change the way diversity is both viewed and practised in Britain, so that we get rid of the simplistic and catch-all term 'equal opportunity employer' and have good practitioners who are actually doing something. It only takes one person to make that difference and I feel like a campaigner. I would die for these principles. I have to be honest: a couple years ago I wanted to close my business for financial reasons but I was steadfast. I deal with big companies who sponsor our work, but they can take four or five months to pay.

'There's a black middle class.'

There's black middle class, and a black working class. I would think there's a solid middle class, an educated one, which obviously has the same goals and objectives as the white middle class. That division has never been acknowledged by society because we tend to lump communities together without seeing that there are different facets, just like the mainstream.

Now that I've been in Britain for thirty three years I feel I belong. But when I first came here, I wouldn't change my passport. I was afraid of losing touch with Jamaica. People ask us how we feel about being in this country but we can only feel the way the host country treats us. For various reasons including the fact that I went to Cambridge University, people find me more like 'one of them'. So it's easier for me to gain entry to any circle I want. My children are here, my husband is here, so I think this is my country now, whether I like it or not.

My own family background was male orientated. My father was not interested in girl children so he praised my brother highly. For him girls were only going to get pregnant, go off and 'do their own thing'. That made me very unhappy and unloved. Then one day my whole outlook changed. The teacher at primary school was reading the best essays, from the topic we'd been given, and I suddenly realised she was reading mine! Somebody actually valued what I had done and I was all perked up! From then on I worked harder. I was the first black woman to go to the Open University and I went from there to Cambridge.

'The sky was the limit when you were thinking about a career back home.'

The sky was the limit when you were thinking about a career back home, because in Jamaica there are black role models all around you. I wanted to be a nurse and a teacher – both of which I later achieved – and everything seemed possible. I won a scholarship to come here and do nursing on the understanding that I would study for three years and go back to Jamaica to help. But I met my husband, and stayed.

I was a nurse in Kings Lynn in Norfolk, a rural area. There were hardly any black people and an enormous amount of racism, particularly among the patients. You would get old people, some of them senile, who would say. 'Take your bloody black hands off me.' The staff were also racist. Black nurses somehow didn't get to be sisters, only staff nurses. I became a senior nurse but because of the unfair treatment of black nurses I left to study to become a teacher.

I studied with the OU because that was the only university at the time that would take me with only two A levels. It was brand new and it was welcoming, even though people were rubbishing it. I was pregnant at the time so it was perfect for me because I could do it from home. I did the degree in the minimum of three years. From there I went to Cambridge University to do a Post Graduate Certificate in Education. At the time my daughter was one, my son was five and I had a part time job as an Information Stewardess with the Air Force.

So I became a teacher and eventually a black head of year in a white school. That was a real turning point for me. There were some white middle class parents who felt I marked their kids too low. I was teaching English, and the attitude was, You don't come and tell us natives how to speak our own language. In the first six months I got it from both sides: from the parents, and from some of the other teachers who thought I was too clever for my own good.

It's a fallacy to think that women are making it more than men. You do hear about a few high profile minority women, and there's enormous activity going on at certain levels, with women like me starting their own businesses. But when the power is allocated, it is still to a black male.

'It's a fallacy to think that women are making it more than men.'

We women have a knack of making ourselves visible. In small businesses, it is women who are now getting ahead, but when it comes to traditional roles such as managers or managing director, that will usually be a man. The only trend which goes against the norm is the so-called equal opportunity officers. They tend to be black or Asian females because the role doesn't have the same status as the others.

As a former English teacher, I love the printed word, which is how I started to write freelance. The magazine I created twelve years ago was not

'The first rule in life is to respect others as you would want them to respect you.'

'I'm not afraid to make mistakes.'

'Someone I really admire is Tina Turner: the sheer energy and style of the woman! There was such difficulty and brutality in her early life, yet she survived it all.'

successful. I was pretty inexperienced then. It had plenty of subscribers but I neglected the advertising aspect which would have brought in the money. I went back to the drawing board and started *New Impact*. As a consequence of this, I had requests to help develop people personally, so I did a few training courses on personal development and started to motivate women, particularly minority women, with a few simple but important tenets.

The first rule in life is to respect others. Then, always have a goal in mind. I have long term goals, short term goals, and today's goals. And I'm not afraid to make mistakes. If we don't make mistakes we never learn or develop. Someone I really admire is Tina Turner: the sheer energy and style of the woman! There was such difficulty and brutality in her early life, yet she survived it all.

At the moment we still have the anomaly of predominantly black schools being led by white head teachers. Yet there is not one with ninety per cent white students led by a black person.

Once again you see the inherent racism and colonialism. It's all very well for teachers to stand up in the classroom and tell their students they will make it, but the kids see a white member of staff, a white head teacher and white governor and they lose hope. In many such schools the pupils who are underachieving are either in deprived areas or are black children. Now they're excluded if they don't perform, because of the league tables. Yet in the West Indies and in Africa, they are not underachieving in any such numbers because their identity, as well as their self-worth, is reinforced.

I am tireless, fearless and too hyperactive for my age – always running around, plotting, planning and introducing. Even my staff can't keep up sometimes! But I wouldn't have it any other way. I have a lot of self-confidence and belief in my abilities, I never try to impress anyone and I love being over fifty because it allows me to be a real rebel with a cause!

I strongly believe in the power of positive thinking to overcome personal odds, especially as a member of a minority group eternally exposed to constant discrimination by a majority culture. I wholeheartedly believe Oprah Winfrey's tenet that, "Where there is excellence and success there is no racism" and I aim to prove it too!

Sybil Spence

Sybil Spence has been a Labour councillor since 1986. She was Lord Mayor of Birmingham between 1997 and 1998, and Deputy Lord Mayor 1998-1999.

Place of birth: Jamaica, West Indies

'We don't have the right structures in place.'

'I was the first black Lord Mayor of Birmingham.'

There are only 25 cities around the country to have the title of Lord Mayor: all the others are just Mayor. The role of Lord Mayor is an ambassadorial one. Because Birmingham has a lot to offer, our aim is to open many doors for the city and help to attract business, bringing in people from abroad and showing off what we have; we hope they can be enticed to invest here.

During my year I had the opportunity to see how the whole gels together: how the private sector works in partnership with the public sector to make things happen in a big way. I quickly discovered that the private sector does give to the community in many ways and that encouraged me to see how everybody is working together. Sometimes we in the black community don't get much help, and it's because we don't have the right infrastructures in place. Things, however, are changing this and many other issues have been recognised as problematic and therefore, must be addressed.

One of the highlights of my year was the G8 Summit, when I had the great opportunity to greet all the Heads of State and show them around the Council. We also hosted the Eurovision Song Contest in 1998, and it felt like the whole world was looking in on Birmingham. Many of the participating countries, commented on Birmingham as a city, its multi-cultural richness and its economic potential. I learned a lot and met many people of influence. It's a glorified role: I was treated like a queen. The biggest challenge is that it's very hectic. You do have to love such work to be able to do it well. But it's a role I would encourage anybody to take on if they get the chance! I was the first black Lord Mayor of Birmingham, and the fourth woman to do the job.

All my education was in Jamaica, but I took A level sociology and law as a mature student in this country in order to increase my knowledge and understanding. When I left school I wanted to be a nurse. I was called to the Kingston Public Hospital for three months and then had the chance to train at the University of the West Indies hospital. But I had met my husband-to-be and he wanted me to come to England, so that's what happened. We arrived in 1961 and I went into nursing. But after my second child was born I couldn't find the childcare I needed when I was on duty, and had to give it up.

I became a councillor here in 1986. But the call to do this kind of work had come to me many years ago in the 1970s. I knew I had to become a councillor in order to help all people. As well as doing that, I worked for 19 years as an administrator in a local company, and I've also brought up three sons.

When I first became a councillor I was only the fourth black person on the council. I was Chief Whip before I became Lord Mayor. The role of Chief Whip was very challenging and required tact, empathy, inspirational thinking and a great deal of patience. Occasionally, it required me to take individuals aside and gently reprimand them, it was important that I did this in private rather than publicly. My work in politics is to help the public. I like to evangelise, if we use the analogy of when you go to the market and see a good bargain you want to tell your friends; well, that's how it is with me, I talk to people and tell them how the Lord can help them. My Christian background influences every aspect of my life.

'Success has to be measured not so much by the position one has reached in life.'

Success has to be measured not so much by the position one has reached in life but by the difficulties encountered while trying to succeed. I thank God when I am successful because I want to spread it to the people. But when I find myself in a particular position where I have the power to help, I always use it for that purpose.

The greatest personal satisfaction is when people write to me to thank me for something I've been able to do to help. In my year as Lord Mayor

I chose Sickle Cell as one of my charities, and I will continue with that work. All those people who care about sicklers including myself are trying to build a respite home in order to help as many sicklers as we can.

'I didn't sit down and plan how to be successful.'

I didn't sit down and plan how to be successful, it just happened. Treat everybody as a person, that's my strategy. If people trust you, they don't see colour. You have to be yourself and do what you think is right.

'Get an education.'

To young black people growing up in this society I'd say, get a good education. We know that many organisations are institutionally racist. But now is not the time to tell them yet again that they are racist. We need to tell them what's needed in order to move on from that racism. The time is ripe, and we all know it, so young people need to keep pushing and saying how the situation can be remedied.

Linbert Spencer

Linbert Spencer works as a freelance management consultant. The Foreign and Commonwealth Office is one of his clients and his role is to help them recruit more Afro-Caribbean and South Asian diplomats into the British Foreign Service.

'I take whatever opportunities present themselves.'

'I think the definition of success is doing everything you can to achieve your goals, being satisfied with what you achieve, and then resetting your goals.'

The scope of the diplomat's work is incredibly wide. At an embassy it's a bit like being the national government, the local authority, the citizen's advice bureau, and the prison visiting service all rolled into one.

I'm a freelance management consultant and was headhunted by the Foreign and Commonwealth Office. I'm fairly driven by a sense of what it is that I want to do and what I want to change. I take whatever opportunities present themselves to enable me to make a difference.

I founded the Windsor Fellowship and was chairman until 1999. I do quite a lot of work with and through the Salvation Army which is my church, and I'm involved in the Salvation Army Housing Association as one of its directors. I'm also a member of the Bedfordshire Committee responsible for appointing magistrates. So I have quite a wide portfolio of activities.

I do a lot of learning and development work. The closer your job can be to your purpose, the more contented a human being you're likely to be. One of the things that I've been very fortunate in for probably all of my professional life, is that there's been a close correlation between what I perceived as my purpose in life and the job that I do and the way I earn my living.

My purpose really, is to inspire individuals so that they give time, effort and energy to taking part in building a world that values diversity. So that's my mission. I think the definition of success is doing everything you can to achieve your goals, being satisfied with what you achieve, and then resetting your goals.

I've got a long way to go to be successful in economic terms by anybody's standards really. African Caribbean people have not made the same advancements economically as have our other migrants of colour.

I came to England in the Fifties, from Jamaica, from a working class urban background, as did many of those who came with me. So we were starting in a totally different place from many of those from South Asia and Africa, who would have been middle or upper class and came here to study, to go to university. Going to school was what my parents had in mind for me, not going to university. Their generation were basically doing work, earning money and spending what they earned. Building up wealth and buying housing and so on was not part of this background. We also came at a time when we couldn't get into local authority accommodation and we weren't able to buy so we ended up in private rented accommodation. That's my thesis of the relative poverty of the Afro Caribbeans when compared to say the African and the South Asians.

When I went to primary school in north west London I was the first black kid in that school. I was obviously highly visible but was reasonably good at things, so there wasn't a massive issue. I failed my eleven plus because it was culturally driven. It had nothing to do with what you learnt in school. It had everything to do with what you knew and understood about the way of life in Britain. So I went to a secondary modern school.

'Luck is just preparation meeting opportunity.'

All I know is that my parents expected me to do well. Although I remained in the A stream throughout my school career I only managed two GCE O levels. Nonetheless my school experience was pretty enjoyable. I played a lot of sport, I captained most of the teams going, I had good contact with my teachers.

When I left school, I went in for cost and works accountancy, as it was then called, and I chose to go and work at the motor car company down the road from where I lived. Then other things intervened. I'm a member of the Salvation Army and I was doing all sorts of work with young people, especially singing and drama. Then out of the blue, someone asked me to do work in a TV drama production – they needed a black cockney who could sing and dance! I got an equity card, and more work came in so I earned my living as an actor for nearly three years. That was a phenomenal experience and most enjoyable.

'I'm a British citizen totally, but not English.'

But I knew that wasn't going to be my life's work. I wanted to do something in the community, but I wasn't clear what. I went and did my community work course for two years at Goldsmiths and then began community development work on two or three estates in Scarborough. I moved from there to Manchester City Council and then to the Greater Manchester Youth Association which is where I began to work as a senior manager. After GMYA I joined Fullemploy and it was during this time that I was approached to help launch the Open College. It was, again, a fairly classic piece of typecasting. We did two series and that was a good experience.

'Dream big dreams and stay focused on bringing them into reality.'

Luck is just preparation meeting opportunity, and lots of times people aren't lucky because they're not prepared when the opportunity comes. It's really about making sure you're prepared. Go with your passions and talk to people about how that might also generate a living for you.

I'm British but not English. Most people in Britain still don't see black British people as being part of a changing Britain. In the main the good guys see us as being totally assimilated to how they are and the bad guys don't see us as being one of them at all. I see myself as part of a Britain that even some of the good guys don't yet understand: one that is multi-ethnic and multi-cultural; what I'd describe as the salad bowl as distinct from the stewing pot.

Shirley Thompson

Shirley Thompson is a composer and film maker.

I was at school in East London in the seventies and then I went on to Liverpool University in the early eighties. I loved learning and largely enjoyed my studies. I was always busy with after school activities such as playing netball and athletics up until I was about 12 and then GCEs and orchestral rehearsals took over. As children we were imbued with the attitude by our parents that everything is achievable if you put your mind to it.

'As children we were imbued with the attitude that everything is achievable if you put your mind to it.'

At junior school I was the only black child in my year and I was in the top stream. But when it came to my going on to the local grammar school my teachers decided I would be "better off" in the secondary modern school. I was in a state of shock. I could not comprehend how it was possible for my teachers to send me to the secondary modern and my class mates, who were no brighter than myself, to the grammar school. After much concerned protestation from my mother to the head teacher and the director of education, I had to attend the allotted school.

A year passed and my mother would not let this go. She enquired again to the director of education about my going to the grammar school. With consistent A+ grades at the secondary modern I was evidently not being academically challenged and was finally given my rightful place at the local grammar school.

This experience at the age of 11, went a long way to shaping my view of the system and left me with many questions about the glaring lack of justice and fair play within it. I was also aware that my parents had to be tenacious in obtaining their rights in the workplace and other walks of life. There's an entrenched and unshakeable perception in the British culture of what being black means. The real decision-making positions aren't being filled by black people and it doesn't seem to be getting easier.

'It's a real challenge to achieve.'

There's a lot of responsibility upon parents to instill self-esteem into their children. It's a real challenge to achieve this here in England and I've seen many people of my generation take their children to the Caribbean and Africa to assist in this purpose.

I achieved good A level results and took up the place offered at Liverpool University. I decided to take a music degree because I had spent a lot of time in this area of study, and I enjoyed it, although taking history was also a strong consideration. In fact I found the opportunity and took musicology and modern history at university.

I knew I wanted to work in TV in some capacity and to use my musical talents in some way. When one of the lecturers suggested pursuing my talent in music composition by taking a masters' degree, this seemed like a great idea. I applied and was offered a place at Goldsmiths College, London University.

I started off in TV as a researcher for documentaries in the independent film sector and then on to the BBC in 1989. I began directing my own films in 1992. *Memories in Mind*, a dramatic documentry broadcast by the BBC, is a film about womens' experiences of migrating to England during the Windrush period and one of the first to be made about this period in British Caribbean history.

During this time I was also getting commissions to compose orchestral pieces which were performed at the South Bank Centre, the Royal Albert Hall and other venues around London. I also composed music for various TV programmes, for film, ballet and contemporary dance.

I was fascinated by the idea of writing an opera, when in 1995 a tender went out to several composers to write an opera for the Theatre Royal in Stratford East, I won the commission. I composed the music for my first opera *A Child of the Jago* which was performed by eight soloists, chorus and my ensemble, The Shirley Thompson

Ensemble on the South Bank in 1997. My production company, Indigo Music, produced the event.

'If you want to be heard you have to work at it.'

As well as the creative side of my work, there is much development, marketing and production work to be done. Getting projects off the ground takes a great deal of time and energy. I work in two competitive industries and if you want to be heard you have to work at it.

I feel successful in life because of the wonderful relationships I enjoy with my parents, family and friends and through having exciting, varied and challenging creative work experiences. I also feel that I have a rich heritage with both Europe and the Caribbean as cultural bases.

Vincent Thompson

Vincent Thompson has been an architect for over 20 years. He is also a town planner by qualification and a visiting lecturer at the London Institute and University of North London

Architecture involves a combination of disciplines. I like investigating the situation. I enjoy the creative act of design and the chance to roll my sleeves up and get involved in all sorts of practical things. I now run my own practice. I also enjoy lecturing, especially relating to students. I like giving something back; I like to see them coming through.

Date of Birth: 24 May 1953
Place of birth: Portland,
*   Jamaica*

'I always had in the back of my mind, the idea of setting up my own practice.'

At the beginning of the 1990s I had been working for a series of nationally based practices. I had always had in the back of my mind the idea of setting up my own practice, and had already taken the steps to do that, so when redundancies started coming through, I decided that now was the time.

I think in my teens, it was very difficult to decide what I wanted to do. I eventually chose architecture because it was a balance of my interest in art and design. But there were other things that I enjoyed, and I couldn't see how I could manage it. I was interested in art and in drama, I was in the National Youth Theatre, and I loved sport.

I didn't have any career guidance but coming from a Caribbean, matriarchal society, the single most influential person was my grandmother. She laid the foundation of mental discipline. Also, some of my teachers took a particular interest in me; an English teacher who took me to an audition at the National Youth theatre, for example.

On reflection I was dissatisfied with the options that black kids were being offered as potential careers. I had decided myself that I wished to study to gain further education instead of pursuing the jobs on offer, and only then my careers teacher said to me that O levels would be worth their weight in gold.

I was born in Jamaica, and I came here at the age of seven. For two years I was the only black kid in my primary school and that was quite traumatic for me. I had to make my presence felt, both physically and mentally. I would say 'Yes ma'am' to the teacher, and both she and the kids thought I was saying 'Yes mum.' They couldn't understand that I was being polite. Little things like that started to make you realise the difference. But it settled down when more black kids came.

I was the school's first black head boy. I also did two seasons with the National Youth Theatre, which exposed me to kids from all over the country. For the first time I went abroad - to Germany – and this also expanded my outlook.

Then I went off to do A levels with the idea of following that with an English/drama degree; but in the end I still wanted to do architecture.

'I refuse to give up and be pigeon-holed.'

I know I've got a sort of bloody-mindedness that comes from my family background. It's a refusal to give up and be pigeon-holed. I say to my students, 'Take something and run with it, exhaust that thing, and bat it around. Don't be told by anyone that it's an impossibility'.

I went to North London Polytechnic. The way architecture works is that you do a three-year degree and then you do a year's placement. I did that at Enfield borough council. They looked after me, and I was able to see how other departments worked throughout that year. So it was a good grounding.

Then you go back to college for a further two years, and then another year with an employer before taking professional exams. My first year after college I returned to the council during which time I applied for various jobs with the usual mail coming back; 'We'll keep you on file ...'. However, one company did write back about six months later, interviewed me and offered me a job. I stayed with them for over four years and during that time I learned a great deal about architecture. They're the people who designed the London Mosque, so I was getting very good experience from an early stage.

There are a lot more black architects coming through now, but still not as many as there ought to be. I think black people going through this society learn to cope; learn to function within work situations. I am used to being in the minority.

I think my approach to it is a sort of defiance. You can go into a situation where you are in the minority and think, I'm in this position because of my merit. If you have confidence, you won't let your race put you in a pigeon- hole.

'You've got to look at things in a positive light.'

You've got to look at things in a positive light – you know, the glass is half-full rather than half-empty, and say: 'Ok. If I'm in a particular situation, why am I here? Am I here for positive reasons? What gives me the right to be here?' For instance, I have the right to call myself British, not just because I've lived here since the age of seven, but also because there are certain shared histories that cause me to be here today. One of those is the history of the people I come from, myself and my family. Being in touch with those things is very important to me.

'You can learn from other people's experience.'

It was only after I left school that I actually read black history, and then during one of many casual chats with my grandmother, she told me that her father – my great grandfather, fought in the First World War! That was an amazing revelation to me. What does that say about my ability to belong? You learn from your own experiences but you can also draw on other people's experiences.

In any new situation you've got to 'break the ice' but as a black person, you know you've got to do it differently. It's always assumed that the senior person is white.

Self employment has given me an element of control over my destiny, about the type of work that I want to do, and how I want to do that work. There's more satisfaction in producing the product for yourself and of yourself.

It's important to me that I'm a loving example to my family and I think a sense of black community is something we mustn't lose. If you're

'A disappointment is a blessing.'

not reinforcing it, thinking about it, feeding it, getting kids to talk and read about their history, we'll lose it. It's right that things move on, but it would be a shame for things to move on so much that you lose that link. When you learn enough about your own community then you can get strength out of it.

I look back at my career so far, and it's all about taking the best of what you can out of each stage – even the bits that are not successful, even the things that have not worked. There's an old Nigerian saying: 'A disappointment is a blessing'. So if things go wrong, use the situation differently. It's not easy, but you can learn from it.

Barbara Tomlin-Lindsay

Place of birth: Kingston, Jamaica

Barbara Tomlin-Lindsay is a civil servant and deputy team leader in the Office of Science and Technology (OST) a business unit within the Department of Trade and Industry in London which funds the United Kingdom Research Councils.

I am the Deputy Territorial Team leader for the NERC. My work is essentially concerned with monitoring NERC's activities which deals with issues relating specifically to the environment. This involves providing briefings for Ministers, in particular the Minister for Science and other senior staff; responding to questions raised by Members of both Houses of Parliament; advising on Ministerial and senior staff visits to organisations associated with the Research Councils; drafting speeches and representing the department at inter-departmental meetings with senior management, and responding to correspondence from external organisations and individual members of the public. In addition, I am responsible for managing the process of making Ministerial appointments to the Council's Management Board; developing performance objectives of the Chief Executive and making end-of-year critical assessment of them.

My job requires a great deal of involvement with scientists, both within Government and in the Research Councils, and although I do not have a science background, my level of interest in the subject enables me to grasp the issues as they emerge and follow the debate taking place around them.

The most challenging aspect of my job is getting the briefing completed on time or the response to a Parliamentary Question. Getting it right is crucial, especially responses to Questions in Parliament to which an oral response is required. It is essential that the Minister is thoroughly briefed so that she or he understands the issues and does not feel threatened by any follow-up questions.

I have always been in the Civil Service and, looking back, I sometimes wonder what it would have been like if I had left and worked in the private sector. One thing I do know is that although I have remained in the Civil Service, I have had a varied career. I think that had I been in the private sector, I would have had to resign several times in order to move on to different jobs to gain the wide experience and expertise I now have. In the Civil Service you can apply to work in a variety of areas across departments and, in addition, you can gain further experience through secondments to the private sector.

I know I have learned a great deal. My work has enabled me to become more assertive and not be afraid to challenge anyone or an organisation especially if I felt that I was in the right. I do not allow for example any of the utilities to intimidate me or commit me to doing something I am unsure about.

I remember when I was at school and spoke to the Careers Adviser, I was being directed towards secretarial work. This was because in those days (over 20 years ago) black children were not seen as particularly intelligent. They used to direct most of us to the service industries, or nursing, and as I said before, secretarial. I made up my mind that I was not going to be anybody's secretary, plus at that time I hated typing anyway.

What I really wanted to do was to train to become an art teacher. My father thought that art was for drop-outs! Since I was not going to become an art teacher, I decided to take the advice of one of my school friends and apply for a job in the Civil Service. The interview went very well and I was offered the job on the same day. It meant doing clerical work, but I thought, 'oh well, I am not going to stay here permanently so it doesn't matter'.

'Promotion was terribly slow.'

'Looking back I have no doubt that on numerous occasions, this was more to do with being black and in some cases being female.'

'I am currently a middle manager and yet people often ask me if I am a secretary or a clerical grade.'

I later got married and had three sons. I continued to work full time, taking several months maternity leave each time. I remember the first time I became pregnant, I was called to a promotion board for a post as a manager. To be quite honest, I did not think the board would promote me because I was pregnant and I thought to myself, the Board members are bound to think, 'oh well, she might not come back anyway'. I was so wrong. I was the first to receive the result of my interview – and yes, I was successful. Promotion was terribly slow after that. Looking back, I have no doubt that on numerous occasions, this was more to do with being black and in some cases being female. I say this because there were managers – and I mainly worked for men – who did not believe that black people were capable of senior positions and often your staff appraisal report was written as though you could not get beyond say the first rung of the management ladder.

Civil Service statistics still show that most of the lower grades are occupied by visible minority ethnic staff. Within the DTI, Sir Michael Scholar, the Permanent Secretary, is trying to address this through a programme of action to improve racial equality. I am a member of the Department's Advisory Group for Racial Equality (AGRE), advising Sir Michael on taking forward the programme of action.

I am currently a middle manager and yet people often ask me if I am a secretary or a clerical grade! This is so typical of many white male managers but I must admit that on some occasions the same view is held by white females. On the other hand, there are many others – both colleagues and managers – who often believe that I am actually two levels higher than I really am. I know that I have been kept back because of a general perception of black people. I have always felt that I have to work ten times harder than my white counterparts. I know my work is good, but unfortunately you are only as good as your line manager says you are on your staff report.

I do not remember anyone being particularly nasty to me because of my colour while I was at school. There were a few teachers, as well as some pupils, who would ask the most extraordinary questions relating to where I was born. I remember one pupil asking me where in Africa was Jamaica! Another had asked me why the palms of my hands and the soles of my feet were never the same colour as the rest of my body! My reaction to the latter question was: 'perhaps it is because I do not walk around with my hands or feet turned up to the sun'! All of my friends at school were white; this was because there were so few black pupils there at that time. In fact, apart from two, possibly three, there were very few minority ethnic pupils at the school. In a way I don't think I was really that bothered because in Jamaica, where I was born, we lived in a multi-cultural society, as it is now; and Jamaica's cultural boundaries continue to narrow. The country's motto is, after all, 'Out of many one people'. I had Indian friends – we did not use the term 'Asian' – and white friends. In fact I remember my sister's best friend at school was so pale – she was white (but we did not use that term either) – and blonde that we actually called her 'Goldilocks'. Just about every race comes from Jamaica. There are white Jamaicans, Jewish Jamaicans and people of mixed heritage.

I remember quite vividly, my first real encounter with racism. I was living in West London (Bayswater) and was looking for a flat to share with two or three others. It was quite hurtful at times when I turned up to view an apartment – especially as I would actually telephone beforehand. I would then go along to view it only to be told it was gone. This was often half an hour after I had agreed to view it.

'I do not take things for granted.'

I must say that I do not take things for granted. I challenge things and that is how I have brought up my three sons. I tell them that you cannot always change how people perceive you as a black person, but you can always change the way in which you react to them. One of my main concerns is the police. I always advise my sons to 'kill them with kindness'. I also say to them, you can challenge everything, but it is how you go about doing it.

'You cannot always change how people perceive you as a black person, but you can always change the way in which you react to them.'

I have often been asked how I would define 'success'. To me, success is not necessarily about what has turned out to be the way you wanted it to be. To me, so-called failures or negative things can be successful if we have learned from them. In other words, even if it did not work out the way you had planned it to be, as long as you had a go and you learned something from it, then you could see it as successful. Having said that, I am a bit of a perfectionist and believe in working hard and getting things right! I will not stop until I think I have got it right.

'I see myself as a black person full stop.'

I see myself as a black person full stop. I do not like the term 'black'. I loathe the tag 'Black British'. It is as though by having the British added on, you need it to make yourself sound better, more British, more acceptable. The two words can be used separately; they do not necessarily have to be used together.

'I loathe the tag Black British.'

To help get me though my working life I have had to learn to adopt a variety of strategies. One of which is to be one step ahead of my managers, and in some cases my peers. However, I endeavour to think before I speak.

'I endeavour to think before I speak.'

I firmly believe that one of the things we need to do is to teach our children about their history, 'black history', and also to get schools to include black history as an integral part of the curriculum. Both black and white children would benefit from learning about black history. Black children should feel proud of being black, not ashamed nor embarrassed. White people need to know we have a history and many great achievements to our credit. I recently learned about a variety of inventions by black people. Did you know that these included: traffic lights, mop, pencil sharpener, clothes dryer, fountain pen, refrigerator, elevator and the filament within the light bulb and may more. There are a lot of famous black people who have made   enormous contributions. Too often these have not been recognised.

Since writing this article, Barbara has again been promoted and is now one of the DTI's two recently appointed Career Development Advisers, providing career advice for staff below senior management level.

Dr Clinton Valley

Date of birth: 22 December 1953
Place of birth: Trinidad

Dr Clinton Valley was the Headteacher of the John Loughborough School, a mixed secondary school with a Seventh Day Adventist religious ethos.

'You have got to be excellent to be equal.'

My role as headteacher was the overall management of the school. We had 300 students and a staff of 25. The high point of the job was seeing our students come through the system, successfully. The difficulties are trying to meet the demands and expectations of various different constituencies: the parents, the governing body, the staff, the public. The school has been very much in the public eye so expectations are high. Sometimes fulfilling them all can leave you gasping for breath!

John Loughborough has been an independent school since 1980 and we became grant maintained in 1998. The school is one where black students are achieving, where they build self-esteem, where there is motivation and where boys are doing equally as well as girls. This differs from the national statistics for the Afro-Caribbean sector.

'The school is one where black students are achieving.'

The Seventh Day Adventist Church operates a strong education system around the world. It is the largest Protestant church school system in the world and the vast majority of members within the Greater London area have an Afro-Caribbean or African background.

'I've come in sideways.'

My initial preparation was for pastoral ministry. My first degree is in theology, my masters is in Church Leadership, and when I came to England 15 years ago I started off as a circuit minister in the Willesden area of London. Although I did complete a doctorate in Education Administration in the United States before coming here, in a sense I've come in 'sideways' rather than through a career in education.

Before I came to John Loughborough I was working at our head office as an administrator for our education network across the country. But there was a need at John Loughborough. The morale was low: we had low academic achievement and financial problems. I came in as a 'Mr Fixit', I suppose. Over the past five years we have been able to pull things together. Flagging morale has been restored, we've sorted out our finances, our position in the league table has dramatically improved and we've moved into the grant maintained sector. So I think the school has a secure future.

I was born and educated in Trinidad. Then I went to the USA to do my masters degree but returned to Trinidad and served for about seven years as a church pastor and educational administrator. I went back to the States to do my doctorate and from there came to England. When I landed I felt like I was back in the Caribbean and over the years that feeling has strengthened. The style of life in London reminds me more of the Caribbean than the United States.

'You have to be careful how you present yourself because it could be misinterpreted.'

Yet life has been more difficult in England than in the USA. I'm a 'get up and go' person, and that fits in more easily with the American culture. The British are more reliant on group consensus and don't like to demonstrate leadership; don't go ahead of the pack. In the States, the person who goes ahead of the pack is paraded, is serenaded. In Britain they get, 'Well, who do you think you are?' You almost have to hold yourself back, rein yourself in, because you don't want to be too different. You have to be careful how you present yourself because it could be misinterpreted. Look how we regard the boss at Virgin.

'Society is threatened by the extrovert young black male.'

You're still thought of as 'Black' here, no matter what you do. You may have the trappings of the middle class but I'm not sure you have their acceptance. I think this society feels threatened by the extrovert young black male and he is quickly regarded as aggressive and a potentially violent criminal. So they try to cut him down to size as much as possible from a very early age. The climb for the black male is always a more difficult one, and after a while he sometimes just throws his hands up and says, What's the use? He loses interest in school, doesn't get qualified, ends up on the streets. The story is a pathetic one. You will find so many more Afro-Caribbean women in the middle class.

Every child has innate ability that has to be nurtured and encouraged. We don't write off any child, irrespective of their background. Many children have ability but their minds have been screwed up and a lot of work has to be done to re-focus their emotions, their attitude towards work and towards themselves. Whatever culture teachers come from, they need to be able to understand the background of the child.

'Parents have a responsibility.'

Parents also have a responsibility. They should become more involved in the child's educational process and be aware of what's happening at school. Parents tend to look only at the academics but you also have to look at what's happening to the child emotionally. There is a need for our black community to become more united and pro-active in challenging the stereotype of black under-achievement. Blacks are achieving!

We need to celebrate the positives, not just have tokens. It needs to become the norm that black people who achieve are talked about rather than those few who disgrace our culture. I think a lot of polarisation still exists in the black community, such as inter-island rivalries. People are still within their little cells, failing to recognise that they're going to be destroyed if they don't come together.

Sometimes I have the feeling that I'm still constantly having to 'get breadcrumbs from the white masters.' In a sense I do feel alone in my endeavour. All the other secondary headteachers in Haringay are white; pretty much all my professional colleagues in education are white!

'It's your mental attitude that influences your path.'

I grew up in a single parent family. We had a pretty stable upbringing but I know what poverty is, and it's not necessarily a negative thing. It's your mental attitude that influences your path more than your circumstances.

In the Caribbean we don't know what it is to be in a minority and we don't know what it is to feel rejected. We may have poverty - we have to walk to school, and sometimes we didn't even have shoes! – but when you get to school there's a sense of achievement. Children are encouraged to excel and teachers take a personal interest in their success. These factors are more important than filling the school with IT resources. The more important thing is the interaction between the teacher and the child.

'We need to be contributors rather then just consumers.'

I believe that every person has been created by God with infinite potential and possibilities. Their purpose in life is to fulfil their potential and contribute to the betterment of society. We need to be contributors rather than just consumers. Young people have a responsibility.

Life could be thought of as a business for achieving personal excellence. Make sure that your life is a wise investment so that when the balance sheet comes out showing how much you give to society and how much you take, it will be a positive balance sheet.

'Young people have a responsibility.'

Everyone needs to be prepared for when the door opens. Opportunities are there and the important thing is to be prepared. Growing up in the Caribbean has helped me. I can come into this society and not feel apologetic for my existence, for my background, for my hair. If people have problems with that then tough luck on them.

Robert Van Loo

Date of birth: 21 March 1954
Place of birth: St Vincent, West Indies

'Being told that I would never make the grade. This made me angry and more determined. I would not give up despite numerous rejections. Eventually I sat in the reception of the top residential chartered surveying companies until I spoke to the chief surveyor. I managed to convince him to give me a chance to prove myself. He did.'

Robert Van Loo, BSc, MCIOB (Member of Chartered Institute of Building), is Chief Surveyor for the London Borough of Barnet, heading a department with responsibility for building surveying and maintenance. He left school with an O level in art and now heads a section of over 20 surveyors and administrative staff, managing an annual turnover in excess of £5million.

My background is in building surveying and I've effectively been in this business since 1971, so where I am now is the culmination of many years.

I wasn't born in this country. I came here in 1957 when I was three years old. Like many West Indian families in the late 1950s we were very poor and experienced a lot of racism. By the time I was five or six years old and going to primary school, issues about me feeling different from my peers had started to arise. I couldn't understand why they wanted me in their football team as their first choice but nobody wanted to walk down the street with me.

At comprehensive school there was a lot of disruption in the class. I felt alienated and the teachers all thought I was a hopeless case. People had written me off at seventeen and I was told I ought to go and work in the local leather factory. I kept telling them I didn't want to do that because I saw myself in the professional arena, but no-one seemed to listen. These experiences made me realise that it was important to review my image. I brushed up my appearance. I learnt how to communicate with a wide range of people.

In school, I would describe myself as bright, curious and a daydreamer. My escape from the torment of school was to take every opportunity I could to skip school – that's not something I feel proud about – but I didn't waste my time. I wanted to learn and I decided to give myself an alternative education, so I spent my days at the museums and libraries.

The only qualification I did achieve at school was art. I liked drawing buildings and landscapes but it never occurred to me that I could make a living of it till my mother suggested architecture.

In my very first job I looked at the Chief Surveyor and thought that's what I want to be. This inspired me to work hard and absorb everything I could. At first I couldn't afford to go to college and then as I progressed in the world I found I had to make career moves in order to be sure that certain things happened. I believe that every single experience I had stood me in good stead. I achieved my goals but not without luck playing its part.

I say luck because on reflection I believe that being talented is not the only criteria for success.

'If talent was the main element then inequalities that we see wouldn't be as great. Many talented people don't find success in their lives.'

If talent was the main element then the inequalities that we see wouldn't be as great. Quite often talented people don't find success in their lives. They haven't been able to market themselves or be in the right place at the right time and most of all know the right people.

The professional world I came into was a culture shock for me because I'd come from a working class background. I was raised in a cockney culture. From an early age I was sensitive to cultural differences and felt comfortable socialising with both white and black people. It wasn't unusual for me to drop in to a white party and then go onto a black rave at three o'clock in the morning. Both of these things were important in my life although I was never able to reconcile the isolation from my roots and culture. My experience here has always made me aware I was not born here and I knew that no matter what, I would never be totally accepted.

At first it felt strange that everywhere I went I never saw another black face professionally. It was okay for them to be at the clerical level or to work in administration but I never saw them at the professional level. I believe the professions themselves still have some soul-searching to do. It seems implausible that there are so few black people there, although there has been some progress over recent years. However, black professionals have broken through to the top rank of the construction industry.

I would say my mother and father are the most significant individuals and supported me through the most difficult times. There have been people who have encouraged me along the way to whom I am grateful, although there were no real black mentors or role models in my life other than sporting heroes. I had to learn to adapt to the circumstances that presented themselves, which meant going back to the one place I tried to avoid for years...school. For the best part of 15 years I studied part time and went to evening classes. On reflection I am self taught.

'We're not talking instant gratification here.'

My life experiences are obviously personal to me. However looking back at my ambition at seventeen to one day be Chief Surveyor it seemed impossible without the qualifications, background or network. I knew it would take hard work and determination just to survive.

'To survive I've had to do a lot of compromising, to be very single-minded and at times thick-skinned.'

We're not talking instant gratification here. There is a career path that must be followed which includes academic study. I have found that there is no alternative easy solution.

It is amazing how provocative to other people the melanin in your skin can be. To survive I've had to do a lot of compromising, to be very single-minded and at times thick-skinned. You need to have a vision about how you see yourself and how you intend to make it happen.

'You need to have a vision about how you see yourself and how you intend to make it happen.'

Black parents need to be far more supportive. Just being there, being interested, is enormously important. And schools can instill the idea that we come from a very great culture that has a long history. In fact, the first book that had an impact on me and made me aware of black history was *Destruction of a Black Civilisation* by Chancellor Williams.

It is important that young people have faith in their abilities. To never give up – to keep their eye on the prize.

Tony Wade

Date of birth: 13 November 1932
Place of birth: Montserrat

'The business really started in the boot of my car.'

Tony Wade is chairman of Dyke and Dryden Ltd. He pioneered the development of the ethnic hair care industry in the UK and introduced the Afro comb. He has been awarded an MBE in recognition of his contribution to business.

A business career was always my first love. My own business began when I spotted a gap in the market, to meet the needs of the black community for hair and skin care products. In the early 60s there was very little available. We imported cosmetics over from the States and made up a price list. In fact, the business really started in the boot of my car. I was going round to shops that were selling food and saying, "If people are coming in for food they'll also buy these things". That was the beginning of the hair care industry. I was literally doing this all by myself, before I decided I needed more staff for my company. I oversaw the company's growth from a £35,000 turnover in 1968, to one of £4.7m.

Mr Dyke and Mr Dryden then one day said to me, "We need somebody, you've got the experience, why don't you come and be part of Dyke and Dryden?" So I joined them in 1968 and I've progressed from the bottom end of the company to the top.

We've generated a pioneering company and we are an enabler in the broad sense. I can think of at least 20 companies that owe their beginnings to us because of the opportunities that we've given them. We've also helped many students with work experience who couldn't get jobs elsewhere.

Dyke and Dryden were at the forefront in the setting up of a business development agency in north London, funding over 3,000 small businesses. This was a government initiative resulting from the Scarman report on the Brixton riots. I'm also a founding director of the North London TEC, which covers the boroughs of Haringay, Enfield and Barnet.

'You're not going to get where you want without strategies.'

Most of my education was in Montserrat. I left the island when I was 21. When we came here the idea was that I would study, improve my education and then go into public work back home. For three years I went to evening classes at what was then Tottenham Tech. I read all sorts of subjects: some I did well in, some I didn't. Through all this, in the end, I found my job.

'Education in the widest sense of the word, is the one method of really fighting discrimination, whatever form it takes.'

You're not going to get where you want without strategies. You have to use stepping stones. At this time I worked in a kitchen, pushing plates into the dishwashing machine. The first thing you need is shelter, food, clothing. You get that in place and you move to the next step.

You want to further your education so you go to evening classes. The job doesn't pay enough so you move on to the next job. When we reached that stage at Dyke and Dryden we set up another company called 'Afro Hair and Beauty' which became the marketing arm of the company, promoting the ethnic haircare industry in the UK and abroad. This created hundreds of jobs in the ethnic community.

I am part of the British community. When we moved to Southgate in 1973 we were probably the first black family in the neighbourhood. My friends said, What will happen to the kids?

You're moving them to a white area where they don't belong. But I don't see it like that. If you stayed where you are then there would be no progress. You've really got to move out and break down the barriers. I don't believe that we can be isolationist.

I have tried through my own children to encourage determination and commitment. We have had our difficulties along the way with UK manufacturers, suppliers, banks, but you have to have double determination. You need to keep your eye on the goal you've set yourself and never be deflected.

I've been involved in many community projects over the years. I was director of the Prince's Youth Business Trust in the east London region, and also a non-executive director of Enfield and Haringay Health Authority. I chaired the Stonebridge Housing Action Trust, one of six major government inner city housing projects.

Any community, to be a good community, does require each member to make their contribution. If we could do that, we would succeed in healing the wounds. Black history should be part of the curriculum, not just for black kids but for everyone. Education, in the widest sense of the word, is the one method of really fighting discrimination, whatever form it takes.

Young blacks have to acknowledge that they are part and parcel of society. This 'one nation' does exist, and you don't change it by confronting it. Get out there and work hard. Show that you are a team leader. Those people who try to block you – don't be afraid to show them how foolish they are. Let the talent shine through, then nobody can deny you your place in society.

'Young blacks have to acknowledge that they are part and parcel of society.'

'Let the talent shine through.'

Dounne Alexander Walker

Date of birth: 28 January 1949
Place of birth: Trinidad, West Indies

'My attitude has been, that if there is a wall, you should keep chipping at it until you break it down.'

'You are the only one who can make your dreams come true.'

Dounne Alexander Walker is the managing director of GRAMMA'S, a company based on spirituality, herbal foods, education and commercialism. Gramma's, produces high quality traditional herbal foods, previously sold to department stores such as Harrods, the major supermarkets and Ireland, but has now moved into the exclusively mail-order global markets.

Everything you do comes with hard work.

I started this business in 1987, after my marriage broke down. I came to the realisation that this is not the way 'life or love' was meant to be. From a very shy, nervous, frightened, insecure young woman, I became a single-parent, moved into a council flat with my daughters and thought:- "This is my life and I'm either going to make a mess of it or a success of it". I knew from the outset that the chances of failure were much greater than the chances of success. But I also had this absolute determination to survive. My attitude has been, that if there is a wall, you should keep chipping at it until you break it down. I'm a black woman, I may be poor and don't have a great education, but I have faith in God and believe in myself.

No one can really teach you business, because it comes from your own divine dreams or inner vision. When I started, I did not realise the amount of potential, talent or ability I really had. This to me means more than making money, realising that you are the only one who can make your dreams come true. I'm determined to break the myth that it is so easy to succeed. Everything you do comes with hard work. Your own hard work. Your own determination. I liken it to an athlete. When you see someone win a big medal, you don't see the many years of pain, sacrifice, pressure and dedicated hard-work they have had to put in from day one.

My business is also very, very spiritual, because I am a spiritual person. It took hindsight to realise there was a reason I was directed into the food industry, to produce 'healing foods' for the nation.

I always felt that I had more to do in this life than I was doing; I've always had a bigger vision. Initially, I used to make my herbal pepper sauces and just gave them away to my family and friends, but everyone wanted more and more. So when I decided to go into business, I wanted to create the most luxurious and highest quality black products on the market; as well as, to educate the nation about the values of ancient cooking, ancient herbalism and the nutritional benefits of black-foods.

So here I was in my little council flat in East London, with two children, no money, no confidence and working full-time, saying that I'm going to make these wonderful healthy products. Because they were 'the best' I wanted them to be in 'the best' stores. The first place I thought of was Harrods and within six months I had personally negotiated them onto these prestigious shelves. It all happened through prayers, intuition, spiritual guidance, courage and hard-work.

'Don't put off for tomorrow what you can do today.'

My grandmother always said, "Do everything with love and God will bless you". This is how I've always lived and worked. She also used to say, "Don't put off for tomorrow what you can do today". "God never gives you more than you can carry", "hard work don't kill but strengthens", " the more you give with love the more you will receive". So in my business, I always give a lot. If someone comes to me for advice, I tell them all I know. This principle is not always for receiving rewards, but mainly to help and support others in need.

'Don't look outside, look within you.'

I always pray, meditate and seek spiritual guidance in everything I want to do. In business you need to be flexible. If I don't get what I go for, then I don't say, "It's because I'm a woman or it's because I'm black". I question myself and ask, "what did I do wrong"? I will sit down and go over the whole interview, the whole process and pick out my mistakes. But I never leave a door closed. So I could always go back. It has taken ten years to go through my self-education in business and to also realise that we are all born highly gifted. Gifts, which no one can actually teach or take away from you, as these are your natural (unique) gifts from God. Unfortunately, the majority of us don't use or apply or develop them. If I did not go through this difficult process, I would not have developed myself to where I'm at today. Because of this, I am determined to let everyone know, that regardless of what race or gender you are, there is untapped potential within us that we don't use and must try to use. Don't look outside, look within you and you'll find whatever hero or shero you want to create, is in there for you.

Everyone has a purpose in life; regardless of how small or how grand it may look. When my mother passed away, I started to appreciate the strength it took for our parents to bring us here, and the fantastic life they gave us, which was a direct result of their hard-work. I also suddenly realised that life is very short and so precious - you can kill yourself working so hard and what was the purpose of it all? Therefore in 1994, I came off the treadmill and went back home to Trinidad, where I met my new husband and rebalanced my life.

'Racism is not our only barrier.'

My business experience was absolute hell. I came through it unscathed realising that although there is racism, but it is not our only barrier. Our main barrier is ourselves and fear. Even with all the racism, I've reached the highest level within my field, achieving far more than many of my white counterparts. I'm the recipient of seven national awards, featured extensively on television, magazines, newspapers, radio, in eighteen books and was included in the BBC's national history project called 'the Millennium Memory Bank', which recorded my experiences for posterity. I get more calls from the top circles of the white community for business advice and motivation. I also lecture at Westminster University to professionals and advance students in business.

Racism will always exist because it is nurtured from birth. You must realise that racism is not just amongst white people. Racism is also within our own community. You even get discrimination within our homes (i.e. skin colour). So don't make racism an excuse for your lack of effort.

'Everything comes from hard-work and most success doesn't come easy.'

Overcoming slavery shows our absolute determination, strength and ability to overcome adversity and survive. Our forefathers fought and died in all the world wars to preserve this country's independence and sovereignity – giving us 'an inherited right to be here'. We should never undermine what they had suffered for our sakes. Collectively, we can become a force, but we are too divided and need to unite.

Everything comes from hard-work and most success doesn't come easy.

Education is not the be-all-and-end-all. You have to have inner strength and single-mindedness. Believe in yourself and treat others with respect. Treat them exactly how you'd like to be treated. Everyone won't give you back the same love or respect, but the majority will. It doesn't mean that you have to compromise. Be strong, be polite, be assertive but not aggressive. Use your experience to try to remove barriers and do it in such a way that the person who is holding you down understands that they have misjudged you. Apart from helping yourself, bear in mind that you are also helping others, including your children and the children to come. Don't be selfish.

Unfortunately, some of our successful black people believe in trying to hug it all to themselves, so learn to share. Do not be pigeon-holed; I don't think of myself as an 'ethnic business'. My official title is a 'British Speciality Producer'.

'Not everyone can be chiefs.'

Stereotypical prejudice was not in the African minds, but in the white man's head. Afro-Caribbean's don't have a cultural problem. What I tell my children about education is, "don't tell me you've failed because you didn't try hard enough". "It's down to you, because I can't carry you all your life". "There comes a time when you've got to pick up your own burdens and also accept and take responsibility for your own actions". Children must learn to think and act positively, and also realise that everyone cannot be chiefs. Whatever you choose to do, be good at it. It takes all sorts to make a world. Be the finest in the place that you have made for yourself. Be passionate and love what you do.

'In life there are no limitations.'

In life there are no limitations, with faith, all things are possible. Whatever your mind can conceive, you can achieve. But remember you have to work hard to make it happen. Never give up on yourself.

I have achieved far more than I ever imagined. I had no previous business experience, training or

'Your destiny is always in your own hands.'

qualifications – yet I've made myself one of the most inspirational and successful business-women in Britain today. I'm not a professional writer, but I also self-publish my own books. This proves that the only training you really need in life, is not to be afraid and simply to try your best. No one holds you back, but yourself. So take the initiative, create your own opportunities and realise that your destiny is always in your own hands.

'Rise above yourself.'

I'm an ordinary working class woman. If anyone wants to put any other classification on me, that is their choosing. It's what people see from the outside. I call myself a child of the universe. I was born in the Caribbean, came to Britain at the age of 16, but I am open to any country. Wherever I choose to live, I will try to assimilate. I try my best not to become too hung up about everything. If you believe in love, you'd appreciate that life's hardness is only a training process you are going through. Learn from it rather than become angry about it. Rise above yourself.

Charlotte Williams

Date of birth: 11 January 1954
Place of birth: London, UK

'It is an achievement, but in some ways I'm probably where I should be.'

Charlotte Williams is a lecturer in social policy at the University of Wales in Bangor. She is also director of women's studies.

My job entails teaching, training and research, and what's nice about it is that I have a lot of autonomy. I can make my own choices about what I want to research and I design my own courses. So I shape my own job and that is what I like about it.

It is an achievement, but in some ways I'm probably where I should be given my background, my education and my parents' aspirations for me. I do put pressure on myself and I think that's a feature in the lives of many black people. I didn't grow up with a black community or with any exposure to black people achieving. I grew up with the assumption that black people were not that bright. So we had to be more than good, more than well behaved and more everything to demonstrate that we weren't the stereotypical underachievers.

My father was a university lecturer so there was an academic ethos in the family, and we were expected to go to university and enter one of the professions. My mum is Welsh and Welsh-speaking and my father is from Guyana. We lived and were brought up in Wales but did travel back and forth because my father's work was in West Africa. There were no other black kids in my school besides my sisters but I didn't think anything of it. There were five of us girls being brought up by a white mum in an area where we rarely saw black people.

When we think of people as successful we imagine they must be at the top of an organisation or way up in the hierarchy. But I think of success in terms of things I set for myself

'I think of success in terms of things I set myself and that I'm happy to have done.'

'There is a sense of not being recognised.'

'My parents felt that education was the most important way of combining racism and of fending off disadvantage.'

and that I'm happy to have done. In terms of being black there are probably many hidden obstacles that I didn't realise before. My aspirations were that I would have a university education and a good job. So I'm knocking on the door to be part of it and I'm doing all I can to contribute, yet there is still a sense of not being recognised. We still have a lot of work to do before we're accepted as the norm in society and not as a peculiarity.

My mother only spoke Welsh until she was 19 and she often says my father, being brought up in a British Colony, was more British than she was. All immigrants, whether Irish, Welsh or from the West Indies, found themselves in similar kinds of lodging houses in London in the late 40s. My mum had to fight because she'd married a black man and had black children. She also had to fight to be Welsh outside Wales. Now we have to fight to be recognised as Welsh.

As a black person, you have to carry a responsibility for the whole black nation. You can't do anything wrong, bad or mad, because it'll mean that all black people are like that. People take you as representative, and that's quite onerous. So you work very hard to be liked and accepted; to be perfect all the time.

I went to a selective grammar school. We were the only black family there but no attention was paid to that fact. We were totally invisible even though we had quite an affluent background and were often travelling. No-one ever asked us about it. The ignorance of adults and people that you thought should know better was disappointing. For example, there'd be ignorant statements about people in Africa, when we'd been there and knew it wasn't the same as the stereotype perception. As we grew up we understood that Africa was part of our origins. My parents felt that education was the most important way of combating racism and of fending off disadvantage.

We grew up as black people in total isolation. If you've never seen anyone who looks like you at 15 or at 20 or at 35 then you lack all the usual references. At 16 I had nine O levels and began my A levels, but at 17 I met the man I was to marry, and in educational terms I lost my way. I married very young, and had my first child at 18. I'm still married to the same man 28 years later so it was a positive experience! But I was terribly young for

*'It took me a long time
to get back on track.'*

that level of responsibility and it took me a long
time to get back on track. I'd left school before
finishing A levels so I had to start again at evening
classes. Evening classes were my way back in.
They're great for anyone who's been
disadvantaged or hasn't made it at school.

So, I didn't go to university until I was 26 or 27
and by that time I'd had another daughter. You
find yourself in a situation where you have two
children and want to improve your situation. I
decided to do a degree in social science so it
would lead to social work. I did become a social
worker for a while and it was horrendous. I ended
up leaving because of racism. Social work is not
easy for a black person. The clients find it hard to
accept that you're credible. They see you as a
foreigner and an outsider. You have colleagues
who are either patronising or tokenistic. So I
decided to go and get some teaching skills.

*'I had high expectations
for myself partly
because I knew what
was expected of me.'*

We went to live and work in Guyana for a
couple of years. It was wonderful to realise that
there were 'black people' there, with similar sorts
of experiences yet when I went to Guyana I
realised I wasn't Guyanese and when I came back I
realised that Wales was my home. I knew I had to
make other people realise that it was my home as
well as acknowledging it to myself.

*'One should never be
indifferent.'*

When my father's generation came to Britain
they had a first class citizen mentality. They had
been brought up in their own countries with a
strong sense of self. Then we, the next generation,
were brought up with second class citizenship. We
experienced the Britain that didn't want black
people even though we'd been born here. Now my
daughters' generation have a first class citizen
mentality again. They're not going to beg for
acceptance. They have a stronger sense of who
they are and they have role models, which we
didn't have.

That's not to deny that racism is still a problem
and that we have a climate where people are
vulnerable to violence and abuse. It depresses me
that black people compete against each other and
fight each other and try to keep each other down
but then, white institutions pitch you against one
another. We have to resist this.

I'm part of a black middle class but there isn't a
public perception of a black middle class in
Britain. The perception is of inner city

degradation and disadvantage. Black women get on because we're seen as less threatening. We more readily fit the 'good black' category than black men do. There are lots of very subtle racisms like this that we experience.

'Believe in yourself.'

One of my realisations about life, was accepting earlier on that things don't always go right, you just have to do your best and enjoy what you're doing and believe in yourself, your own skills and abilities. Look at other black people as allies not competitors.

You just can't afford to be indifferent.

Lola Young

Lola Young is Professor of Cultural Studies at Middlesex University and project director of the National Museum and Archives of Black History and Culture.

'I'm ambivalent about role models. Everyone's experience and circumstances are unique.'

Date of birth: 1 June 1951
Place of birth: London, UK

Part of what a professor is meant to do is enhance the reputation of the institution in terms of research and scholarship. It involves a great deal of writing and giving papers at conferences both here and abroad. I also broadcast on radio and television as a cultural critic about race, gender, sexuality and class.

Another part of my work is the supervision of PhD students and I find this incredibly energising. It's also a way of mentoring and facilitating people who want to come into the academic world.

My own particular field of interest is 'representation', especially representation on television and in film. My most recent book was about race, gender and sexuality in the British cinema.

I love my job. I couldn't say that has always been the case, but it has grown into something I find immensely pleasurable. Middlesex has been very supportive, letting me grow and be flexible in my work. Currently, for example, I've been seconded to a new project, setting up the National Museum and Archives of Black History and Culture. This will contain black historical documents available on-line.

'Be clear about why you're doing things.'

Many black students look up to you in this position. Some think they'll get a better mark from me because I understand their situation. Others, when I don't take part in every black event, say I've sold out. You just have to ride that and be clear about why you're doing things.

'Personal identity is closely bound up with the work we do.'

I'm at the level now where I think, I know what I want to do; I know what my objectives are, so whatever you think doesn't bother me. Personal identity is closely bound up with the work we do. If you think you're hard done by because someone else has been promoted and you haven't, then you'll say that it's because they're black, or they're a woman, or passive or whatever... There's so much envy and insecurity, and gender and class seem to be driving forces.

I get exhilarated by working hard and having a lot to do. I chaired the judging panel for the Orange Prize for fiction, which meant that I had to read 120 books and then facilitate the discussions. It was a lot of work and also a great honour, because it's a very prestigious prize.

One of the good things about having a number of academic black women around now is that when I'm asked to go on *Woman's Hour* say and I'm busy, I can actually refer them to someone else. When I first started, I did feel a burden of representation and didn't like to say no. It's important to have a black presence.

Financially the rewards are okay, though it doesn't compare with any kind of corporate salary. I didn't realise at first that it was possible to travel so much as an academic. I do like meeting colleagues from abroad and having a productive conversation. It's a great perk, which isn't to say that it doesn't entail hard work. I write something new every time I speak, which is one way of keeping up my production of publications.

I've achieved a lot of what I wanted to do in my career. One of the things that I'd still really like to do is a key television or radio series that would place black arts, culture and history on the map in a way that hasn't been done before.

'My first job was with the Gas Board!'

I can scarcely remember my first job. It was with the Gas Board! But that was because I didn't get good enough A levels to go to university. I did some drama at evening classes and decided that I wanted to act, much to everyone's amazement. So that's what I did for eight or nine years. Eventually I got fed up with acting a nurse, a prostitute, a bus conductor and never being given the chance to stretch myself despite all the experience I'd had in theatre and television.

I then went into arts development and really enjoyed it. But people around me were discussing things I didn't understand – aesthetics and culture – and I realised these were things I had to learn about. So I decided to do a degree. My employers supported me and gave me time off. When I'd finished, a tutor suggested I carry on and do a PhD. I was shocked, because I hadn't been brought up to think I could achieve such things.

'On reflection, I wasn't expecting to be here at all!'

After I'd completed my PhD I started to do part-time lecturing. When people look at my career path they think it's rather chequered, but now all of those things are coming together in an interesting and gratifying way. But on reflection, I wasn't expecting to be here at all!

I was born here in the UK and my parents are from Nigeria, so in terms of thinking through what it means to be black it was mostly via images from the Civil Rights Movement. There are certain things I felt I had to do because I'm a black woman, so that's been a strong motivational force. I have the material benefits of success but often the term 'black middle class' is used pejoratively by black people. However I do think there is a small and growing black middle class.

Sometimes from quite young black people you get the feeling that you're not being allowed to be part of the black community. There are so many exclusions set up: if you've had a mixed race kid; if you have a white woman friend; if you don't wear your hair plastered to your head. So there is a sense of conflict, dispute, conversation over what it means to be black. I think what's emerging is that it has to be much more plural. People read that as a diminishing of what it means to be black, but to me it's just change. If we were all in Africa or the Caribbean we would still be changing.

'We all need to set goals for ourselves.'

We all need to set goals for ourselves. You need to have in your head some things that you want to do and the type of person you want to be... and then try and keep to that and achieve a level of contentment within yourself. It's about trying to be decent to people, and not making other people's lives a misery – including your parents! When you're in difficult circumstances you can be tempted not to take responsibility: to blame the system or your parents – anyone but yourself. Part of deciding what you want is taking responsibility. It isn't easy, and it's not to say that other people aren't still going to try to thwart you.

'Part of deciding what you want is taking responsibility.'

Educational qualifications are important, and it's never too late. I didn't do my degree until I was in my mid-thirties. So if you are feeling thwarted at a particular moment try and think around the problem and see if there are other ways to do it.

We should try to be supportive of each other and accept difference.

Appendix 1

Research background

The book arose from the need for greater public awareness of the contribution that black people make in Britain, despite the widespread media coverage of black under-achievement.

Initially conceived as a resource for young people making life and career decisions (school careers lessons, mentoring, youth services) the project has yielded material of value and interest to a wide readership. It provides a series of accessible and personal narratives of black achievers in the UK.

The aim was to cover a wide range of occupations and involve individuals from across the UK. The sample was monitored by age and gender in order to maintain a representative and interesting balance.

A database of some 300 names was assembled, with an initial mail-out, consisting of an explanatory letter and a questionnaire.

Prerequisites included the need to have been born in the UK or a resident since the late 1940s, and to have achieved a recognised professional status within their field.

Early Results

Returns were disappointingly low, with less than fifty responses. The reasons for poor first returns might have included:-

◆ timing of the mail-out

◆ whilst approving of the idea in principle, being deterred through not knowing the author or the institution involved

◆ requiring more detail as to how the information would be used

◆ not having time to complete the questionnaire.

Follow-Up

Further individuals were then contacted and interviewed.

Interviews

Individuals covered a broad range of occupational categories and reflected many regions of the UK. Those interviewed covered a spectrum of age (25 - 70+), gender and background, and their experiences demonstrate that there is no simple formula to achieving success.

Interviews with seventy two individuals took place over a two-year period, and were based on information from the questionnaires and a question list. The latter was re-designed after initial interviews.

Interviews were of one to three hours' duration and were recorded. They were then transcribed verbatim.

Editing

Full length transcripts were read and key sections identified. A shortened version of each interview was then produced, using as much as possible of the actual words spoken by the interviewee. Drafts were then forwarded to the interviewees for amendment and approval.

Final drafts incorporated the interviewees' alterations and suggestions.

Photographs

Additional funding from the DfEE brought Robert Taylor a black photographer on board. Robert's role was to provide a black and white photograph of each interviewee, encapsulating something of their character and personality.

Index of interviewees

Chief Insp. Martin Harding	Police	Manchester	122
Michael Hastings	Public Affairs, BBC	London	126
Mark Hendrick	MEP	Blackpool	129
Lenny Henry	Comedian/actor	London	133
Jo Hodges	Screenplay writer/ advertising	London	135
Claire Holder	Nott Hill Trust	London	138
Paul Hull	Rugby	Bristol	141
Jessica Huntley	Publisher	London	145
Keith Kerr	Gen Manager, BA	London	148
Andrea Levy	Novelist	London	152
Chris B Lynch	Surgeon	Milton Keynes	156
Chief Insp. Dalton McConney	Police	London	159
Penny MacDonald	Editor-in-chief, Redwood	London	163
Sidney McFarlane	RAF	Cranwell	167
Bazil Meade	Leader, Gospel Choir	London	173
Errol Murray	GLR	London	175
Chris Nasah	Architect	London	179
Rev Ronald Nathan	International Religious Consultant	London	182
Lloyd Newton	Opera Director/singer	London	186
Dele Ogun	Tax Solicitor (own firm)	London	190
Bruce Oldfield	Designer	London	195
Herman Ouseley	CRE	London	197
Elsie Owusa	Architect	London	202
Carl Palmer	Journalist	Manchester	205
Prof Geoff Palmer	Cereal/brewing	Edinburgh	209
Alex Pascall	Writer/Broadcaster	London	213
Trevor Phillips	Broadcaster	London	220
Sybil Phoenix MBE	Refuge Admin etc	London	224
Bob Purkiss	TGWU	London	227
Heather Rabbatts	Local Auth. Chief Exec.	London	231
Trevor Robinson	Quiet Storm Agency	London	234

Index of interviewees by occupation

Syan Blake	Actress	London	62
Yvonne Brewster	Theatre Director & Admin.	London	73
Desune Coleman	Actor, Eastenders	London	87
Lenny Henry	Comedian/actor	London	133
Jo Hodges	Screenplay writer/ advertising	London	135
Andrea Levy	Novelist	London	152
Bazil Meade	Leader, Gospel Choir	London	173
Lloyd Newton	Opera Director/singer	London	186
Shirley Thompson	Composer	London	255

Banking, Business, Administration

Dounne Alexander Walker	Business founder (Gramma's)	London	277
Mervyn Archer	Bank Manager	London	39
Yvonne Foster	Training/HR	London	104
Keith Kerr	Gen Manager, BA	London	148
Heather Rabbatts	Local Auth. Chief Exec.	London	231

Civil Service, Police

Chief Insp. Martin Harding	Police	Manchester	122
Chief Insp. Dalton McConney	Police	London	159
Linbert Spencer	Foreign Office	London	252
Barbara Tomlin-Lindsay	Board of Trade	London	262
Sidney McFarlane	RAF	Cranwell	167

Clergy

Rev Ronald Nathan	International Religious Consultant	London	182
Rt Rev John Sentamu	Bishop of Stepney	London	237

Community Work

Sonia Bassey	Project Coordinator	Liverpool	51
Sybil Phoenix MBE	Refuge Admin etc	London	224
Eleanor Grant	Community Arts	Bristol	116

Computing, IT

Luna Frank Riley	IT Consultant in EU	Manchester	107
Janet Campbell	HR – SCO computer software	Watford	81

Fashion, Beauty

Tony Wade	MD, Dyke & Dryden Cosmetics	London	274
Bruce Oldfield	Designer	London	195

Law

Chris Cleverley	Lawyer	London	85
Claire Holder	Nott Hill Trust	London	138

Media

Abiola Awojobi	Producer, BBC	London	43
Pogus Caesar	Windrush Prod. Co	Birmingham	76
Michael Hastings	Public Affairs, BBC	London	126
Jessica Huntley	Publisher	London	145
Penny MacDonald	Editor-in-chief, Redwood	London	163
Errol Murray	GLR	London	175
Carl Palmer	Journalist	Manchester	205
Alex Pascall	Writer/Broadcaster	London	213
Trevor Phillips	Broadcaster & Labour Chair of Greater London Assembly	London	220
Elaine Sihera	Publisher/writer	Marlow	245
Patrick Berry	Choice FM	London	55
Trevor Robinson	Quiet Storm Agency	London	234
Brenda Emmanus	Journalist/TV Radio Presenter	London	97

Medicine, Science

Dr S Prince Akpabio	Dentistry	London	22
Chris B Lynch	Surgeon	Milton Keynes	156
Prof Geoff Palmer	Cereal/brewing	Edinburgh	209
Denise Everett	Embryologist	London	102

Politics

Valerie Amos	Baroness	London	30
Paul Boateng	MP	London	68
Mark Hendrick	MEP	Blackpool	129
Herman Ouseley	CRE	London	197
Bob Purkiss	TGWU	London	227
Sybil Spence	Labour Councillor	Birmingham	249

Sport (Management)

Paul Hull	Rugby	Bristol	141